19

02 1997

GOVERNORS, LEGISLATURES, AND BUDGETS

GOVERNORS, LEGISLATURES, AND BUDGETS

DIVERSITY ACROSS THE AMERICAN STATES

Edited by

Edward J. Clynch

and

Thomas P. Lauth

Contributions in Political Science, Number 265
Bernard K. Johnpoll, *Series Editor*

Greenwood Press
New York • Westport, Connecticut • London

Library of Congress Cataloging-in-Publication Data

Governors, legislatures, and budgets : diversity across
  the American states / edited by Edward J. Clynch and Thomas P. Lauth.
     p. cm.—(Contributions in political science, ISSN 0147-1066 ; no. 265)
    Includes bibliographical references and index.
    ISBN 0-313-25930-5 (lib. bdg. : alk. paper)
    1. Budget—United States—States. 2. Legislative oversight—
United States—States. 3. Legislative auditing—United States—
States. 4. Governors—United States—States. I. Clynch, Edward
J. II. Lauth, Thomas P. III. Series.
HJ2053.A1G83 1991
353.9372221—dc20   90-38524

British Library Cataloguing in Publication Data is available.

Library of Congress Catalog Card Number: 90-38524
ISBN: 0-313-25930-5
ISSN: 0147-1066

First published in 1991

Greenwood Press, 88 Post Road West, Westport, CT 06881
An imprint of Greenwood Publishing Group, Inc.

Printed in the United States of America

The paper used in this book complies with the
Permanent Paper Standard issued by the National
Information Standards Organization (Z39.48-1984).

10 9 8 7 6 5 4 3 2 1

Copyright Acknowledgment

Figures 3.1 and 3.2 are reprinted with permission from *Public Administration Review*
by the American Society for Public Administration (ASPA), 1120 G Street N.W., Suite
500, Washington, DC 20005. All rights reserved.

Contents

v

Acknowledgments

It would have been impossible to produce this book without the contributions of our colleagues who wrote the state chapters, and without the cooperation of state budget officials who shared information and insights with each of us.

We thank Glen Cope, Ellen Dran, Syd Duncombe, Gloria Grizzle, Merl Hackbart, Ted Hebert, Jim Jernberg, Jack King, Dick Kinney, Carol Lewis, Susan MacManus, Jerry McCaffery, Irene Rubin, Steve Wagner, and Marcia Whicker for writing their respective state chapters. Their budgeting expertise and sound professional judgments are the *sine qua non* of this volume. We also wish to thank Lisa Aplin for her valuable help in assembling and editing this book.

On behalf of all of the authors, we thank the many state budget officials who granted formal interviews, participated in informal conversations, and provided requested data. They contributed substantially to our efforts.

Budgeting in the American States: Important Questions about an Important Activity

Edward J. Clynch and Thomas P. Lauth

Budgeting represents a central activity in state government. Budget decisions determine not only how much will be available for state spending, but also which policies will be implemented and which social values will prevail in state governance. Executive branch recommendations portray the governor's policy goals and objectives and constitute a plan for state disbursements. Legislative appropriations determine which agency programs and gubernatorial policy initiatives receive financial support.

The separation of powers principle, which divides policymaking authority between the executive and legislative branches, complicates decision making in the American political system. Budgeting requires continual executive-legislative interaction because governments begin each budget cycle anew and produce a new product. Research on the budget process reveals a struggle between the executive and legislature in which neither branch ever completely eclipses the other.[1]

At the beginning of this century, the traditional standard operating procedure in many jurisdictions led to legislative dominance and a minimal role for presidents, governors, and mayors. Departments presented spending requests directly to the legislative body.[2] Agencies normally submitted lump-sum budgets and bargained directly with appropriations committees over their spending desires. Chief executives lacked the authority to coordinate or revise those estimates, consider them in relationship to each other, or balance them against an estimate of available revenue. Furthermore, agency estimates were sent forward at different times, in a variety of forms, and adhered to no common classification scheme. Many government reform advocates such as Frederick A. Cleveland, Frank Goodnow, and William F. Willoughby regarded these practices as inefficient, likely to lead to excessive spending, or even worse, to abuse in the handling of public funds.[3] These problems were exacerbated in state government by the large number of agency heads who were either directly elected or appointed by independent boards and commissions.

Early budget reformers, such as A. R. Hatton and William Willoughby, as well as their later brethren, argue that democratic responsiveness undergirds arguments for increasing the power of the chief executive. They suggest that the executive budget serves as a tool of governmental accountability.[4] Popular control in the majoritarian sense is enhanced when a political executive, who is chosen by the entire electorate, uses the budget to strongly influence the expenditure of public resources. Increasingly large and complex governments will be responsive to the citizenry only when the executive organizes the distribution of public benefits. As the 1921 congressional report advocating a federal executive budget states, "He [the president] is the only officer as a whole rather than in one particular part. He is the only administrative officer who is elected by the people and, thus, can be held politically responsible for his actions."[5]

Notions of democratic responsiveness also underpin arguments for legislative control of budget decisions. Despite problems created by dispersed power, supporters of strong legislative influence maintain that diffused power over spending decisions represents the lesser evil. In their view, placing too much power in the hands of the executive leads to abuse.[6] To the extent that lawmaking bodies maintain substantial influence, budget decision making reflects pluralist politics with multiple points of access. Decisions emerge as bargains and accommodation among the diverse groups with a stake in the outcome. In effect, the legislature serves as the critical policymaker. Rather than leave the job strictly to the executive, the legislature, with a membership that mirrors divisions in society, should play a major role in apportioning public resources.[7]

Reformers propose bringing the chief administrators into the budget process as the priority setter and coordinator. Under an executive-centered system, agencies submit their spending requests to the chief executive who, in turn, sends a single budget to the legislature. The executive modifies spending requests to fit within available revenue. Furthermore, preexisting executive program priorities allow the chief administrator to evaluate the desirability of each request and to modify agency submissions on a rational basis. As a result, the consolidated budget, which is proposed to the legislature, pronounces executive program priorities. Instead of working directly with the spending units, the legislature reviews and reacts to the unified executive budget. Generally, the legislature stays within the spending ceiling set by the executive and makes minor spending modifications. Budget reformers envision the legislature using the budget process for oversight of ongoing programs and agencies. In effect, executive-centered budget advocates expect the president, governor, mayor, and other officials, to set the basic spending parameters, and the legislature to tinker with the recommendation. Lawmakers should use their approval authority to oversee agency operations rather than to set expenditure priorities.[8]

Eventually, many lawmakers at all levels of government accepted a consolidated executive budget as a better alternative to the existing system. Even though a chief executive with strong budgetary powers may represent a formidable adversary, legislative bodies benefit from the executive budget in important ways. By relying on the executive to define and present agency budget needs within the framework of a comprehensive plan, legislatures relieve themselves of the burden of dealing directly with competing claims for resources. Lawmakers also believe that placing the central administrator between spending units and the legislature curbs rising government spending and establishes meaningful controls. With lump-sum submissions, legislators lack detailed information to evaluate agency actions. Furthermore, no one exercises control over spending to insure accountability to legislative intent. The consolidated budget forces the collection of data in a form suitable for legislative review. Moreover, the legislature assigns the duty of monitoring spending to the chief administrator in order to guarantee conformity with appropriations statutes. In essence, the concentration of budgetary responsibility turns the chief executive into a legislative control agent.[9]

The concept of a unified budget first emerged as a feature of the municipal reform movement early in this century. The federal government installed an executive budget in 1921. At the local level, evidence seems to support Louis Friedman's conclusion that ''the distribution of influence varies from executive to legislative dominance.''[10] During the 1980s, students of federal budgeting debated whether an executive budget even existed. Executive-legislative gridlock and large chunks of expenditures committed to interest on the national debt, entitlements, and defense abrogate the utility of the president's budget as a priority-setting tool.[11]

At the state level, the executive budget movement constitutes an integral part of an integrated administrative system with the governor as chief administrator.[12] The idea of assembling agency requests into one budget spread quickly among the states between 1910 and 1930. Many states gave the governor the authority to assemble and present a unified budget. In some states, however, the legislative leadership or a group composed of both legislators and statewide elected officials were assigned this task.[13] The addition of the governor as a relevant participant in the budget process stimulated scholars to analyze gubernatorial-legislative interaction and the impact of each institution on budget decisions. Generally, most recent research falls into two categories. Many studies emphasize multistate aggregate data comparisons without adequate attention to the institutions, processes, and patterns of interaction found within individual states.[14] Others review budgeting in single states with little concern for comparison with other states.[15]

Nearly all cross-state comparative research uses aggregate financial and demographic data. Although this approach successfully models the relationships among agency requests, gubernatorial recommendations, and legislative appropriations, it gives us limited insight into the institutions, processes, or patterns of behavior that occur during preparation and approval of the unified budget. Moreover, aggregate studies mask the range of reactions to gubernatorial proposals by the legislature. A close reading of aggregate studies demonstrates that the ability of governors to gain acceptance of their budget proposals varies widely among states. Wildavsky suggests that gubernatorial success depends on institutional characteristics, the political party composition of the legislature, and the patterns of interaction among the participants.[16] Abney and Lauth also determined that governors use the line-item veto as an instrument of partisanship.[17]

In addition to the comparative aggregate analysis, the literature contains several single-state studies or comparisons of a limited number of states. These investigations do address institutions, processes, or patterns of interaction, but they were conducted at quite different points in time and without benefit of a common organizing framework. Thus, it is difficult to conduct a meaningful comparison and contrasting of findings. A few of these efforts focus on a state's entire budgetary process, but most concentrate on one facet of state budgeting—such as planned program or zero-base budgeting or budget reviews by analysts.[18]

For the most part, state budgeting studies do not address the question of whether financial condition changes the distribution of executive and legislative influence. Some research focusing on national budgets suggests that tight money acts as a centrifugal force that increases the power of the executive at the expense of the legislature; such a pattern may also occur in the American states.[19] In addition, Wildavsky argues that budgeting in growth states with growing revenue concentrates on ways to dispose of the fiscal dividend. Although budgeting in states with static receipts focuses on avenues to fund current services and to reduce spending unit requests for new money, states with tight revenues also scan the environment for new sources of money.[20]

This book seeks to overcome both deficiencies with a series of individual state studies that use the late 1980s as the standard time frame and that follow a common organizing framework: political structure and fiscal condition. We operationalize political structure as the relative influence of governors and legislatures in terms of both formal powers and actual practice. The various contributors examine an array of actions that take place during budget formulation and approval to ascertain the influence of the governor and legislature. Individual state chapters touch on the structural factors that shape executive-legislative budget interactions.

— Who possesses the authority and responsibility to receive spending requests, sift through them, and formulate a unified budget for submission to the legislature? Does this power rest solely with the governor, or does the legislature collect and analyze spending information independently of details funneled through the executive?

— Who makes revenue estimates? Does the governor control this process, or does the legislature or some other independent body generate information on revenue availability?

— Who formulates the budget that serves as the working document during the legislative session? Does the legislature react and tinker with the governor's budget? Conversely, does the legislative leadership substantially revise the governor's proposal before legislative consideration, or does the leadership even develop its own budget proposal to serve as the legislative operating draft?

— Do partisan differences between the governor and the legislature affect legislative consideration of the governor's budget?

— What role does the governor's veto play? Does it help the governor shape spending decisions in a meaningful way, or does structure or tradition render the veto ineffectual?

The book operationalizes fiscal condition through conventional measures of revenue growth and decline, with attention given to the impact of the revenue situation on budget processes and budget decisions. The various state chapters address revenue conditions and their effect on budgeting.

— As Wildavsky asserts, does budgeting in cash-strapped states focus on ways to increase revenue while budgeting in cash-surplus states centers on ways to spend the fiscal dividend?
— Given the conflict that arises when budget cuts are necessary, do states use smoke and mirrors to postpone the day of reckoning?
— Who takes the initiative to address revenue scarcity, either through increased taxes and fees or cuts in spending? Does the governor or legislature put solutions on the table? Does financial shortfall increase the leverage of the governor or the legislature over budget decisions?
— Who determines the content of budget revocations during revenue shortfalls, and do rescissions enhance the influence of the governor or the legislature?
— In states that have surpluses, what roles do the governor and the legislature play in determining surplus dispersal?

This book includes states from all areas of the country. Demographically, they range from very rural to heavily urban, from resource rich to resource poor, from high-population growth to declining population, and from high-tech economies to workforces dominated by unskilled and semiskilled labor. They also differ from each other with regard to the strength of their executive, their experience with fiscal stress, and their history of rational budgeting reforms. This volume provides the contextual richness needed to understand the executive-legislative interaction that occurs during the recurring process of budgeting. The following chapters add to our understanding of who has power and how governors and legislators use their influence to shape spending priorities. Chapters 2 through 4 focus on strong executive states, with gubernatorial domination approaching the executive-centered process envisioned by reformers. Chapters 5 through 9 concentrate on mixed states in which the legislature retains the ability to challenge executive assumptions in a meaningful way. Chapters 10 through 13 highlight strong legislative states in which legislative leaders prepare the budget document to which the legislature reacts. Chapter 14 outlines the fused government arrangement that exists in South Carolina.

2

California: Changing Demographics and Executive Dominance

JERRY L. MCCAFFERY

California is a study in contrasts. It is the nation's leading agricultural state, but 90 percent of its people live in cities. It has both the highest and lowest geographical points in the continental United States. It has more miles of coastline than any other state except Alaska, and its population tends to cluster on the coast, around San Francisco and Los Angeles. It is the most populous state in the union, but vast areas in the east and north have sparse populations. Its leading industries tend to be aerospace and to be high-tech oriented, yet its agricultural industries demand backbreaking stoop labor. It is known for good movies and bad earthquakes, good wines and bad traffic, and good government and weird ideas. Some residents of the state have a sense that anything is possible; others fear they may be right.

California is an annual budget state. Its budget is the largest of the state budgets, with over $44 billion for FY1989. The governor is the chief architect of this budget, ably assisted by the budget groups in the Department of Finance. As is common in many states, the legislature is a powerful modifier of the budget. Although it begins with the governor's budget, the legislature does a lot of independent analysis. Its principal assistant in this effort is the office of the Legislative Analyst, a highly professionalized and politically neutral staff unit that analyzes and reports on the governor's budget. These recommendations concern both grand questions of policy and the minutiae of management.

The governor has a line-item veto which he or she utilizes with regularity to shape the budget to his liking. Policymaking in California is also played out within an environment of direct participation. Public initiatives in the last decade have capped local tax revenues, forced the state to bail out local governments, and linked state spending growth to changes in the cost of living and population growth. Other initiatives have been proposed which would directly control the maximum salary payable by governmental units in California and constitutionally dedicate portions of state taxes to local governments based on where the tax originated.

California has been called a state of mind. One is tempted to remark that it is a confused state of mind, but in the main California is a progressive, well-governed state with a multiracial population and a seemingly inexhaustible supply of new ideas. Lobbyists are an important force in state policymaking, but publicity about government issues is so widespread that almost everyone who wants to know can find out what's at stake. The task of this chapter is to describe the budget mechanism of this state.

THE EXECUTIVE BUDGET PROCESS

The budget process in California is an executive-dominated process that features program budget categories organized along a line-item base. In the 1978 Budget Act, the legislature established funding for the California Fiscal Information System (CFIS), an automated fiscal database that is equally open to the executive and the legislature for budget development and execution activities. CFIS was designed to include the development of a centralized fiscal and program database; improved program performance and expenditure data; expanded accounting and fiscal reporting capabilities; and on-line computer access to state budget, revenue, and expenditure data.

The idea was to provide decision makers with more timely and better fiscal information. The CFIS database was designed to be the critical tool in this system, organizing detailed accounting system data and high-level fiscal information into a coherent system. The data to be provided included revenues and expenditures by line item, program, governmental unit, and fund source. In addition to fiscal data, the system also provided for performance data such as workload measures.

Partially as a result of this system, the budget process in California has been automated. Normally in early July, the Department of Finance provides baseline budget estimates for the coming year from the CFIS system. These estimates contain the official budget for the current year, any additional appropriations or changes, and the automatic roll-in of certain statutorily obligated cost-of-living adjustments. In August and September the individual agencies modify the CFIS baseline budget. They do so by creating budget change proposals. The baseline budget reflects the anticipated costs of carrying out the current level of service or activities as authorized by the legislature. It includes adjustment for cost increases but does not include changes in level of service over that authorized by the legislature. A budget change proposal (BCP) is a proposal to change the level of service or funding sources for activities authorized by the legislature, or to establish new program activities that are not currently authorized.[1] Budget change proposals either change the intensity with which old programs are administered or create new programs. Standard budget routines occur in late summer and the fall. Agencies compile their own budgets, hold internal hearings and reviews, and submit the budget to the Department of Finance for review. After the governor's decisions are made, the budget is printed and transmitted to the legislature in January.

In general, this is an open process, and much of the information is in printed form. A lot of good staff work is performed by the substantive committees, the money committees and their staffs, and the Office of Legislative Analyst. The governor's budget is a major cue, with focus on the increment of change. Both the Department of Finance and the legislative analyst are highly respected, as are the committee staff members. They look at the budget through different lenses. The committee staff, for example, tends to reflect the political viewpoint of the committee or party member they work for. The Department of Finance has budget compilation and review functions as well as analysis. The Office of Legislative Analyst has gained a reputation for neutral expertise. As "professional question askers," they can draw different conclusions using the same data as the Department of Finance.

The legislature (1979, 1983)[2] required the Department of Finance to report annually on the methods and procedures used in establishing budget priorities. The Program Base Analysis is utilized to provide the necessary information. Within a three-year period each department has to prepare justifications that substantiate the maintenance of program service levels within its baseline. This is part of zero-based budgeting logic which attempts to investigate the budget base. However, it does it on a staggered basis over three years, exempts some functions—administrative programs in 1984—and waives the requirement if another party, for example, the legislative analyst or a legislative committee, is already analyzing the function. If a budget change request was submitted, however, then a base evaluation has to be done.

The analysis has six parts. Part one focuses on the reason for the program's existence, its history, and its benefits and beneficiaries. Part two relates to goals and objectives and requires that performance information be related to the accomplishment of objectives and goals. Part three asks for alternative means of achieving goals and objectives. Part four asks for alternatives, requiring first a description of the status quo and then reasons why other alternatives have been rejected. Part five is a complex schedule relating tasks to be done and the personnel years required to do them. Part six asks for a quantification of workload statistics so that a reviewer can check part five. For example, with fifty inspections per person and two hundred inspections to be done, "one could conclude that four inspectors would be required to handle the anticipated workload."[3]

The stated intent of the governor's budget letter for FY1986 was to improve the quality of service, increase productivity, and lower the overall cost of government by decreasing its size through effective management and innovative techniques. Departments were called on to review the level of staffing for all programs, with the ultimate aim of reducing the number of positions and personnel years.

Thus, budget change proposals were to be accepted only for priority program needs. New programs or program expansions would not be accepted unless the agency secretary requested them. Two criteria were identified for use in prioritizing programs:

1. BCPs that proposed a redirection of existing resources, thus trading old programs for new programs.
2. BCPs that resulted in a more efficient provision of services or a more effective way of managing state programs or that produced significant long-term savings through more cost-effective alternatives.[4] An additional emphasis in 1984 was a stress on BCPs that addressed increased automation and personnel reduction.

Although the base analysis forms did not appear to make a difference in budget review, the budget change proposals do. For the administration they are the heart of the budget process. Most BCPs concern workload change; some concern new initiatives. The fact of life for the California state budget is that enrollment, caseload, and population drive most of the budget; educating children and young adults, providing health services, providing welfare assistance, and running correctional institutions and interest on indebtedness account for 92 cents on every dollar spent. Health, education, and welfare programs alone account for 87 cents out of every state dollar.[5] Thus, there are no easy marks for budget reduction or cutbacks, and most of the money is in areas where emotions run high. Changes in population demographics directly impact the California budget. Thus, as part of the budget guidance, the Department of Finance provides population growth estimates by age bracket for the budget year and a book of price inflation estimates.

Compounding the budget equation is the fact that when times get bad, caseloads get higher. As revenues fall, demands for services increase. Moreover, many of these demands in health and welfare are backed by the force of law because they are entitlements or legally mandated payments. Here is a budget that is arguably 92 percent mandated and tied by law into doing more when times are bad. The budget is also dominated by cost-of-living adjustments. Many of these adjustments are statutory; some are discretionary in the sense that the percentage given may change, but the expectation is that a cost-of-living adjustment will be given. For example, over 55 percent of the general fund increase from FY1984 and FY1985 was mandated by cost-of-living adjustments in health and welfare and K–12 education and civil servant and university employee pay raises, with percentages ranging from 3 to 10 percent.[6] Even within this seemingly mechanical environment, however, choices must be made. For example, the budget begins with the base year adjusted for price increases. Departments may take a fixed percentage as stipulated by the economic studies group in the Department of Finance, or they may follow a guide list by category. In 1985 this price list showed a range of over twenty points: heating oil increases were estimated at a 3.1 percent increase and laundry price increases at one of the state hospitals at 24 cents a pound. Since not everything increases at 5 percent, agencies may seek to take an across-the-board rate that benefits them.[7]

THE MAJOR PLAYERS

The Department of Finance is the governor's budgetmaker. It has responsibilities for budget formulation and analysis, budget implementation, and revenue estimation. It also provides estimates of population growth for caseload-driven functions and estimates of price inflation for components of programs so affected. Earlier examples ranged from periodicals to a pound of laundry. It is the central control agency, and the expectations placed on it are very high. Although it must routinely process a great deal of paper, it meets most expectations for analysis. It does, of course, see the budget through the governor's eyes. That is its job. Analysts cite key skills such as communications skills, listening, and writing, particularly in doing bill analysis. There are seventy to eighty budget analysts in the Department of Finance. For roughly eight weeks they work seven days a week twice a year—in October through December and again in April through June. Their slow months tend to be February and July.

The governor's involvement in the budget process varies. In December the governor spends two weeks of five-hour days on the budget. In 1984 this meant reviewing two issue notebooks of some 650 pages. This concentrated period of time represents a colossal amount of the governor's time. Governor George Deukmejian had a reputation for always being prepared and for having looked at the issue books in advance. Jerry Brown, the previous governor, was said to have paid attention the first two years, then only focused on pet projects, a profile not unlike that of many presidents who find the budget filled with intractable issues. The governor also looks very carefully at all legislative augmentations—that is, what the legislature adds to the budget. The governor spends approximately a week working up his or her vetoes when the legislature finally sends the chief executive the budget bill. The present governor, being more conservative than the legislature, has used the veto frequently in his two terms, whereas the previous governor did not use it a lot.

The governor has a good reputation for absorbing information quickly, for growing as a technician, for arguing on both sides of an issues, for not making snap decisions, and for giving budget people the time they need with him.

The legislature basically defers decisions on the budget to the Assembly Ways and Means Committee and the Senate Finance Committee. Most of their work is done by subcommittees. William Hamm[8] suggests that California's legislature has effected two dramatic changes in the last decade: (1) the election of legislators who had previous experience working for the legislature in a staff capacity—perhaps a third of the group—and (2) the increase in legislative staff. The Office of Legislative Analyst was the only legislative staff until the late 1960s. Today committees are served by highly capable staff. Even the minority members have staff. Hamm believes that policymaking has become more complicated, since staff spend more time working with staff.[9]

One principal committee staffer, called a consultant in California, has characterized the legislature as an independent legislature that takes a close look at the governor's budget. Exceptions to the budget have to be negotiated with the legislature, and the legislature insures that the governor cannot spend money he does not have. Technical data analysis is performed in the subcommittee hearings, and although some items are put in the budget on the floor, most budget issues are shaped in subcommittee hearings.

The Office of Legislative Analyst has an outstanding reputation in Sacramento and nationwide for analytical staff work. It produces (1) a detailed analysis of the governor's budget, identifying issues, analyzing facts, and making recommendations; (2) an analysis of every piece of legislation that would have a fiscal effect if enacted—some 3,500 bills in 1985; (3) and, finally, a written analysis of all measures proposed for the state ballot like Proposition 13, the property tax freeze.

The Office of Legislative Analyst employs seventy to eighty budget analysts. Their tasks range from computing workload adjustments to focusing on broad policy issues—for example, future consequences of the fact that the prison system is growing faster than state revenues are growing. As Hamm says, "Broader issues such as this are very important to address when there still is time for making changes in the underlying trend."[10]

Hamm emphasizes that analysts must take an analytical approach to the world and be tough minded; at the same time they must be willing to listen and be convinced by a good case. The analyst must be an excellent communicator—able to "distill months of effort into a paragraph or page that is easy for a decision-maker to understand."[11] The analyst must be able to think on her feet and be able to give an answer when asked, rather than providing an answer later, after the opportunity to shape policy has passed. Analysts believe a timely good answer is preferable to the perfect answer too late.

Watching subcommittee hearings makes it obvious that legislative analysts have done their homework.[12] Their recommendations range from the broad to the specific. For example, in one department the analyst recommended adding an EDP position and had detailed knowledge of the job to be done. In another the analyst and the agency had apparently conferred before the hearing, because they were able to agree on a numerical discrepancy between the budget bills and the budget itself. In another hearing, the analyst chided the agency for "not doing what we said last year," as he pointed out that their reimbursement was understated by some $53,000 and their workload was less than projected. Thus, he recommended that six vacant positions be dropped. In some cases the hearing becomes a subtle joust between the Department of Finance analyst and the analyst from the Office of the Legislative Analyst. In this way issues are exposed, mistakes aired, and viewpoints expressed. Because it serves everyone, the Legislative Analyst Office is able to raise questions about everything, from the most routine to the most powerful. Executive branch work has to be analytically sound, and the taxpayer is well served since there is an organization that acts as a brake or a buffer on spending.

The main point of the legislative budget process is to move the budget to conference committee. Conference committees are typically small—perhaps six members, with four from the majority and two from the minority party. They meet in an intense format: six days a week from 8:00 A.M. to 12 midnight; they may even take meals together. There are rigid rules about who attends. There is one staff person for each member allowed, and secrecy provisions govern the process. One representative speaks for each of the following groups: committee lawyers, Legislative Analyst, Department of Finance, Senior Committee staff. Hundreds of issues are aired, and all must be resolved and an official record made of the decision. Next, the Conference Committee report is sent to each house where it must be passed by a two-thirds vote. Then it is sent to the governor for a signature and line-item vetoes which he exercises against legislative positions with which he disagrees.

THE FISCAL CLIMATE

State budgeting in California is dominated by incremental change, accommodation to fluctuating revenues and a deteriorating fiscal situation in the early 1980s, and the long-term impact of the local government property tax freeze. For three years in a row the budget showed a constant dollar decrease, averaging a negative 4 percent from FY1981 through FY1984. In real dollars the budget hovered around $21.5 billion from 1981 through 1984. Per capita spending decreased steadily from 1981 through 1984.[13] The impact of Proposition 13 which limited local property taxes was an extreme shock for the state budget. In FY1978–1979 California state expenditures increased 25 percent on a per capita basis in constant dollars.[14]

Although California is not a poor state, the period of the late 1970s and the early 1980s gave rise to high uncertainty and a pattern of continuous budgeting and repeated and incorrect forecasts of revenues and expenditures as resource uncertainty prevented orderly planning and budgeting. In addition to limits on revenues and growth, California was also affected by a recessionary economy at the same time it decided to index its income tax. The result was unpredictable revenues and revenue shortfalls while obvious needs had to be met in a process of continuous rebudgeting with no fiscal cushion.

The 1982 budget was balanced by a series of ad hoc actions, mainly by one-time tax increases or decreases in the money passed from state to local governments. One-time revenue increases totaled $514 million; one-time expenditure cuts totaled $208 million. The 1982 budget was reopened in the fall because a deficit threatened once more. The governor was forced to implement a 2 percent across-the-board cut and to delay capital projects. November brought further deterioration, and the state borrowed over $900 million to meet general fund obligations. In January the legislature, in special session, enacted an accelerated withholding schedule to speed up revenue collections. February saw the enactment of increased penalties for late tax filers and a speedup of corporate sales tax collections. Another measure cut aid to families with dependent children. Still another bill cut $107 million in programs, and raided special funds for their revenues. Capital construction and energy and resource projects were again reduced. But the crisis was not over yet. The legislature had to be reconvened again and pass one more budget-saving bill, worth $481 million. The bill was an amalgamation of one-time cuts, pension deferrals, sales tax collection accelerations, and suspension of cost-of-living adjustments. The last move saved about $350 million and affected the first three months of the following fiscal year. The day the bill was signed the governor froze all state personnel actions that had fiscal consequences. The budget had been saved.

This series of crisis-containing actions had done nothing, however, to avert a crisis in the next fiscal year. After a series of negotiations, the governor was finally able to strike a balance for FY1983 at a current dollar level less than the previous year by cutting aid to cities, increasing student fees at all state colleges and universities, eliminating all state employee salary increases, and cutting a state medical insurance welfare program by about $400 million. These had longer term consequences, but they appeared at the time as a series of ad hoc decisions designed to keep the budget afloat until the economy turned and preserved the narrow ground of political consensus.[15] What now seems like a relatively quiet period in California budget history is indeed the calm after the storm. In 1987 the state had a surplus for two years in a row, and the governor decided to return that surplus to the taxpayers, despite vehement protests from local school groups and the state superintendent of education that the surplus should be used for local education. Other groups also made calls for their share of the surplus. In the end the governor won, but the debate was so bitter that the budget was not passed on time. The governor signed it on July 7, and the surplus issue was decided later in the fall as California gave back part of its surplus in late 1987. In the spring of 1988 the rest of its surplus simply evaporated under the impress of unforeseen economic conditions

The governor's item vetoes of the state superintendent of education budget— about 10 percent of the total—were seen as punishment for the superintendent's speaking out on the surplus issues.[16] Nonetheless although the governor and the legislature differed over spending priorities, these later years were a period of relative tranquility and not fiscal crisis adaptations.

HEALTH AND WELFARE FUNCTIONS AND EDUCATION

Health and welfare functions and education make up about 85 percent of the state budget. They are basically driven by population, enrollments, and caseload. The secretary of health and welfare is responsible for caseload-budget-driven programs that range from social services through public health, aging, mental health, and aid to families with dependent children. Many federal requirements impact the budgets of these programs. Estimating costs is a problem because most of these programs are entitlements and are set by law. If estimates of costs or units of service are incorrect, a deficiency will occur, and perhaps a deficiency appropriation will have to be passed. A small estimation error can lead to a large dollar effect since the population is large and benefits have to be paid. Court cases also have impacts: one case alone cost the state $50 million.

In 1986 California was the only state that had automatic cost-of-living adjustment for welfare recipients. Most recipients get benefits as entitlements; to change those costs the law must be changed. In the discretionary programs, such as mental health, alcohol rehabilitation, and job welfare, clients and their associated interest groups resist cuts. The governor's last review in May gives the department one last chance to check the present-year indicators against the budget year, which will begin in two months, to see if any drastic modifications are needed. History with the program this year is an aid to calculation for the next year.

Education makes up a little over half the state budget. It has been one of the present governor's high priorities. Moreover, the educational establishment is not "beholden" to the governor in the same way as the secretary of health and welfare is. If California's state universities get cut, they go to the legislature to get the cuts restored, whereas health and welfare cannot easily go to the legislature, since their secretary is appointed by the governor.

If the sense of fiscal control is different, the decision criteria are just as concrete. Education budgets are driven by average daily attendance, full-time equivalent positions, and workload. Price inflation is also a crucial budget factor for the education budget. Thus, the price inflation guidelines issued with the budget letter are an important tool for this area. In 1986, for example, price inflation for periodicals was estimated at 17.6 percent and serials at 20.7 percent. In a lean year the university system may have to absorb the cost of inflation.

In general, in a lean year, where education has come up with a rational budget but revenues are inadequate, cuts have to be made. Since cost-of-living adjustments are easiest to revise, they are cut first. Cuts are then made in new programs, followed by program expansions before going into the base. Base evaluation takes more time. In education, workload increases are automatically included; new programs and changes in program intensity are therefore the most vulnerable. Price adjustments are the easiest to make; the more difficult decisions involve deciding on new programs where no one can tell one way or the other and turning back "turkey" proposals that have a lot of political support. Typical issues in the education area involve student fees, faculty salaries, facility maintenance, deferred maintenance, replacement of instructional equipment, K–12 student performance on standardized tests, student aid programs, the role of the community colleges, Proposition 13, and who should now pay for what. Although the level of commitment may be altered from year to year, the demand for service will not disappear.

SUMMARY

California is like a giant in shackles, but the shackles are of its own choosing—caseload, enrollment, population. The budget tends to change incrementally with the economy since the factors that make it up change with the economy in a countercyclical fashion or with demography as more or fewer people go to schools or universities. Although California does spend on infrastructure and other functions, the operating budget is dominated by a commitment to caring for people. The political argument between left and right is the argument between how much care should be given and how much people should be left to do for themselves. Even here the range of choice seems narrow. Whereas the federal government is a distant checkwriter that provides defense and audits tax evaders, the state is an intimate partner in the daily life of its citizens. The issues in that partnership surface in an annual budget process governed by incremental rhythms safeguarded by professionalized politicians from the governor through the legislature and their professional staffs.

3

Illinois: Executive Reform and Fiscal Condition

Irene S. Rubin, Jack King, Steven C. Wagner, and Ellen M. Dran

THE ILLINOIS BUDGET PROCESS

Illinois is a strong executive state. The power of the governor over the budget includes not only a line-item veto and a reduction veto, but also an amendatory veto. Earlier descriptions of budgeting in Illinois as primarily reflecting legislative desires to deliver benefits to constituents and lacking all central policy direction are no longer true. The governor's powers have been used not only to curtail legislative excesses and keep the budget in balance, but also to impose the governor's policies on the budget. This chapter discusses the evolution of budgeting in Illinois, to reflect the origins of the current configuration of power. It then shows the current process, emphasizing the relative power of the governor and the legislature. The chapter concludes with an evaluation of the state's fiscal condition.

The Executive Budget: An Evolutionary Process

Thomas Anton's well-known case study of budgeting in Illinois described in rich detail the budgetary process in Illinois for 1963.[1] His description of budgeting in the 1960s was incrementalist. The Illinois governor had an executive budget, but he had limited power over the executive branch, budgets did not deal with policy issues, and there was no public debate on the issues. Review of agency budget submissions was carried out by a Budgetary Commission. The composition of the Budgetary Commission was a legislative power elite. The motivations of the members of this commission were often geared toward delivering a share of the tangible benefits to their districts. The procedure for review of budget proposals was unlikely to produce adherence to an overall plan.

Although Anton's study of Illinois in 1963 suggests considerable stability in budgetary process, budgeting processes had changed considerably both before and after this study. Looking back to the 1800s, the Illinois constitution of 1848 greatly limited the power of the legislature.[2] As the power of the legislature was curtailed, the power of the governor was somewhat increased. The governor was given a veto, but only a simple majority was required to overturn.

The 1870 constitution gave a stronger veto power to the governor, requiring a two-thirds majority to overturn. The number of private and special laws and the governor's apparent inability to control them helped strengthen his veto powers.[3]

Another major change took place in the early 1900s. Governor Frank Lowden proposed more centralization, recommending departments headed by single persons rather than committees, and he included the executive budget as a cornerstone of reform. He proposed identical accounting systems for every department, a central purchasing agency, and competitive bidding. Lowden believed that industrialization had created new centers of power, such as banks and corporations, but their growth had thrust on government the unfamiliar role of guardian of the common weal against mighty and conflicting forces. Power alone could check power. The governor should have ample discretion and funds to carry out his duty. His proposals were passed speedily by the legislature in 1917. They reduced the number of departments to nine, creating a new Department of Finance. Lowden created cabinet government.[4]

The reforms of 1917 brought tax reduction and a virtual end to calls on the legislature for extra appropriations to cover administrative deficits. These things worked in favor of keeping the reforms.

The next major change was the creation of the Illinois Budgetary Commission in 1937 by Governor Henry Horner, to study revenue problems. He created this committee when his proposed tax increase (3 percent on utility sales) was defeated. Although its initial charter did not include any budgeting functions, it came to review department requests and give informal advice to the governor. The committee included the governor and legislative elites and, hence, became a liaison between the governor and the legislature. Its raison d'être was to give the governor advice on spending proposals. When governors chose not to use it, it had no legitimate source of power. If the governor accepted its recommendations, legislative/executive cooperation was established.

In the mid-1950s, as a result of a financial scandal, the committee was given more responsibility and a staff and resources were assigned to it. By 1969, however, the governor, with the reluctant consent of the legislature, abolished the commission and set up an executive Bureau of the Budget. Each governor has strengthened the bureau since its founding.

In the mid-1960s the legislature began to reform itself. It created a bipartisan staffing system, as well as standing committees for policy development and oversight, and it initiated annual and interim sessions. This period of reform culminated in the constitutional convention of 1970 and a new constitution for the state. The 1970 constitution added a reduction and an amendatory veto to the governor's veto, giving the governor tremendous power to reduce the budget and implement his own budget request. The constitution helped to integrate the executive branch but took only moderate steps in that direction. It eliminated only one of the elected executive offices, but made the governor and lieutenant governor partners. The constitution tried to balance the powers of the governor by increasing somewhat the power of the legislature. The auditor of public accounts was replaced by the comptroller, who provided an alternative channel for public accountability on matters of finance. In addition, the constitution gave postaudit powers to the legislature.

In the 1970s efforts to implement zero-based budgeting (ZBB) and other techniques to make budgeting more policy oriented and less incremental and across-the-board usually failed. Under Governor Richard Ogilvie (1968–1972), however, the Bureau of the Budget (BoB) got to make some policy. "Ogilvie's BoB and the often intimidating 'whiz kids' who ran it were usually at the center of, and the source of, major controversies over State expenditures and their policy implications. For the first time, Illinois had an executive budget process and a staff to run it, which could accommodate serious analysis of issues, alternatives, spending levels and finances."[5]

Ogilvie's successor, Dan Walker (1972–1976) reined in BoB staff, arguing they should "help solve problems and achieve financial accountability, but, under no circumstances, were they to speak for him or to make decisions on matters of program and policy."[6] Walker, doubting the usefulness of the planning capacity built into BoB under Ogilvie, largely dismantled it.[7] Under Governor James Thompson (1976–) BoB remains fairly strong, with considerable policy as well as budgetary power.

Contemporary Budgeting: The Governor's Tools of Control

The governor, rather than the departments, dominates the budget preparation stage in Illinois. He maintains that control over the departments after the budget has been presented in order to prevent his proposals from being undermined or overturned. When his proposals are cut back or the legislature presents alternatives, he can, and often does, use his extensive veto powers. The governor also has considerable control over budget implementation.

The Bureau of the Budget is a major tool of control over the departments during the budget preparation stage. It is organized into three divisions: the fiscal analysis division, which is responsible for monitoring state income and expenses; the program division, which analyzes state programs under the various categorical subheadings; and the planning division, which is responsible for information gathering and analysis and acts as a clearinghouse for intergovernmental grants.

BoB sends the agencies a specific reporting format for submitting requests. During this first phase BoB has the most control over the budget. In dealing with the FY1987 budget, the process began with a BoB staff retreat in September to begin looking at budget issues.[8] In October, agency heads submitted preliminary budget proposals to BoB, which according to Director Robert Mandeville "are always too high."[9] The preliminary budget proposals include information on how the agency would reduce its programs if it received less funding that the prior year, the cost implications of new program initiatives, requests by or requirements of the agency during the upcoming fiscal period in some type of priority order, and any special or significant issues, trends, or problems that require attention by the governor. Agency directors must not only justify fiscal and programmatic increases to BoB, but also give philosophical reasons for program initiatives. If these proposals are not consistent with BoB's philosophy, they may be eliminated.[10]

There is, however, some give and take between the agencies and BoB. After the forms have been submitted, a process to resolve disagreements occurs. Agency heads have some limited ability to appeal decisions made by the BoB director. However, frequent requests to overturn BoB decisions signal to the governor the agency's unwillingness to get on the team.[11]

The entire budgetary process is kept confidential until after the governor delivers his budget message in March. Once the budget becomes a public document, agency staff have the opportunity to lobby for additional programs or resources.[12] The governor's office maintains control of agency lobbying through the use of agency liaisons. Appointees of the governor, these liaisons are responsible for managing the agency legislative activity. According to the employee handbook of the Illinois Criminal Justice Information Authority, the legislative liaison is responsible for explaining and representing the Authority's position both on bills recommended by the Authority and on bills affecting criminal justice information policies. According to the public information officer for the Office of InterAgency Cooperation, the legislative liaison has the responsibility for managing the agencies' relationship with the legislature, as long as there is no conflict with the governor's overall policy agenda. Although the governor is able to monitor the agencies' legislative activities, he is not able to curb them completely. Agency staff members still lobby, overtly and covertly, through professional associations and interest groups.

While the budget is being evaluated by the legislature, much of the formal and informal negotiations occur among the various players. Legislative priorities may differ from gubernatorial priorities. Partisan agendas regarding fiscal support or manner of expenditures are negotiated. If the results of these negotiations are not to the governor's liking, he can use his veto powers either to reject legislation (ordinary veto), portions of legislation (item veto), or rewrite parts of legislation to conform to his goals (amendatory veto). The most powerful of his tools at this point in the process is the amendatory veto, added to his powers in the 1970 constitution.

Under this process, the governor may return a bill together with specific recommendations for change to the house in which it originated. The bill shall be considered in the same manner as a vetoed bill, but the specific recommendations may be accepted by a record vote of a majority of the members elected to each house.[13]

The original intent of the amendatory veto was primarily one of procedural expedience; specifically, it sought to provide a vehicle for simplified technical change. In practice, the uses for the amendatory veto include the following: to correct mechanical errors due to lack of coordination between the two houses; to correct typographical errors; to coordinate separate amendments to the same sections of a statute; to allow for substantive changes in a bill; to make a bill conform to other definitions and uses; to create order out of chaos; to correct abuses of the conference committee by allowing the amendatory veto to act as a device for passing important legislation, or to delete or add important sections to bills produced by conference committee; and to effect major change in a bill that the governor may not approve of, that is, to sponsor a rewritten bill to advance the governor's legislative policies.[14]

The amendatory veto as an administrative tool was used approximately two hundred times from 1971 until 1975. During that period, the Illinois General Assembly accepted the amendatory veto 75 percent of the time, even though 130 of those amendatory vetoes dealt with substantive policy changes. During those early years, six of the bills were overridden by the general assembly, while an additional forty-one died owing to a lack of a majority to accept the governor's recommendations.[15]

During his first three years in office, Governor James Thompson authored more vetoes than his two predecessors wrote in six years.[16] In the first six years Thompson vetoed 335 bills. This use of the amendatory veto to effect major change or to advance his own legislative policies led to an October 1983 debate (on Senate Joint Resolution 2) on a need for a constitutional amendment limiting the amendatory veto to technical corrections.[17] It also led to a legislative council study of the 161 amendatory vetoes in 1983. House speaker Michael Madigan convened a task force to examine and recommend changes to the amendatory veto in June 1984.

Concern with the use of the amendatory veto for his purpose centered on representative fairness. Unlike the legislative process, which occurs in the open, the use of the amendatory veto happens in private and allows the governor and those with access to him to rewrite not only the principle of the bill, but also the details. Despite the legislature's discontent, the governor's power remains intact.

The governor's control extends to the period of budget execution. After the governor signs final legislation, the agencies must file a quarterly expenditure plan. These plans force the agencies to refine their budgets in a way that is manageable and can be monitored. Budgets that are not expended in the quarter planned are lapsed and are not available for use later in the fiscal year. The lapsing of allotted but unspent funds prevents the buildup of excess funds at the end of the fiscal year when heavy expenditures would otherwise create annualization problems for the following fiscal year. Generally, annual spending is limited to 98 percent of the appropriation. The remaining 2 percent is placed in reserve.

Contemporary Budgeting: The Legislative Role

On the first Wednesday of March, the governor formally presents the proposed budget to the legislature. Part of the formal presentation is the introduction of approximately eighty budget bills. Each bill represents a spending plan for an individual executive agency, for example, the Department of Transportation, and for ancillary institutions, such as state colleges and universities.

The department's budget bills combine elements of program budgeting and line-item budgeting. Each department's bill represents a spending plan for the department's specific programs, such as roads, bridges, and highways, and is broken down into line items, such as facility costs, personnel, and travel. The bills are prepared by BoB and approved by the Legislative Reference Bureau.[18] Although the governor is clearly in command of determining an agency's budget, the legislature is not completely locked out of the initial preparation. Close allies of the governor in both legislative chambers have access and can succeed in lobbying the governor on behalf of a special project or for an increase in a department's operating budget, especially if the legislative revenue estimates are higher than BoB's and there is substantial constituency or interest group support. Committee or floor activities are the only options available to those legislators who are not close allies of the governor. The governor has allies in both parties.

Of the eighty budget bills, approximately half are referred to the House of Representatives and half are referred to the Senate. The governor identifies individual legislators to sponsor the bills. The bills' sponsors in the Senate are of the same party as the governor (currently Republican), even though the opposition party holds the majority of the seats. In the House, the majority party (presently Democrats) ruled that it alone could introduce budget bills. Nevertheless, the governor has been able to identify allies who will introduce his spending plans. Once the bills are introduced, they are automatically referred to committee for review, analysis, and possible revisions.

Each chamber has two standing appropriations committees, each with approximately twenty members. Individual members request seats on the appropriations committees, and they are appointed by party leaders, not the leadership of each house. The selection procedure allows the committees to reflect individual members' goals while ensuring that the committees are highly partisan. The jurisdictions of appropriations I and II in both chambers are fixed roughly according to capital and service expenditures.

Each appropriations committee must act on about twenty budget bills, almost regardless of the substantive nature of the bill. At this point in the process, each bill is considered independent of all other spending and revenue-raising efforts. Near the end of the legislative session (June 30), the spending bills are brought together and considered in conjunction with available revenues. Party leadership and committee staff bring together the separate spending and taxing resolutions into a single state budget.

Once the governor's spending proposals are referred to committee, the legislature can initiate changes and adjustments. If the governor's opponents do not favor the original bills, contrary budget bills are introduced. As a rule, the opposition bills offer incremental adjustments to the governor's spending plan. Changes made in the governor's budget bills reflect the goals of committee and chamber members and party leadership, the revenue estimates of the Economic and Fiscal Commission, and the input of lobby groups that represent executive agencies. The impact of aggregate anticipated revenues and the governor's initial spending proposals clearly guide committee deliberations.

During each of the last fifteen years, the governor's aggregate spending plan has been modified an average of 5 percent. The governor's budget proposals were reduced during severe economic downturns. In more affluent years, the spending proposals were increased. Among both Republican and Democratic legislators, the notion of economizing prevails, which clearly reflects member reelection goals. Raising revenues (especially through taxes) and expenditures has spelled electoral defeat for many Illinois politicians.

When reductions are deemed necessary, the House tends to cut according to its assessment of the worth of each program expenditure, whereas the Senate tends to reduce aggregate expenditures by a set percentage. During the last two weeks of the session (June 15 to June 30), differences between the House and Senate on specific spending proposals are resolved in conference committee. Before the close of each session, both chambers must approve all budget bills. Final approval generally occurs with remarkable speed and little debate. The members of both chambers assume that the appropriations and conference committees have resolved all problems and differences, which allows final floor approval to become almost perfunctory.

The sponsors of the governor's budget bills and the sponsors of the opposition spending plans guide the bills through the decision-making process in committee, on the floor, and, if necessary, in conference committee.[19] Each of the four appropriations committees is assigned partisan staff that has the responsibility to analyze the budget bills, prepare written reviews, and inform committee members of problems and opportunities with the bills.[20] The staff tends to be loyal to the committee chairs and party leadership, facilitating party control over information and committee decision making. Once the staff reviews the bills, hearings are held on each bill.[21] This is the first and only formal opportunity for affected individuals, groups, and executive agencies (working through client lobbies) to argue for an increase beyond the governor's proposals or to justify past efforts to avoid a decreased largess.

The localism of individual legislators in the General Assembly is clearly evident during committee hearings. Committee members tend to center their attention on issues that affect their districts and their substantive policy concerns. Hearings for each bill are short and usually conclude within ten minutes. Committee members yield to the knowledge and wishes of the committee chair, the bill sponsor, and the staff.[22]

Every attempt is made to refer the bills out of committee with unanimous approval. Less than unanimous approval often results in questioning and debate on the floor. If excessive floor debate occurs, committee members recognize that the power they enjoy over the appropriations process will be forfeited. Furthermore, owing to the time constraints imposed on the process, coupled with the multitude of regional, party, racial, and ethnic divisions that exist in Illinois,[23] the committees must produce budget bills that include the input of all relevant interests or the process will break down. Unanimous approval of budget bills in committee is a way to show to both chambers and the governor that all relevant interests have been heard and accounted for in the final version of the budget.

Once the General Assembly approves the budget bills, they are forwarded to the governor for approval or veto. Although the whole process is loose and somewhat unorganized, communication and cooperation are clearly evident. Party leadership in the legislature works closely with the governor to ensure that the budget bills are either approved or minimally subjected to the governor's line or reduction veto.[24] Here again, it becomes clear that the governor has immense power in the budget process. The governor provides a road map for the legislature to follow and then has wide use of the item and reduction vetoes to reinstate his priorities if the legislature makes changes. Unless the governor and the legislature reach agreement prior to bill passage, the legislature can become a significant loser. A three-fifths vote is required to override an item veto, and a simple majority vote is necessary to override a reduction veto. Considering the slim majority of seats held by the Democratic party, it can be virtually impossible to override a veto.

The governor's power exceeds that of the legislature in budgetary decision making. The governor initiates the budgetary process by proposing a plan of expenditures. The legislature utilizes the governor's proposals as its primary decision-making tool. If the legislature changes the governor's spending plan, the governor can restore his proposals through the item and reduction veto. The budget, therefore, represents the governor's version of what needs to be accomplished in Illinois. This is not to say the legislature is powerless, just that the governor dominates the process from beginning to end.

FISCAL CONDITION

On June 30, 1985, the fiscal year ended in the state of Illinois with a record year-end balance of $479 million. Some politicians soon followed the announcement of this large surplus with a call for tax reductions. The governor's plans for a major infrastructure spending program were met with enthusiasm. By the end of the next fiscal year, however, the balance was down to $288 million. Less than a year after that, the governor was calling for more than $1 billion in increased state taxes. How could such a rosy picture turn so rapidly to gloom?

The answer lies in the way Illinois indicates its fiscal status. The commonly used year-end balance is seriously flawed. Alternative measures suggest that the fiscal status of state government is not so rosy and is probably worsening.

The Bottom Line in Illinois

The most important users of fiscal information in a democratic system—generalist legislators and even more generalist citizens/taxpayers—usually want a single "bottom-line" indicator. Consequently, like other governmental units, Illinois tries to sum up its fiscal status with a year-end, bottom-line figure, the balance available in the state's general fund.[25] The available balance is the cash on hand at any time. As such, it has a fiscal role to play by providing information on whether the state can pay its upcoming bills, but, as a fiscal status indicator, it can be misleading for several reasons. For one thing, a surplus or deficit may merely be the result of random ups and downs or of idiosyncratic events at the time the balance is reported. The FY1985 "surplus" in Illinois was at least partly the result of one-time occurrences as the state benefited from "an unusually high level of nonrecurring revenues."[26] A reference to that surplus in isolation from this consideration dramatically distorts the status of the state's fiscal health.

As a cash balance in a fund accounting system, the available balance is susceptible to administrative manipulation. Like most states, Illinois requires a balanced budget. At the end of the year, this is determined by whether the available balance shows a surplus or a deficit. Because of this purpose, there is an incentive to "play games" with that balance.[27] The balance can be built up by delaying payments to vendors, by delaying transfers into other funds, by speeding up collections, or by adding borrowed funds. It can be lowered by speeding up payments out or transfers to other funds, and by delaying collections or transfers into the General Fund. In sum, "When an administration commits itself to a specific end-of-year available balance, it can manipulate the revenue processing system to bring about an available balance consistent with its prediction."[28]

One would expect a good indicator to point to deficits as well as to surpluses. But the available balance is always positive. This happens because Illinois is on a cash accounting basis for receipts, and any cash on hand goes into the available balance, even if its source is a loan. In some years the "surplus" in the end-of-year available balance has existed only because of borrowed money in the account.

Another problem with indicating fiscal status with the year-end available balance is a possible padding of the financial condition by including the first $200 million. The comptroller considers that amount necessary to allow for cash flow and economic uncertainty. If that $200 million is "not there" in the sense of not being available for allocation, then the state has really been in a deficit position on numerous occasions when a surplus was reported. Since FY1980, the available balance has been below $200 million on three occasions. Prior to FY1980, $100 million was considered the necessary cushion, and the available balance was below this amount in five out of the eighteen budgets between 1954 and 1979.

Finally, the available balance at the end of the year does not give an accurate accounting of the dollar amount available for allocation for another reason. Like revenues, expenditures are reported on a cash basis, which means that the available balance as reported does not account for liabilities. This permits the presentation of an inflated picture of fiscal status at any given time. Nonetheless, disbursements during July, August, and September for liabilities incurred in the previous fiscal year are credited to that year's budget. This is referred to as lapse-period spending. The available balance at the end of a fiscal year, then, always has obligations against it. A more accurate picture of the state's fiscal position would take account of these accruals. For instance, in FY1985, the record surplus of $479 million was, in fact, virtually wiped out by the $450 million in lapse-period spending.

Alternative Concepts

It should now be clear that, as the indicator of the state's financial health for an entire year, the story told by the end-of-year available balance can be misleading. Because the end-of-year balance represents just a single point in time, it does not necessarily reflect the typical cash-flow position over the whole year. The average available balance can be looked at instead.

The Average Available Balance

It turns out that, from 1954 through 1984, the average end-of-year figure ($202 million) overestimated the state's average end-of-month cash status ($180 million) by 12 percent.

A good indicator should not only accurately portray the current status, but should also point to future fiscal trends. The fiscal stress experienced by the state of Illinois in FY1983, for example, would have been better predicted by an average available balance indicator than it was by the end-of-year balance. Although there had been a precipitous drop in the year-end balance from 1980 to 1981, that balance then appeared to stabilize in 1982. The average end-of-month balance, however, had continued the steep decline in 1982, better presaging the problems of 1983. Using the average instead of the year-end available balance gives a more useful picture of the state's fiscal status, but it does not account for lapse-period spending. The budgetary balance, provided by the Comptroller's Office, does not include this spending.

The Budgetary Balance

Under the budgetary balance concept (which is modified accrual accounting), fiscal status is reported as the available balance minus lapse-period spending. The budgetary balance tells a radically different story than the available balance concept. The mean budgetary balance since 1955 is negative, −$2.7 million, compared with an average monthly available balance of $180 million and an average end-of-year available balance of $202 million. A graphic comparison of the average available balance and the budgetary balance vividly displays the different fiscal stories these two concepts tell. (See Figure 3.1.) The positive slope for the average available balance implies that Illinois is building up its surplus over time. The budgetary balance, however, shows a clear and precipitous decline in the state's fiscal health.

The political importance of these alternative concepts is clearly reflected in the Illinois governor's change in 1978 from reporting the budgetary balance at

Figure 3.1

Average Available and Budgetary Balances: Fiscal Years 1955 to 1984, Current Dollars

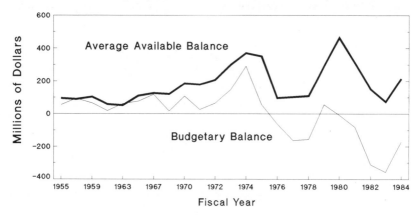

Avg. available balance slope = 7.6   Budgetary balance slope = –13.9

year-end to using the available balance. This maneuver enabled him to define a surplus into existence, following two years of negative budgetary balances.

A Fiscal Picture Over Time

Even using an improved indicator, trying to assess the state's fiscal health on an annual basis, presents some problems. There is nothing inherently logical about a period of twelve months for showing a state's fiscal situation. In addition, the year-end balance often includes borrowed funds which are made up in the next fiscal year. Looking at the budget over time averages out these borrowing and paying back situations to give a clearer overall picture of the state's fiscal status. Given the governor's importance in the executive budget process, it seems useful to look at the moving average of both the budgetary and the average available balance over four-year periods, the length of the gubernatorial term.

The four-year cycle smoothes out the curves considerably (see Figure 3.2), but the picture of the state's fiscal status worsens for both balances. For the average available balance, the slope is still positive but not as steep; for the budgetary balance concept, the steepness of the negative slope increases.

The Surplus in Real Terms

Viewing the balance as a moving average improves our understanding of the state's fiscal status. What really counts, however, is not dollar amounts but purchasing power. The average monthly available balance for the years 1954 to 1984 is only $158 million in constant 1972 dollars, or 12 percent less than the current

Figure 3.2
Average Available and Budgetary Balances over Moving Four-Year Average: Fiscal Years 1955 to 1984, Current Dollars

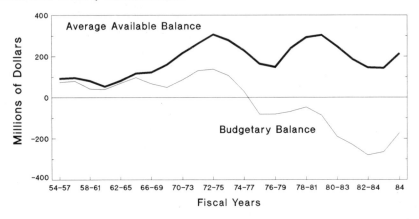

Avg. available balance slope = 6.4   Budgetary balance slope = 16.0

dollar mean of $180 million. Since 1970, the constant dollar mean has been relatively even less—$161 million compared with $229 million in current dollars, a decline of 30 percent. There has been a distinct decrease in the purchasing power of the Illinois surplus, especially since 1974.

CONCLUSION

The power of the governor in budget preparation has been extraordinarily strong in Illinois. The state also has a constitutionally mandated balanced budget. However, the state has not avoided executive manipulations of the budget balance and has not achieved a really balanced budget. The finances of the state have been deteriorating in recent years, at least in part because of a declining economy. The agricultural sector remains weak, as in the rest of the nation, and Illinois shares in the economic decline of heavy industry in the Midwest. Budget reforms to strengthen the governor have had relatively little effect on this long-term trend. Moreover, when the governor misrepresented the state's fiscal health, he was among the first to try to take advantage of an illusionary budget balance by spending on a capital distribution program that would enhance his political popularity. Pork barrel projects are not limited to the legislature; curbing the legislature and creating superpowerful executives is not a formula for fiscal health. In fact, one element in Illinois which was never effectively reformed, the independent election of some of the cabinet officers, is responsible for part of the openness of the budget process. Without the independently elected comptroller, who is often of the opposite party to the governor, the governor's distortions of the state's fiscal health might be less transparent.

The period of reform in the second decade of this century brought with it more efficiency and lower tax rates. However, continued increases in the governor's powers and the continued relative weakness of the state legislature have not had positive effects on the state's fiscal condition.

4

Ohio: Impact of Economic and Political Conditions

SUSAN A. MACMANUS

The need for more sophisticated policy analysis and for rational approaches to budget formation and execution intensified in the late 1970s and early 1980s as Ohio and its local governments experienced severe fiscal pressures to a point near bankruptcy.[1] Even though the state's books have now been balanced (and there is a substantial surplus as well as a new rainy-day fund), its economy is still pressured by the transition away from a manufacturing-dominated economy. The political reactions to these severe economic pressures explain the state's changing tax structure and its expenditure priorities as well as the adjustments to both its formal and informal budgetary processes. Moreover, Ohio's budget process is continually affected by changing political and economic climates which are themselves interrelated.

Historically, Ohio's economy has fluctuated more than the national economy.[2] The problem is that the differential is negative and widening. Three major factors have contributed to this problem: (1) a nondiversified economy, still heavily dominated by manufacturing jobs in smokestack industries; (2) a population decline, including a significant (37 percent) outmigration of the state's college graduates; and (3) a reputation as being a "bad place to do business." It is not surprising, then, that for Budget Biennium 1985–1987, the programmatic goals focused on accelerating Ohio's economic recovery, creating more jobs, improving the quality of education at all levels, and controlling the costs of running the government.[3]

Ohio's political environment has remained a competitive one as measured by levels of interparty competition.[4] The prevailing pattern has been for the balance of powers to tip slightly in favor of one party and then the other. This trend parallels basic economic trends. Democrats initially gain control when the economy has been in decline or recession. Republicans tend to gain control when it is overheated or inflationary. Predictably, the "out-party" blames the "in-party" for the prevailing economic trend.

We now look at how the budgetary process works.

THE BUDGETARY PROCESS

In the words of three-time Ohio budget director, Howard Collier, "Budgeting is more than numbers, it's people and power-oriented. . . . A state budget is a power scorecard."[5] The words reflect the informal dimension of the budgetary process which is as critical to understanding the state's budgetary process as are the formal structural and procedural characteristics. This section highlights both the formal and informal dimensions of Ohio's budgetary process.

Budget Preparation

The budget-making power of Ohio's governor is regarded as strong in comparison with that of other governors.[6] Typically, the governor's role in the budget preparation stage is to set the parameter within which the budget is prepared: Will it be a growth, no growth, or cutback budget? Will there be a tax increase? What are the high-priority policy areas? In what format will the budget be presented? Will it include line-item, goal and objective, and performance data at a detailed program and activity level? Political and economic realities of the day dictate these decisions.

Ohio's governor is heavily dependent on the forecasting staff of the Office of Budget and Management (OBM) to prepare the initial fiscal outlook for the state's next biennium. Ohio's fluctuating economy has made this task more difficult, despite staff use of more sophisticated forecasting techniques (regression and econometrics) and use of outside forecasting firms such as Chase Econometrics. Although forecasting is an ongoing OBM activity, the first "semiofficial" projections are usually transmitted to the governor around late August or early September of the even-numbered year immediately preceding the odd-numbered biennium. The governor uses these projections to formulate budget strategies.

Historically, there appears to be a partisan pattern to how governors establish their priorities. Democratic administrations have preferred a very bottom-up method. The technique commonly used is the formal Issue Paper. For example, in preparation for the executive budget for the fiscal years 1987–1989, state agencies were asked to identify and propose issues that would (1) be of high gubernatorial priority; (2) have a direct and significant impact on the budget; (3) be capable of being analyzed within a two-month time frame; (4) result in recommendations that could be implemented; and (5) be related to the implementation of the agency's strategic plan.[7] In contrast, Republican administrations (all headed by the same individual, Governor James Rhodes) have used a more centralized prioritization process, projecting priorities from the top down.

For quite some time, state agency budget submission documents have included elements of program, performance, and zero-base budgeting. The submission documents require statements of goals and objectives, workload and output measures, cost-benefit analyses, and ranking of alternatives and contingency spending plans.

The starting point for agency spending projections is the computed continued funding level calculated by the state Office of Budget and Management. This computed-continued-funding-level figure is the actual budgeted amount for the previous biennium plus an inflation factor. In other words, the most commonly used base is an actual dollar base. Seldom does the computed-continued-funding level approximate a current services base, but it would be possible during a robust, expansionary economic cycle.

The use of rationalistic elements in both the agency submission and executive budget documents has paralleled changes in the composition and professional training of OBM and Legislative Budget Office (LBO) personnel, namely, the hiring of more individuals with master's degrees in the social sciences.[8] Agency submissions are formally due to OBM no later than November 1 of the even year preceding the biennium, or on December 1, if a new governor has been elected in November.[9]

The Office of Budget and Management plays another key role in the budget preparation stage in addition to the preparation of revenue estimates, the establishment of budget submission formats, and policy development and prioritization.[10] OBM holds a series of executive budget hearings that focus "on potentially controversial items in the proposed budget and upon proposals for new, expanded, or improved program items."[11] Executive budget hearings usually begin in early November with small agencies going first. Larger agencies are intentionally scheduled for after the general election. Executive budget hearings are monitored carefully by key agency clientele groups and legislative officials, often through LBO personnel.

Following a revised revenue estimate and some last-minute budgetary adjustments, the governor formally transmits the executive budget to the General Assembly no later than four weeks after the Assembly convenes in January.

Budget Adoption

The General Assembly has formal responsibility for adopting the budget. In recent years the legislature and its budget staff have played a much stronger role in the budgetary process, most noticeably during the adoption and execution phases. This trend parallels a national trend in which fiscal pressures have been a major stimulant:[12]

States [have] found it necessary to adjust revenue estimates, reduce budgets and increase taxes several times during a year. Legislatures are increasingly reluctant to cede the authority to make such budget adjustments and their consequent policy implications to the governor and administrators. This is particularly true in states with a legislature controlled by one party and a governor from the opposite party [Ohio Senate and Governor].[13]

Richard G. Sheridan, the first director of the Legislative Budget Office, who held the position for almost ten years, has identified a number of differences that distinguish the legislature's outlook on appropriations from those of the governor and state executive agencies.[14] First, he claims that the executive branch tends to be reproductive and repetitive, and the legislature, creative, innovative, and committed to change. Second, executive branch personnel, especially agency personnel, are more permanent than legislators. This dichotomy has been minimized because of low legislative turnover rates, especially among Finance Committee members, and by a change in gubernatorial administrations. Third, the executive functions on the basis of a hierarchical organization more so than the legislature, although legislative leaders do have some influence with individual legislators. Leaders assign committee work that is often critical to constituencies served by an individual legislator and collectively adopt the budget. The executive budget, on the other hand, is unilaterally approved by the governor. This means that more bargaining, compromising, and trading-off will occur within the legislative branch. In other words, politics, more than process, dictates outcomes, and politics is never absent from the process, no matter what stage of the budget.

There is also a difference in the time frame used by decision makers in the two branches. Legislators think short term, whereas executives, namely, agency personnel, think long term. Much of this difference is attributable to the terms of office associated with each: two years for the House and four years for the Senate and the governor. Midlevel civil service agency personnel are less affected by political and election cycles, which helps explain their proclivity to think long term.

There is also a sharp contrast in the loyalties of the two branches. Sheridan found that the legislature is usually loyal to individuals, such as legislative leaders and popular individuals, whereas members of the executive branch are more loyal to the organization than to their superiors, including the governor.[15] Finally, legislators are more public relations oriented and are more prone to succumb to emotional appeals, especially with cameras whirring and the press corps present en masse during the heat of legislative budget hearings. This, too, can work to the advantage of the executive agency, if staged properly.

Recognizing the growing complexity of the budgeting process and the widening advantage held by the executive, in 1973 Ohio's legislature created the Legislative Budget Office and a twelve-member bipartisan Legislative Budget Committee. LBO has historically been charged with performing a wide range of services for the General Assembly, usually as directed by the Legislative Budget Committee composed of members from each house's Finance Committee. During the biennial budget adoption process, LBO prepares independent revenue estimates, analyzes the executive budget, drafts the appropriations bills, prepares fiscal notes for pending legislation (required by statute since 1977), and provides independent estimates of public welfare caseloads and education enrollment projections. Throughout the biennium, LBO provides regular reports on issues affecting state finance, monitors state finances for compliance with legislative intent, acts as staff to the Controlling Board, and interacts with OBM to share data and concerns.

The relative effort spent on these activities varies across time as issues, finances, politics, and personalities change. For example, the agency's first director took an aggressive, public relations posture—a more political role. His successor took more of a low-key technician's approach, which was important during the revision of the state's financial accounting system. However, the general feeling of most legislators and executive agency personnel was that the low-key approach diminished LBO's influence both inside and outside the General Assembly.

The newest director is committed to recapturing that influence. He feels that greater LBO influence will also be promoted because of professionalization and expansion and continuity of the staff now that the General Assembly has authorized higher base salaries. Up to this point, LBO salaries had been considerably lower than those of OBM.

Similar to OBM analysts, LBO agency analysts play a key role in checking the mathematical accuracy of agency submissions and their statutory legality. Analysts are also responsible for developing pertinent questions for the Senate and House Finance Committees to ask of agency personnel during the legislative budget hearings. These questions are formulated following a standard checklist of questions: (1) Are all personnel in a new or expanded program likely to be hired immediately upon passage of the appropriations act? (2) Are the assumptions used in the current services budget (continuation level of funding) reasonable or can they be altered? (3) Was allowance made for the "washout" factor (promotional costs versus retirement and attrition costs)? (4) Can there be a savings by contracting for a government service instead of using state employees to provide the service, or vice versa? (5) Are all the budgeted services really required by law? (6) Is there duplication within the same agency or between agencies in performing a service?[16]

Once into the hearings, legislators can expect to confront the same types of maneuvering employed by agencies during OBM's executive budget hearings. Only the mix and the audience change. The LBO staff also plays important followup roles. If a legislator asks for additional data from an agency, and it is "allegedly" forthcoming, LBO makes sure the information arrives as promised.

In spite of LBO's legislative character, at times the General Assembly does not unilaterally accept its estimates. In recent years, as revenue and expenditure forecasting has become more difficult, the legislature has tended to adopt an informal rule of "splitting the difference" between OBM and LBO estimates. Surprisingly, perhaps, both OBM and LBO forecasters generally agree that this strategy has worked well, and both share economic databases such as Chase Econometric forecasts and meet informally to discuss interpretations.

The major role in establishing legislative budget priorities lies with each house's Finance Committee. The legislative appropriations bill customarily, but not necessarily, originates in the House. This means that the House Finance Committee typically plays the lead role in revamping the governor's executive budget. The House Finance Committee breaks up into three subcommittees (Education, General, and Human Resources), each of which holds hearings and solicits briefings and analyses by LBO staff. Eventually, the chairperson of the Finance Committee, in consultation with subcommittee chairs, the speaker of the House, other majority leaders, and key minority leaders, drafts the legislative version of an appropriations bill which is reported out of the Finance Committee for full House floor debate. The usual approach is to start full committee deliberations with a dummy or mock version of the bill, which can be marked up and down throughout the debates, a process taking up to five months.

Once passed by the House, the bill moves to the Senate and its Finance Committee, which usually sits as a small committee of the whole rather than breaking into subcommittees for budget hearings. LBO staff members share summaries of each agency's House testimony with the Senate Finance Committee. This does not necessarily produce House–Senate consensus, especially when the majority party in one house is the minority party in the other. This situation puts a lot of extra pressure on the "neutral" LBO staff, and increases the likelihood of a major rewrite of the House version by the Senate's Finance Committee.

Actually, a number of appropriations bills are introduced and adopted each biennium, but there are just a few main ones: an operating appropriations bill for all state agencies, except those financed by gasoline tax revenues, an operating appropriations bill for the Department of Transportation and Highway Safety, and a capital improvements appropriations bill. The bulk of the legislative session prior to the beginning of the fiscal July 1 year focuses on the operating appropriations bill. Historically, the capital improvements appropriations bill is not passed by both houses until after the fiscal year begins.[17]

The governor still has one more significant input after the appropriations bill is finally ratified by both houses. Ohio's governor can veto not only specific appropriation items, but also substantive provisions in the appropriations bill. This broad interpretation of Ohio's gubernatorial item veto emerged from a state Supreme Court decision. Over time, it has become a very substantial source of power for the governor because the General Assembly has increasingly added substantive language to its appropriations bills.[18]

Ohio's governor has ten days during the session or ten days after the session to veto all or part of an appropriations bill. A three-fifths vote of each house is needed to override a governor's veto. There have been very few overrides of gubernatorial item vetos but many instances where governors have exercised this power. Appropriations for current operating expenses go into effect immediately, in contrast to capital appropriations which typically go into effect 90 days after the governor has filed the bill with the secretary of state unless, there is an emergency clause.

Roles of the Governor and the Legislature

The governor, five executive agencies, and two joint legislative-executive boards (Controlling Board and Emergency Board) have formally assigned responsibilities for overseeing the administration and expenditure of the appropriations bills, many of which are checks and balances on the others. Like all governmental entities, Ohio has a multitude of funds and special accounts. Pragmatically, however, most general observers of state spending patterns focus their attention on the General Revenue Fund, since over one-half of the total operating expenses for state government comes from this fund. It is financed by the largest share of tax revenues (sales and use, personal income, corporate franchise, cigarette, public utilities, excise, alcoholic beverage), as well as earnings on deposits, liquor and lottery profit transfers, and certain federal reimbursements. By statute, any revenue that is not earmarked for a specific purpose is deposited in the General Revenue Fund.

The power to transfer monies between these funds during the biennium is statutorily granted to the Controlling Board, a joint legislative-executive body composed of six legislative leaders and the OBM director (or designate thereof), who serves as the president of the board. Three members from each house are appointed by the leadership of each house (two appointees from the majority party and one from the minority party, which statutorily includes the chairpersons of the House and Senate Finance Committees). Requests or transfers between funds may be made by the auditor, any state agency, or the OBM director and must be approved by a majority of the Controlling Board.

The Controlling Board's power to transfer appropriated funds extends beyond interfund transfers. State statutes also authorize the board to transfer appropriations within an agency, between state agencies in the case of a reorganization, and from one fiscal year of a biennium to the other. The board can make permanent or temporary transfers. Temporary transfers are sometimes made as "loans" to agencies or programs just starting up, in anticipation of receipt of revenues (and repayments) by the agency at a later date. Temporary transfers are also made to "balance" the books at the end of the fiscal year, since Ohio's constitution requires a balanced state budget.

The power of the Controlling Board is greatly enhanced by its Emergency Purposes fund (the All Purposes fund), from which it can transfer monies to agencies requesting additional funding during the biennium. The General Assembly determines the size of this unearmarked, discretionary pool of money in its appropriations bills. Predictably, the dollar amount of agency requests exceeds the appropriated funding level. This means that the board has to pick and choose who will get funding, making the process a very political exercise.

The board meets every two weeks and handles fifty to one hundred requests each meeting. By the time the request comes up for formal approval, consensus has generally been reached (95 percent approval rate). Much of this behind-the-scenes consensus building is through the efforts of OBM and LBO staff responsible for overseeing the same agencies.

The Office of Budget and Management plays equally important roles in tracking revenues and expenditures. OBM must transmit to the governor, on a monthly basis, accurate statements of revenue intake and drawdown rates. The governor often calls on OBM to make revenue forecasts, particularly if the economy is worsening. It relies heavily on tax collection data generated by the Department of Taxation, the agency responsible for administering most state-collected taxes and several locally collected ones. It also relies on receipts data generated by the treasurer, who collects sales, gas, and utility taxes. These forecasts may be the basis for the governor's decision to issue an executive order to state agencies mandating them to cut back spending levels in the current fiscal year to meet new gubernatorially certified revenue estimates. In the past when this power has been exercised, it has sometimes triggered legal challenges on bases not unlike those raised with regard to the Gramm–Rudman–Hollings legislation at the national level—namely, the constitutionality of executive exercise of the appropriations power. The state Supreme Court has not been consistent in its interpretation of this issue, which arose several times between FY1974 and FY1987.

On the expenditure side, OBM has considerable control over the expenditure rate during a biennium. It can establish allotment periods (e.g., monthly, quarterly) for individual agencies. This is perhaps one of its strongest cash management tools. OBM's role in financial management is much stronger than its role in performance-related management. OBM has the statutory authority to prescribe and require uniform financial reporting forms and procedures for submitting statements of proposed expenditures or expenses, orders, invoices, claims, vouchers, or payrolls.[19] Without OBM approval, the state auditor is not permitted to issue a warrant for payment.

The real responsibility for performance monitoring will continue to be with the individual agency and with interest groups, clientele groups, the legislature, LBO, and the governor's office since OBM's budget analyst staff is so small. A popular alternative in recent years has been the use of private sector management evaluation teams. Typically, the problem with such studies is the lack of followup to determine how many recommendations are ultimately implemented and their effectiveness. The Emergency Board is composed of the governor or the governor's designee (an OBM official), the auditor, and the attorney general (or their representatives), and the chairpersons of the Senate and House Finance Committees. The board meets quarterly, a recent change from its former biweekly schedule. Prior to 1985, its sole function was to authorize any out-of-state travel by state agents at state expense. This was statutorily altered by the General Assembly, such that the board is now charged with establishing policies and procedures governing out-of-state travel and setting an annual travel expense ceiling for each agency. The board also has the power to raise an agency's ceiling within the agency's current appropriations. The board's functioning is another example of mandated legislative-executive cooperation in the execution phase.

Several other departments and elected officials play important roles in the implementation phase. For example, the Department of Administrative Services (DAS) reviews agency requests for waivers of competitive bidding and advises the Controlling Board on their legitimacy. DAS also establishes state guidelines covering purchasing, personnel, competitive bidding, and architectural standards, to name a few. DAS monitors agency compliance with these guidelines throughout the fiscal year. The state treasurer, a separately elected official with a four-year term, collects most state revenues, pays all state debts, invests state monies, and supervises the sale of state bonds. The state auditor, another separately elected official with a four-year term, serves as the state's chief accounting officer. During the budget implementing phase, the auditor is responsible for pre-audits and the maintenance of a complete and accurate accounting of all state revenues and expenditures.

The interactive responsibility of Ohio's "split executive" (governor; treasurer; auditor), and the tendency for these elected officials to be from different political parties, makes the dynamics of Ohio's budgetary process particularly intriguing, especially during election years and periods of economic distress.

CONCLUSION

The budgetary process in Ohio will continue to evolve in response to changes in the state's political and economic conditions. In light of the projected slow rate of economic revitalization[20] and further cutbacks in federal funding,[21] the focus of the budgetary process will continue to be on the development and refinement of revenue enhancement strategies; on expenditure reduction strategies, including cost containment and productivity; and on better financial management of cash and long-term investments. The election cycle and the political composition of the executive and legislative branches will undoubtedly produce different taxing, spending, and borrowing programs, but the final goal toward which all are headed is revitalization and diversification of the state's economy. The quasi-legislative, quasiexecutive nature of Ohio's budgetary process increases the likelihood that the final goal will be reached.

5

Connecticut: Prosperity, Frugality, and Stability

CAROL W. LEWIS

THE CONNECTICUT TRADITION

By geographic destiny, Connecticut stands at the gateway to New England. Town greens and wooden church spires keep New England traditions alive to the eye. They are alive as well in elements of the political rhetoric and administrative style and in important facets of the budgetary process. The governor, in office since December 1980, echoed this political value in his 1989 budget address to the state legislature (General Assembly) by saying, "We have promised you consistency and stability in government and that is what we have given you."[1]

Nevertheless, critics charge that the budget resembles the Barnum circus, another famous Connecticut product, which entertained and awed with a dazzling display of skill, pomp, trickery, and smooth talking ringmasters. Connecticut's financial operations are considered on a "modified cash" basis, and only beginning with FY1988 (after years of annual audit recommendations) was the independently elected comptroller to issue a financial report in accordance with generally accepted accounting principles (GAAP). Reports of operations as budgeted by the legislature and the budget as appropriated currently do not comply.[2] Allegations of using "smoke and mirrors" to balance budgets by using the budget reserve and one-time revenues to fund continuing programs[3] and shifting spending off the general fund[4] provide other examples of a system apparently so Byzantine, partisan, and mysterious that one of the more powerful actors, formally House co-chair of the joint Appropriations Committee, suggested that "the budget becomes a novel" during implementation.[5]

In Connecticut, old-style partisan politics and organization are slowly fading as overworked, underpaid, and understaffed, part-time legislators "deliberate" under a media spotlight in three- or five-month frenzied sessions.[6] The budget vote remains very much a partisan issue. Despite the noise and attention devoted to the public forum, the governor evidently is the ringmaster. The process unquestionably is dominated by the executive and, secondarily, by the majority party.

"The budget is the policy statement of the executive and the majority party in the legislature."[7]

The budget is in center ring, as policymaking is absorbed into budgetmaking. In the governor's view, "Nothing less than the history of our democracy has defined our task in government. The budget is the principal governmental tool we have to accomplish it."[8]

FISCAL CONDITION

An assessment of ability and willingness to pay lies at the center of the state's budget process. Perhaps foremost among the state's political traditions is the Yankee frugality that emerges in the budgetary process as deliberate fiscal conservatism. For example, in his budget address seven years earlier the same governor remarked, "I am convinced that we must balance our hearts with our wallets."[9] State budgeting occurs in an environment marked by a long tradition of relative prosperity coupled with official and public resistance to taxes.

Prosperity

Per capita personal income in Connecticut has consistently outstripped the national average for as long as the majority of Connecticut residents can remember. Despite a relative decline in the postwar years and especially in the 1970s, per capita personal income increased 43.9 percent from FY1982 to FY1987 and is now about one-third again the national average.[10] Personal income averaged an annual growth of 9.5 percent in the period FY1980–FY1987. It increased more rapidly throughout the 1980s than the national average and outperformed the Gross National Product (except in FY1984). These trends drove per capita personal income to second only to Alaska in 1984 and 1985 and to first among the states in 1986.[11]

Approximately 3.2 million residents enjoy the consequences typically associated with these trends. The tax burden is lightened and the debt burden reduced when weighted by personal income and other indicators. For example, Connecticut's relatively high indebtedness per capita is offset somewhat when income and property values are taken into account. State tax collections represented 6.53 percent of personal income in FY1987, a figure that put the state thirty-first among the states.[12]

No Constituency for Taxes

Neither governmental leaders nor public attitudes are especially receptive to altering the level of tax effort. The governor reiterated his position by announcing "For the fifth year in a row, I can stand before you and say: this budget does not contain a general tax increase! In essence, it follows my long-held belief, and a belief deeply ingrained in the Yankee heritage of this state, that we should do what we can afford to do."[13]

According to a public opinion poll conducted during the hue and cry over accelerating deficits projected during the 1988 legislative session, there is no constituency for higher taxes among Connecticut residents. Although a majority of respondents (53 percent) considered state taxes already too high, about two-fifths (41 percent) judged them "about right." Only 1 percent answered "too low." Opinion about policy options is less clear-cut. There was no majority for "cutting programs" (41 percent), "raising taxes" (35 percent), or a combination (13 percent).[14]

REVENUE STRUCTURE

Economic growth, rather than new or increased taxes, is responsible for the remarkable revenue growth in recent years. Budget expansion has been largely cost-free politically but utterly dependent on economic performance. Because economic conditions differ substantially, even across this small state, significant regional and jurisdictional variations in wealth, economic growth, tax capacity, and tax effort complicate budgetary politics, in which distributional issues frequently play a large role.

Total general fund revenues grew almost 47 percent in the five-year period between FY1983 and FY1987. (The general fund accounts for almost 90 percent of the state budget.) The governor's FY1989 budget recommendation projected almost $5.5 billion, bringing the increase since FY1983 to almost 69 percent. However, subsequent economic developments and forecasts from the legislature's nonpartisan professional staff, the Office of Fiscal Analysis, raise questions about the reliability of that projection.

Taxes consistently generate over three-quarters of the revenues, and their weight is increasing somewhat. The sales tax, adopted in 1947[15] and notable for the highest rate in the nation of 8 percent, is the backbone of the revenue structure. Reliance on this source has recently been increasing. The governor's FY1989 budget recommendation counts on the sales tax to produce over two-fifths of all general fund revenues or over one-half of total tax revenue. Corporation taxes were projected to contribute almost 15 percent of collections in FY1989, compared with less than 11 percent in FY1983. Nontax revenues play a relatively modest role, and federal grants have accounted for less than 12 percent of general fund revenues over the past decade.

Ranking highest in per capita income, the state nevertheless makes use of only a limited income tax.[16] Adopted in 1969, it is levied only on capital gains, interest, and dividends.[17] Although its growing yield generated almost 10 percent of revenues for FY1987, recent modifications[18] reduced the yield to 6.9 percent ($390 million) of general fund revenues projected for FY1989.

In a revenue response to budget deficits, Connecticut flirted with a more broadly based individual unearned income tax in 1971. After only several weeks and much vocal protest—and with not one dollar ever collected—the new tax was overturned by the General Assembly in its reconsidered collective wisdom. This experience and the continuing expression of negative opinion encourage few politicians to advocate its adoption today.

SPENDING PATTERNS

The past decade saw budget growth in Connecticut in real terms and an average annual nominal increase in FY1979 compared to FY1988 of over 10 percent. Despite a revenue structure that is something less than highly progressive, the state is able to use its fiscal dividend to pursue its equity and social purposes through the expenditure side of the budget. Overall, state expenditures parallel some general patterns in other states, with education, welfare, health, and transportation emerging as significant functions. Education and welfare together represent just about one-half of state spending. Education is central to budgetary politics in Connecticut. "Equalized" public school financing, via state funding, has been a major issue in state politics from an initial court order early in the last decade. A radically redesigned distributional formula adopted in the 1988 legislative session activated little public debate on this complex arrangement, which, evidently, will generate spending obligations well beyond current tax collections. The 1988 formula for state aid to public education may ultimately be the engine to drive through a new revenue structure.

Baseline Budgeting

The concepts underlying budget formulation affect the interpretation of budgetary outcomes. When claims are made on state resources in Connecticut, formal budgetary procedures have institutionalized history and given past decisions a special legitimacy. Limiting current choices—and conflict—to proposed changes from the previous year in effect "holds harmless" the vast majority of dollars spent.

Program Budgeting

Connecticut joined the majority of states in 1981 when the legislature mandated a programmatic format for the governor's budget submission; appropriations, the legal basis of most state spending, are still by line items. A program is "a set of activities devoted to a common purpose, result, or problem,"[19] and the statute initiating the change defines a program budget as "an estimate of proposed expenditures expressed as major functions and activities or projects of the budgeted agency and the means of financing them."[20] "The informational basis of budget choices has been altered by the six components of the program budget in Connecticut: program structure, explicit program objectives, program and performance measures, analysis, consideration of future-year costs, and management involvement in developing and maintaining the program budget."[21]

The goal was to increase and improve information available for the allocation of inevitably constrained resources, that is, to clarify choices. More is involved than a technical change in format.

People recognize the increasing difficulty of budget decisions; they want better information to understand the impact of such decisions on the state's citizens; and they therefore endorse the distinctive purpose of program budgeting—to define the specific results expected from each proposed expenditure.[22] The program budget was phased in as participating agencies increased from three in FY1984 to thirteen in FY1985. By FY1986 statewide conversion was completed for the more than eighty budgeted state agencies.

Focus on Changes

The fact that the core of the program process is the "option" is confirmed by executive and legislative participants and the terms in which current budget choices are phrased. According to the governor, "the options process is at the heart of budget decision making. It has lead to a more open dialogue regarding budget choices, better data and articulation of needs and anticipated results. It has made choices clearer and more reasoned."[23]

An option is a proposed change in the current services budget, meaning a prioritized recommendation for an increase, decrease, reallocation, or revenue change over last year's budget. Critical to a recommendation's success are priorities (agency, gubernatorial, or legislative), cost information, and justification. State priorities that fit the agency's mission are identified as important elements.[24] A major agency's internal directions instructed: "Think of the option as a sales/marketing document."[25] The number of options doubled from FY1984 to over eight hundred in FY1986 and has remained stable since. The quality remains mixed.

The current services budget is last year's actual expenditures adjusted for a variety of factors, including inflation according to directions from the executive budget office; past year wage settlements, wage adjustments (e.g., annual increments), and retirements; revolving fund rates; and annualized cost for new positions or program changes subsequent to approval of the prior budget.[26] This figure quickly became the starting point for discussion. As an executive budget staff member remarked, "When we talk about an agency's budget in 1985, in fact we talk about the current services budget."[27]

The options element divides budget analysis, formulation, and discussion into two broad categories: current services or base, and recommended options or changes. This distinction is built directly into the formulation process and is also incorporated into legislative review. "The use of options has changed the framework and language in agencies and in the legislature."[28] The legislative budget office "makes its recommendations on an options format that is tied to programs; using options, the analysts put together policy alternatives for appropriations subcommittees.[29] Significantly, agency budget submissions go to the legislative budget office as well as to the governor's budget staff, and the legislature may resurrect and fund an agency's suggested programmatic change.

Through this process analytic and allocation attention is directed primarily to change, and past decisions and spending habits are relatively insulated. By virtue of starting from the current services budget, past practice—history—is the most compelling argument for current spending. The options process represents a powerful tool that can be seen as dangerous or stabilizing, depending on the observer's political values. "The process of developing and reviewing options is potentially the most powerful, enduring component of program budgeting, because it offers decision makers a menu of choices and helps to identify policy issues."[30]

THE PLAYERS AND THEIR POWERS

Executive Dominance

The governor, his policies, and his budget staff are in center ring. Even a legislative assessment pronounced, "In Connecticut the Governor has the greatest impact on the budgetary process since she/he presents the executive budget to the Legislature, and it is with this budget that the Legislature must work."[31] A participant for four decades on both the executive and legislative sides of Connecticut budgeting described the situation in these words: "[The budget] is the governor's plan through which he puts forward his goals, objectives, and the tone of his administration. The legislative appropriations act records the General Assembly's acceptance, rejection or modification of the governor's policy proposals."[32]

The opening political step occurs when the governor's budget call goes out to state agencies in the summer. The central importance of the governor's policy position is reflected in his budget staff's directions for developing options. His budget office directed that agency budget submissions for FY1986 be justified by specific criteria, the first of which is "Implementation of Governor's policy directive."[33] The same point is repeated for FY1988 in a major agency's internal directions.[34]

The fiscal policy arm of the executive branch is the central staff agency, the Office of Policy and Management (OPM), created as a "superagency" under the Reorganization Act of 1977. Other responsibilities include management analysis, energy policy, planning, and intergovernmental relations. "Operationally, the staff is an extension of the governor's office. OPM's work on the budget is continuous."[35] According to Secretary Anthony V. Milano, its current and only head since its creation, "the primary objective of any head of OPM in budgeting is to carry out the governor's policies and this is unchanged from the years before 1977. Ready access and a good working relationship between the two officials is essential to the smooth functioning of the entire administration and particularly the budget process."[36] This office reviews agency requests for accuracy, comprehensiveness, inclusion of legally required changes, and conformity to gubernatorial guidelines.

The governor is also empowered constitutionally to veto all legislation and can line-item veto any individual account within an agency's appropriation. There is no pocket veto; a bill becomes law if the governor fails to sign it within specified time limits. (Should the governor veto a bill after adjournment, the legislature is called back into veto session.) Because the veto can be overridden by two-thirds vote of each legislative house and suggests unmade or unraveled compromises, it may be more powerful in potential, as a threat, than in use. In fact, the line-item veto has not been exercised in recent memory.

The Legislature

The legislature's role formally begins when the governor's proposal is submitted early in each session. The bicameral General Assembly directly receives agency requests, including proposed options, and, in this way, significantly restricts executive prerogative and extends agency participation to the appropriations phase of the process.

The governor's proposal is separated into its functional components and referred to the two joint (with both House and Senate members) fiscal committees' subcommittees. The basic work of reviewing proposals for state spending agency by agency and line by line occurs in subcommittee, although eventually only one big appropriations bill is passed. (Review of the prior year's spending is far weaker, except for the legal-and-compliance type postaudit.) According to one agency budget officer, "The depth with which an agency's budget is dealt with by the legislature is largely a function of the subcommittee and its chairman."[37] The House co-chair of appropriations in the 1988 session made the following observation from the same leadership vantage point in the 1983 session: "It's not the name of the subcommittee but the guy who runs it—the expertise and information—that gives it credibility and influence . . . the subcommittee is as powerful as the subcommittee chair is good."[38]

Although described as "the weakest of the main actors,"[39] the legislature can make any increases or decreases in spending or revenues that it wishes. A decade ago, a legislative budget office's paper remarked, "Although the legislature can make any changes it wishes, it has been tradition in Connecticut that it has made relatively few major changes in the budget."[40]

The tradition holds today, with most of the budget left intact and rarely substantially altered, as shown in Table 5.1. Part of the explanation lies in the fact that so much of the budget is devoted to continuing obligations and is treated as nondiscretionary. Another part of the explanation lies in perceived roles. It has been, and still is, the legislature's fundamental role to respond to the governor's proposal.

The legislature authorized spending from all funds for FY1989 at a combined total of over $6 billion. Using the legislative staff's identification of new and expanded programs of over $1 million, it is apparent that the legislature authorized

Table 5.1
Governor's and Legislature Budgets Compared

Fund	FY 1987–88 Estimated Expenditures	FY 1988–89 Governor's Recommended	FY 1988–89 Legislative Budget
General Fund			
millions	$4,958.07	$5,580.97	$5,547.52
% change*		11.7 (14.35)	13.69
Combined Total			
millions	$5,678.94	$6,324.76	$6,289.70
% change*		10.6 (12.21)	11.60

*Figures in parentheses show adjustments in percentage changes made by Office of Fiscal Analysis to maintain bases comparable with FY 1988

Source: Connecticut General Assembly, Office of Fiscal Analysis, "Budget Comparisons," April 15, 1988 and Governor's Proposed Budget for Fiscal Year 1988–89.

a net aggregate reduction in the governor's recommendation of almost $.52 million, or less than 1 percent of all authorized new programs and expansions.[41] Furthermore, all legislative alterations of gubernatorial proposals, including both increases and decreases over $1 million, sum to $23.64 million. In effect, changes emanating from the legislature for FY1989 represent only 0.38 percent of total spending from all funds but 36 percent of all new and expanded programs in excess of $1 million, which were ultimately approved for FY1989.

Much of the analytic work underlying both legislative reactions and initiatives issue from the Office of Fiscal Analysis (OFA). This is the professional, nonpartisan staff for the two joint fiscal committees, Appropriations and Finance. Since its creation in 1969, its function has been to perform research and to analyze fiscal matters. "This office was to take the politics out of the numbers. Surely, no one was so naive in the legislature as to think that this would take the politics out of the policy decisions. But at least everyone would be able to agree on the basic numbers."[42] According to OFA's director, "there is a system of checks and balances today that didn't exist, particularly in the revenue area that is so important in setting budget policy."[43]

Numbers Game

The result has been to change the terms of the discussion by providing numbers based on different (and more recent) analyses and to translate budget battles into sometimes technical debates over analytic assumptions, economic conditions, and validity of forecasts. For example, a 1988 disagreement between the executive and legislative budget offices over defining the base resulted in different figures for percentage change and allegations of "phony" versus exaggerated increases. By adjusting data to maintain a comparable spending base as shown in Table 5.1, OFA's calculations for FY1899 put the governor's proposed increase in the operating budget at 14.35 percent instead of the 11.7 percent cited in his recommended budget, whereas the increase for all funds jumped from the governor's 10.6 percent to 12.2 percent by OFA's analysis. With respect to revenue estimates, executive and legislative budget staffs usually sit down together and try to project likely revenues, but each staff maintains independent estimates, and agreement is not required.

A financial tracking mechanism serves as an alert; the state comptroller (elected for a four-year term) produces monthly updates on the state's financial status. With the reports showing budget surpluses of recent years transformed into substantial deficits, the numbers fight grew especially serious in the 1988 legislative session. The transformation was variously attributed to Democratic overspending, Republican undertaxing, and gubernatorial political sleight of hand. Because the legislature is statutorily bound to pass a "balanced" budget wherein projected revenues match estimated expenditures in a single bill, Appropriations and Revenue were at odds, and leadership could not get the budget out. To cope with the remaining $127 million shortfall (after $33 million in spending cuts), revenue estimates were altered and other funds were tapped to absorb the projected revenue shortfall in the general fund. OFA participated in the Finance Committee's necessary adjustments of revenue estimates where there was "latitude to pick the optimistic end of the range."[44] This effort was different from some memorable past instances in that professional analysis and reality intruded into (but still fell short of dominating) a political and highly partisan process.

Partisan Politics

"Politics, in the sense of electoral designs and party designations is supposed to, and usually does, dominate legislative deliberations and decisions."[45] Although partisan influences have been declining, they are still relatively strong in Connecticut and important for understanding the budget process. Thus, the assistant minority leader noted with evident pride that, for FY1989 "House Republicans offered a more than reasonable alternative to the highest state spending hike in the nation . . . and the use of several controversial one-time revenue sources."[46] Party affiliation especially influences executive-legislative relations, as the following analysis explains:

Depending on the division of political power within the legislature, various compromises are reached among legislative leaders and between the legislative and executive branches. The degree of compromise in the legislature is partially dependent on the ratio of Democrats to Republicans. The smaller the ratio, the more compromise tends to occur. Also, more compromise tends to occur between branches when the legislative majority is of one party and the Governor is of the other party. There is limited conflict between the House and the Senate due to our joint committee system.[47]

Party politics is preserved directly and formally in the budget process through legal requirements for bipartisan representation. For example, legislative appropriations may be modified subsequent to adoption of the budget and on the basis of the governor's request by the Finance Advisory Committee, a body with majority and minority members from both houses as well as representatives of the executive branch. Similarly, the Bond Commission, which authorizes projects for bonding, is another executive-legislative body with bipartisan representation.[48] Furthermore, the postaudit, a legislative function, operates through a nonpartisan staff under Democratic and Republican auditors. Institutionalized through House and Senate rules on committee assignments and leadership selection, the party caucus also reinforces partisanship. The full fiscal committees vote on the budget bill only after it has been approved by caucus and leadership. Voting on the budget and other caucus bills is most frequently along partisan lines, whereas such straight party-line voting occurs more rarely on other legislative matters. The 1988 session was no exception.[49] "[T]he arithmetic is elegantly simple: the majority party is supposed to vote yes and the minority party to vote no on revenues and appropriations."[50]

Stability

The state has witnessed exceptional stability in dominant players, both in the sense of formal roles and in personalities. Institutional calm has characterized state administration since the last major administrative reorganization in 1979. Thus, an observation made in 1980 still holds: "We have a neat little budget process. Everyone has his role to play and the law tells him when to play it."[51] As for individuals, the governor has been in office since December 1980, and both the executive (OPM) and legislative (OFA) budget offices since their inception each have had only one incumbent chief. On the legislative side, the long tenure of some members of leadership also adds to smooth working relationships, expertise, and stability. Credibility, reliability, and trust in informal relationships and across institutional boundaries contribute a great deal to a process that is dependent on timely compromise and mutual accommodation.

THE BOTTOM LINE

In a process marked by continuity, stability, and tradition, only a general assessment that something is very wrong induces change or the contemplation of change. That happened in 1971, when the state responded to deficits by introducing the short-lived income tax and shifting to the still-retained annual budget cycle. It recurred in response to deficits in the early 1980s.

The surplus or deficit is the single most important overall indicator by which the process is assessed, and this single figure is behind most attempts to alter that process. Most players, including the public, appear to agree with the governor's words: "the measure of a budget is the extent to which it achieves an appropriate balance between the services provided by government and the level of taxation necessary to support these services."[52] The level of services and the tax effort at which the balance is achieved are subsidiary concerns.

This approach has the virtue of simplicity and consensus, but little else to recommend it. Although financial tracking continues to improve with computerization and systemization, operations are so complex and economic circumstances so fluid that precision and certainty are frustrated. According to one longtime participant, "fortune, good or bad, usually ranks alongside administrative skill in managing the year-end and surplus statement."[53]

Although the governor submits a balanced proposal and the legislature passes a balanced budget bill, there is no legal requirement for a positive year-end balance. It is customary to add any negative balance to the next budget period. In addition, there is no restriction against bonding an operating deficit. The burden is kept within bounds because a joint executive-legislative body, the Finance Advisory Committee, approves reductions in allotments (recissions) when the projected operating deficit triggers statutorily defined limits.

CONCLUSION

In 1983, just about six months before the fiscal year would end with a small deficit, a bipartisan commission reported: "the projected deficit is not so much the problem as the reflection or symptom of the State's fiscal difficulties over the last decade—difficulties on both the expenditure and revenue sides of the ledger. These difficulties run broad and run deep and must be addressed if the State's budget problems are to be resolved."[54]

The state has not resolved the "budget problems" and seems headed in the same direction. The appropriated budget was balanced for FY1989 by drawing materially on the budget reserve fund and other funds. Because a sizable deficit is predicted for the next round and because the future costs of some programs, notably state aid to education, are high, increased controversy is likely. Accusations of poor management and overspending undoubtedly will vie with charges of inadequate taxes and a search for new or additional revenues. Considering the enduring value of frugality, there will be considerable pressure on the expenditure side. Many players will have learned that "We can't go solving all the world's problems at the same time and that's what we've been trying to do."[55]

The resolution of "broad and deep" problems is bound to elude Connecticut's budget process because resolution is continuous and provisional upon changing conditions. A chief asset of the process is that it produces "appropriate balance" through compromise. That balance is necessarily a temporary phenomenon, to suit the times. Of course, compromise is easiest when prosperity diminishes the impact of tax effort. When projected deficits again constrain budget growth within more spartan margins, compromise will be more difficult and the process more strained. Although the impending deficit may provoke challenges and demands for procedural or substantive change, the budgetary process will remain stable, partisan, dominated by the governor, and responsive to fiscal conditions and political demands.

6

Georgia: Shared Power and Fiscal Conservatives[1]

THOMAS P. LAUTH

The executive budget has been the centerpiece of efforts to strengthen the powers of state governors. Compared with most other states, the budget powers of the governor of Georgia are strong. However, the General Assembly is an influential counterbalance in the state's budgetary process. This chapter delineates the formal budget powers of Georgia's governor and examines their influence on appropriations outcomes. It also assesses the impact of the state's economy and the fiscal attitudes of policymakers on appropriations decisions.

FORMAL BUDGET POWER IN GEORGIA

Strong formal budget powers exist whenever a governor has direct responsibility for budget preparation and execution, the central budget office is located in the office of the governor, and the governor has authority to line-item veto legislative appropriations. Unrestricted tenure in office and the ability to appoint all or most heads of executive branch agencies are formal powers that may indirectly have ramifications for budgetmaking. By these standards, the formal budget powers of the Georgia governor are relatively strong.

Georgia is one of forty-seven states in which responsibility for budget preparation rests with the governor rather than a budget commission or board. This places the governor in the proactive position of presenting the agenda of state spending for the coming fiscal period, while the legislature is, for the most part, in the position of reacting to the governor's budget initiatives.

The Georgia Office of Planning and Budget (OPB) is a staff agency located within the governor's office, rather than within a Department of Finance or Administration as is the case in many other states. Its location facilitates access to the governor for top-level budget officials, and increases the likelihood that budget analysts understand and identify with the governor's programs. Its role in reviewing agency budget requests contributes to the centralization of budget decisions in the office of the governor.

Georgia's governor is one of forty-three governors who possesses the line-item veto. This special form of the veto power has the potential to discourage pork barrel appropriations. It makes it difficult for the legislature to include in the appropriations bill items that are unacceptable to the governor because he is able to veto them individually without having to veto the entire appropriations bill.

To the extent that tenure in office is related to budgetary power, the governor's office in Georgia was strengthened in 1976 when a constitutional amendment made it possible for a sitting governor to seek reelection.[2] Executive branch agencies and legislators now have fewer opportunities to attempt to take budgetary advantage of a lame duck governor.

The governor's formal appointment power is relatively weak. Georgia is one of only twelve states that have seven or more popularly elected agency heads.[3] The Georgia constitution calls for the direct election of seven executive branch agency heads (a total of eleven officials), not including the lieutenant governor.[4] Although shared power within the executive branch is usually regarded as a weakness in the formal powers of chief executives, previous research has demonstrated that the method of agency head selection is not systematically related to agency budget success in Georgia.[5] In recent years a number of Georgia's elected agency heads first attained office through gubernatorial appointment to an unexpired term. For this reason, the governor's appointment power is not as weak as it may appear.

On balance Georgia's governor has strong formal budget powers. This was not always the case, however. Early in this century the governor's budget powers were weak, and the legislative branch dominated the appropriations process. Later in the century, the governor's budgetary control was virtually unlimited despite relatively weak formal powers. Today, budget powers are more evenly shared between the branches.

DEVELOPMENT OF THE EXECUTIVE BUDGET IN GEORGIA

The budget process in Georgia was dominated by the legislative branch until 1931. In that year the General Assembly established the state's first executive budget system. A Budget Bureau was created consisting of the governor as ex officio director of the budget and the state auditor as associate director of the budget and chief operating head. The three decades between 1931 and 1961 were characterized by a shift of budgetary control away from the legislature to the executive.[6]

A major struggle between Governor Ernest Vandiver and the General Assembly over appropriations in 1961 resulted in actions to limit the governor's nearly total power in budgetary matters.[7] Ironically, the 1962 Budget Act and 1962 constitutional amendments, which were designed to curtail the governor's power, also established the foundation for the current strong executive budget system in Georgia.[8] The 1962 Budget Act reconstituted the Budget Bureau in the governor's office, established the position of state budget officer, and authorized professional support staff for the new agency.[9] Since the Executive Reorganization Act of 1972, the central budget office has been known as the Office of Planning and Budget.

STRENGTHENING THE GENERAL ASSEMBLY

In addition to the 1962 limitations placed on the governor's discretionary budget authority, three subsequent actions have helped strengthen legislative influence in the budgetary process. In 1966 the speaker of the House of Representatives became more independent of the governor. Prior to that time the governor hand-picked the speaker and committee chairpersons, and was able to have his budget approved by the legislature without much difficulty.[10] A new era of legislative independence began in Georgia when the House elected its officers without suggestions from the executive branch of government.[11]

In 1969 the General Assembly established the Legislative Budget Office (LBO) consisting of the legislative budget analyst and approximately ten other professional budget analysts. This agency provides the legislature with counterpart expertise to the governor's Office of Planning and Budget. During the twenty years of its existence, the Legislative Budget Office has been headed by a veteran analyst who previously worked in the old Budget Bureau. His experience, expertise, and institutional memory compensate for the lack of financial expertise that is typically found among all but a few members of the General Assembly (which meets for only forty days each year).

The Legislative Budget Office officially serves as a staff agency for both the House and Senate appropriations committees, but in practice it is more extensively utilized by the House committee. The Senate appropriations committee tends to rely more on the governor's Office of Planning and Budget for staff assistance.

Prior to 1975, the General Assembly appropriated in four major object classifications: personal services, operating expenses, lease rental, and capital outlays. Since 1975, the appropriations act has contained approximately a dozen standard object of expenditure classifications and several other subobject classifications. This development was largely an effort to increase legislative control of spending.

During budget execution, legislative control is manifest in the requirement that agency funds cannot be transferred from one object of expenditure classification to another without approval of the legislature's Fiscal Affairs Subcommittee.[12] (Reprogramming of funds within the same object class requires only the approval of the governor's Office of Planning and Budget.) The Fiscal Affairs Subcommittee is composed of four members appointed by the speaker of the House of Representatives, four members appointed by the president of the Senate (the lieutenant governor), five members of each house selected by the governor, as well as the speaker of the House and the lieutenant governor. State law requires this subcommittee to meet at least once each quarter, or at the call of the governor, for the purpose of reviewing and approving budget unit object class transfers recommended by the governor. However, in recent years it has met only once a year, usually in June, just before the end of one and the beginning of the next fiscal year. Although Fiscal Affairs is an instrument of legislative control over the transfer of funds, its agenda is set by gubernatorial recommendations. It is, therefore, a reactive rather than a proactive form of legislative influence.

The history of Georgia's budgeting in this century has been characterized by extreme periods of legislative domination (prior to 1931) and executive domination (1931–1961). Since 1962, gubernatorial power has been strengthened by an enhancement of formal budget powers. During the same period the legislature has sought to maintain parity with the executive branch by exercising greater independence in selecting its officers, acquiring its own staff expertise, and increasing line-item control in the appropriations act.

REVENUE COLLECTIONS

The adequacy of revenue substantially influences the behavior of participants in state budgeting.[13] Georgia receives most of its revenue from a general sales tax of four percent, special sales taxes on such products as motor fuel and alcoholic beverages, and income taxes. Georgia state government revenues grew each year between 1980 and 1989 without the benefit of tax increases. More importantly, the state experienced real growth in revenue collections during this period. Revenue collections from state sources between FY1980 and FY1989 increased by an average of 9 percent per year in current dollars and by an average of 4.2 percent per year in real dollars (Consumer Price Index, 1982=100).[14]

Economic Growth

Revenue growth without tax increases was facilitated by a growing state economy. Between 1980 and 1989 Georgia employment grew at the rate of 3.4 percent per year, compared to the national rate of 1.9 percent per year. Georgia employment grew more rapidly than U.S. employment in every year of this period, and Georgia employment, as a share of U.S. employment, increased steadily from 2.4 percent in 1980 to 2.8 percent in 1989.[15] The Georgia unemployment rate was also below the national rate each year between 1980 and 1988.[16] During the same period, Georgia per capita personal income grew at the rate of 7.4 percent per year, while the U.S. per capita personal income grew at 6.3 percent per year. Georgia per capita personal income as a percent of U.S. per capita personal income grew steadily from 84.8 percent in 1980 to 92.5 percent in 1988.[17] In short, a robust state economy has contributed to the state's revenue growth during the past ten years.

The first indication that budget growth in Georgia could no longer be entirely sustained from a growing economy came in the 1989 session of the General Assembly when a one percent sales tax increase (from three to four percent) was enacted. This was the first state tax increase since 1972, and the first sales tax increase since 1951. Near the end of the decade state revenue collections have been increasing at decreasing rates. In 1984 and 1985, the percent change in revenues from the previous year was 8.3 percent and 9.4 percent respectively in constant dollars (Consumer Price Index, 1982 = 100), but in 1986, 1987, and 1988 the percent change was less than 6 percent each year.

The Revenue Estimate

Georgia's governor is responsible for preparing the annual revenue estimate. Because the state constitution prohibits appropriations in excess of the official revenue estimate, the governor sets appropriations parameters. The governor's revenue adviser, using an econometric forecasting model, estimates the range of likely revenue yields, but the selection of a specific figure which becomes the official state revenue estimate is a policy decision made by the governor. Traditionally, revenue estimates have been conservative, leading to an underestimation of actual revenue collections. An advantage of conservative revenue estimates is that they reduce the risk and political embarrassment of overestimating revenue collections. If a revenue shortfall is detected during the year, the spending plans of state agencies must be revised to keep the budget in balance. The disadvantage of conservative revenue estimates is that they constrain gubernatorial recommendations and legislative appropriations for the improvement of state services.

In practice, conservative revenue estimates are expected to generate surplus funds from the second half of the prior fiscal year and the first half of the current fiscal year which can be distributed as supplemental appropriations (an amendment to the general appropriations act in force) midway through the current fiscal year.

The General Assembly which convenes in January each year, enacts two budget laws during the session—a general appropriations act for the fiscal year that will begin in July, and an amendment to the general appropriations act passed in the previous year's session. The amended general act is the principal mechanism for adjusting the state's spending plan midway through the fiscal year to conditions of a revenue shortfall or surplus. Legislators also view the mid-year budget amendment as an opportunity to fund projects of local interest which do not compete very well with statewide projects in the general appropriations act.[18]

The ability to set state financial policy through the revenue estimate is a very important aspect of the governor's budget powers in Georgia. The legislature may attempt to convince the governor to revise the estimate, but setting the revenue estimate is ultimately the governor's prerogative.

Use of Debt

Most state programs and projects are financed through direct appropriations from the general fund. However, the state may also incur general obligation debt not to exceed ten percent of the previous year's revenue collections.

Like most states, Georgia's financial needs exceed available tax revenues, but unlike other states Georgia has been reluctant to use revenue bonds to meet its resource requirements. All bonds issued by the State of Georgia since 1973 have been general obligation (GO) bonds. The Georgia State Finance and Investment Commission (GSFIC), an agency established to issue GO bonds and manage the investment proceeds from bond sales, may approve the sale of non-guaranteed revenue bonds by state authorities, but prefers as a matter of operating policy that such debt instruments be infrequently used. GSFIC reflects the debt philosophy of fiscal conservatives, occupying leadership position in state government.[19] In general, that philosophy holds that if there is a need to incur debt, GO bonds should be used. They are usually cheaper, easier to control, and because default is less likely the credit position of the state is preserved.

Because state revenue collections recently have been increasing at decreasing rates, and the costs of health care payments and prison construction have been rapidly escalating, it may be difficult to continue to fund new capital projects exclusively through the sale of GO debt which must be serviced from state general funds. The state's recently declining fiscal capacity to service new GO debt may lead to greater use of revenue bonds in the years ahead.

During the past ten years, Georgia budgetmakers have been fiscally conservative in revenue estimation and the use of debt. The state's economy has been growing, but at decreasing rates near the end of the decade. Moderate demands for new programs and the expansion of existing ones were easily accommodated throughout most of the decade from new revenues produced by a growing economy. That pattern may change in the 1990s, however, as Georgia finds its economy caught in the main currents of national fiscal stress.

CONTROLLING AND DIRECTING STATE AGENCIES

In addition to being a vehicle through which the governor sets the agenda for state spending and legislative appropriations, the executive budget is also an instrument for gubernatorial control and direction of executive branch agencies. How effective have Georgia governors been in controlling agency acquisitiveness, and to what extent has the General Assembly taken its appropriations cues from the governor?

Controlling Acquisitiveness

In order to better understand the relative influence of agencies, the governor, and the legislature in the Georgia budgetary process, we have analyzed appropriations outcomes for nine fiscal years from FY1980 to FY 1988. Between FY1980 and FY 1988 the mean agency request (N=262) was for an increase of 49.6 percent over the previous year's budget authority. The average gubernatorial recommendation during this period was an increase of 7.6 percent over agency budget authority of the previous year, and the average legislative appropriation amounted to an increase of 8.4 percent. This pattern is consistent with previous research which found that operating agencies seek to expand their budgets, governors and legislatures reduce agency requests, and legislative appropriations tend to be slightly above or below gubernatorial recommendations.[20] That research also found that governors and legislatures attempt to balance budgets at higher levels of expenditure. Between 1980 and 1988 Georgia's revenue growth permitted budgets to be balanced at a rate of expansion close to that recommended by the governor and approved by the legislature.

At least in the aggregate, gubernatorial recommendations substantially reduced agency requests, and legislative appropriations conformed more closely to gubernatorial recommendations than to agency requests.[21] This suggests that the governor has been successful in controlling agency acquisitiveness and inducing the legislature to adopt his spending plan.

One indication of the governor's relative strength is the degree to which legislative appropriations approximate his recommended spending levels or the spending levels requested by executive branch agencies. Annual appropriations which are closer to agency requests than to gubernatorial recommendations suggest either that agencies are able to circumvent the governor and negotiate their budgets with the legislature, or that the legislature is acting independently of the governor in deciding state spending priorities. Conversely, annual appropriations which are closer to gubernatorial recommendations than to agency requests suggest legislative reliance on cues from the governor. A comparison of appropriations as a percentage of agency requests and gubernatorial recommendations for the fiscal years 1980 through 1988 indicates that in each of the nine years, average agency ($N=29$) appropriations were closer to gubernatorial recommendations. Similarly, appropriations came closer to gubernatorial recommendations than to agency requests for twenty-nine of thirty-one agencies included in the Georgia budget between 1980 and 1988.

In budgetary matters, the road to the General Assembly passes through the governor's office. State agencies are required to submit their budget requests to the Office of Planning and Budget by September 1 of each year. The governor presents his *Budget Report*, revenue estimate, and a draft appropriations bill to the General Assembly shortly after it convenes each January.[22] Analysis of the relationships among agency requests, gubernatorial recommendations, and legislative appropriations suggests that the General Assembly takes its appropriations cues not from the agency requests which go into the governor's office but from the gubernatorial recommendations which emerge.

Managing the Costs of Continuation

As noted earlier, Georgia's agencies are highly acquisitive. Because of the state's balanced budget requirement, the governor must reduce the aggregate of agency requests to an amount approximately equal to the official revenue estimate. This means that the governor's recommendations for some agencies will be the same as agency requests, but that gubernatorial recommendations for most agencies will be less than agency requests. This fact of budgetary life leads to a competitive relationship between agencies, and the executive and legislative budget offices. This is most clearly seen in different institutional estimates of the costs associated with program continuation. Since 1980 Georgia budget documents have included estimates of the cost of program continuation prepared by the major participants in the budget process, agencies, the governor's Office of Planning and Budget, and the Legislative Budget office.[23] Continuation is officially defined by the Office of Planning and Budget as "a level of effort . . . that will support a continuation of the presently budgeted level of output into the next fiscal year."[24] With the exception of only a few agencies, continuation estimates usually exceed 100 percent of the current year's budgetary authority. Between FY1980 and FY1987 the mean agency (N=234) estimate of continuation was 6.9 percent above the current year's budget authority. The average gubernatorial estimate of continuation during this period was 1.2 percent above agency budget authority of the current year, and the average legislative estimate of continuation was 1.3 percent below agency current authority of the current year.

What accounts for agency estimates of continuation? Because they believe the budget base is a relatively safe haven for funds, agencies are usually expansive in their definitions of continuation. However, inflation does increase the prices of many goods and services which agencies purchase, and projected increases in the number of eligible clients or the volume of agency work also contribute to the magnitude of continuation estimates. Projected cost increases attributed to continuation are frequently a sticking point between agencies and the Office of Planning and Budget. Agencies argue that when they request funding for more of what they are already doing, or for the enhancement of an ongoing activity, that is continuation of an already justified activity or program, not something new. OPB analysts are likely to regard increased effort or enhancement as something new, requiring more stringent standards of justification. These distinctions are not easily made, and such matters are frequently settled through hard negotiations.

Capturing Money

What is at stake in definitions of continuation? One of the major responsibilities of the OPB director is to find enough money each year to fund the governor's priorities. If, in the aggregate, agency estimates of the costs of continuation absorb too large a portion of new resources each year, it is difficult to fund the governor's program initiatives. In effect, agencies through expanding continuation would crowd out gubernatorial control of the executive budget. In order to prevent this, OPB analysts seek to contain continuation estimates.

Similarly, a major task for the legislative budget analyst is to find enough money in the budget each year to fund projects of interest to the constituencies and districts of individual members. Just as the OPB director must control agency continuation if there is to be enough money available to fund gubernatorial initiatives, so also must the legislative budget analyst contain agency continuation if there is to be enough money available for legislative projects of local interest.

Legislative leaders have an interest in protecting the budget base of agencies because projects which are important to individual legislators reside there. At the same time, they seek to restrict the expansion of continuation so that sufficient resources will be available for new projects which are also important to individual legislators.

In years when robust revenue growth permits budget expansion, it is possible to fund fully continuation and still be able to fund new gubernatorial and legislative initiatives. In years of declining rates of revenue growth the costs of continuation tend to restrict new initiatives.

USE OF THE ITEM VETO

The line-item veto is an important weapon available to the governor to defend his budget proposals against legislative additions or changes that the governor believes to be unnecessary or unwise. Although it may seem that the item veto gives the governor undue influence over legislation in violation of the separation of powers principle, especially in those instances where the governor also exerts influence through his prerogative to develop and present the budget proposal, it is nevertheless a formal power of governors in Georgia and forty-two other states. How often is that power used?

During the fiscal years 1974 through 1989, with the exception of one year, governors of Georgia did not invoke the item veto very often. In that period they found it necessary to use it less than four times per year on supplemental and general appropriations bills. In four of those years, the gubernatorial line-item veto was not used at all.

Governor Jimmy Carter invoked the item veto eighteen times in 1975. Prior to the Carter administration, Georgia's governors tended not to use the item veto. Governor Carter's item vetoes during his last year in office represented a major departure from that tradition. The appropriations act for FY 1975 and the amended appropriation act for FY 1974 contained approximately ten new standard object classifications as well as several agency-specific object classifications. The new appropriations format was generally regarded as an attempt to protect legislative intent. Governor Carter opposed this move on the part of the legislature, and vetoed a combined total of eighteen items in the two acts.[25]

Since 1975, Georgia governors have exercised item veto power sparingly. Because of the strength of their other budget prerogatives, they have not needed to use it.[26] The General Assembly tends not to take appropriations actions opposed by the governor. Nevertheless, the item veto remains a potential weapon in the budgetary arsenal of the chief executive.

CONCLUSION

The governor of Georgia possesses strong formal budget powers. He has responsibility for fashioning agency requests into a comprehensive set of spending recommendations. The *Budget Report*, revenue estimate, and draft appropriations bill structure the General Assembly's budget deliberations. The Office of Planning and Budget is a policy arm of the governor's office, and the governor has responsibility for management of the operating budget. The governor possesses the item veto.

Yet, the General Assembly is not without budgetary influence. It exerts object of expenditure control over agency spending through the appropriations act and the Fiscal Affairs Subcommittee. It has staff support from the Legislative Budget Office whose head is the senior expert on the state's budget.

Unlike earlier periods in Georgia history, neither the governor nor the General Assembly dominates the budgetary process at the expense of the other. The governor's formal budget powers are strong, and the legislature tends to take its budgetary cues from the governor. The governor is the dominant partner in this executive-legislative relationship, but it is a partnership in which the legislature cannot be ignored.

Idaho: Process and Politics in Gem State Budgeting

H. SYDNEY DUNCOMBE AND RICHARD KINNEY

Idaho is a semirural western state with a population of 1 million (forty-first in the nation) and an economy extensively dependent on agriculture, forest products, and tourism. During the 1980s, the state had a low job-growth rate (2 percent for 1980–1986), a per capita income of only $11,120 (fortieth in the nation), and faced hard times.[1] During most of the recent fiscal years, governors have had to hold back funds from state agencies because revenues fell below expenditure levels.

In politics, Idaho tends to be Republican and conservative, although voters sometimes split their ballots to elect popular Democratic candidates. For the past sixteen years, two Democratic governors (Cecil Andrus and John Evans) have faced overwhelming Republican majorities in both houses of the state legislature, and vigorous battles have been fought over budgets and taxes.

This chapter provides an overview of Idaho's revenue and expenditures, examines the budget process, and briefly analyzes budget outcomes.

A PROFILE OF THE IDAHO STATE BUDGET

Idaho's budget is one of the smallest in the nation. For FY1987, it ranked forty-second in terms of general fund revenues and forty-fourth based on revenues received from all funding sources.[2] General fund revenues increased from $230.9 million in FY1976 to a projected $655.6 million for FY1988. During this period, general fund revenue collections grew annually by as much as 15.1 percent (FY1979) and as little as 2.3 percent (FY1983) with an average of 9.4 percent. Only as recently as FY1985 did total funding from all sources surpass the $1 billion mark.

The state budget has been funded by three main revenue sources. General fund revenues have comprised about one-half of the total; federal funding about 25 percent; and dedicated funds approximately 20 percent. General fund revenues have come primarily from individual citizens through their payment of income and sales taxes, each source supplying about 40 percent of the total in recent years.

General fund appropriations levels increased from $222.6 million in FY1976 to $657.3 million for FY1988. The growth rate ranged from 23.6 percent (FY1985) to −2.8 percent (FY1984). Actual expenditures grew, on the average, at a rate of 8.7 percent. However, when the FY1977 levels are used as a base and the figures for the subsequent years are "deflated" by applying the Consumer Price Index, "real" growth in expenditures took place only in fiscal 1978, 1983, and 1985.[3] For the other years, the actual growth averaged −1.7 percent, ranging from −0.1 percent to −8.9 percent. Even though the state obtained more revenues through tax increases and other enhancements, it has had difficulty just maintaining programs and services and protecting against reductions in operations.

Elementary and secondary education in public schools was most favored in state general fund appropriations during the FY1976–1988 period. The share for the public schools increased to over 50 percent, in part because of the policymakers' interest in keeping down local property taxes and enhancing the quality of education. The portions of other areas declined: university education from 20 to 15 percent; health and welfare, 17 to 12 percent, and natural resources, 3 to 2 percent. The shares were somewhat stable for the other executive departments, elected officials, and the legislative and judicial branches.

THE IDAHO BUDGET PROCESS

Idaho has an annual budget and a fiscal year that begins on July 1 and ends on June 30. The process of preparing agency budget requests begins in March each year in larger state agencies, sixteen months before the fiscal year starts. The requests prepared by field offices and small central office units are reviewed at successively higher levels within the department until the fiscal officer and department director complete their reviews and the budget is submitted to the executive budget staff in late August or early September.

The Budget System and Budget Guidelines

Idaho has a budget document that combines program and zero-base budget features.[4] The guidelines for departmental budget preparation are prescribed in the *Budget and Legislative Development Manual* prepared by the Division of Financial Management each spring. The budget forms request information on agency program goals, objectives, and performance indicators, as well as much line-item detail on personnel and other costs.

The most important set of budget request forms are the decision unit forms that begin with the current-year appropriations base and build first to the current-year estimated expense, then to the budget year base, next to the maintenance of current operations level, and finally to the agency request. Typically, ten to twenty decision units are used to build the budget request for a program, and these decision units usually include increases in employee compensation, inflationary increases in nonpersonnel items, replacement of capital outlay, and sometimes improvements in agency programs and new programs.

Executive Budget Review

The Division of Financial Management (DFM) serves as the executive budget staff of the governor, and its administrator is the state budget director. The nine budget analysts are assigned specific agencies and are divided into four teams—education, general government, human resources, and natural resources.

After they receive agency budget requests, the DFM analysts concentrate first on verifying the accuracy of the figures in the decision units that add to the maintenance of current operations (MCO) level. The analysts are also concerned about fund sources, particularly the shift in costs from federal or dedicated funds to the hard-pressed state general fund. In addition, closely scrutinized by the analysts are decision packages above the MCO level, such as those for increased workload or program enhancement.

The DFM analysts are often given general guidelines for their recommendations. For example, when the governor wants to rely on current revenue sources with a few million in revenue enhancement, the examiner may be told that budgets should be set at the MCO level or a little above. Availability of funds, affordability of the requested decision unit, programmatic considerations, policy issues, and perceived gubernatorial policies are among the considerations that weigh in the analysts' decision making.[5]

Beginning around mid-November, the budget analysts, accompanied by the administrator of DFM, bring their budget recommendations to the governor, who makes the final decisions on each agency budget. By early December, final revenue estimates have been made, and the governor weighs budget increases against tax increases. The executive budget is printed in mid-December and is usually available to the legislature in late December or early January.

Legislative Budget Review

The key agency in the legislative budget review process is the Joint Finance-Appropriations Committee (JFAC) composed of the twelve-member House Appropriations Committee and twelve-member Senate Finance Committee, which meet together to hear agency officials present their budgets and to set appropriations. So powerful has this joint committee been in the past two decades that it has been traditional for 99 percent of all appropriations bills approved by JFAC to be neither amended nor defeated on the floor of either house.[6]

Serving as staff for JFAC is the Legislative Budget Office (LBO) whose analysts begin their budget review as soon as they receive a copy of the agency requests in mid-August to mid-September. The immediate objective of the review is to prepare the *Legislative Budget Book*, which contains a program description of the agency, performance measures, and the cost and description of all departmental decision units. A secondary objective of the LBO analysts' review is to prepare themselves to answer questions on the agency and to provide suggestions or recommendations, if asked. The *Legislative Budget Book* presents important information provided by the agencies. LBO analysts do not include their own recommendations on agency requests in the *Budget Book*.[7] However, JFAC members informally ask LBO staff analysts for their comments on and evaluation of agency requests, and LBO analysts need to prepare themselves to provide this service.

The budget hearings of the Joint Finance-Appropriations Committee usually begin the second week in January and last three to five weeks. Small agencies are given only fifteen minutes, and the director makes the entire presentation. The larger and more important an agency, the longer the hearing and the more likely that the director will call on the other departmental executives to testify. At the conclusion of the departmental testimony, JFAC members may ask questions on the agency request or programs.

While JFAC is holding budget hearings, the Revenue Projection Committee is working on its revenue estimates. The committee holds hearings in which representatives from business, agriculture, banking, and other segments of Idaho's economy testify as to business conditions and prospects. After the hearings, the committee votes on estimates on each major general fund source of revenue for the upcoming fiscal year. A majority vote of the committee determines the estimate for each tax, and several motions may be defeated before a majority is achieved. The Revenue Projection Committee introduces House Concurrent Resolutions with its projections for the current and upcoming fiscal years, and these resolutions have generally passed both houses by early February. Once passed by the legislature, the revenue estimates tend to set ceilings on total general fund appropriations unless the legislature is willing to raise taxes.

After the revenue projections are made and the budget hearings conclude, the majority leaders in both houses come to grips with overall state fiscal policy. In some years, this results in recommendations (or direction) to JFAC on overall appropriations ceilings and attempts to influence the revenue and taxation committees on what tax bills, if any, should be passed to increase or reduce tax levels. While the revenue and taxation committees are working on tax measures, JFAC begins its budget-setting sessions, which in 1987 lasted from February 23 to March 17. In setting appropriations, JFAC members usually base their motions on the decision units shown in the *Legislative Budget Book* and the governor's budget. When the appropriations are set, they may lie before the committee for a few days or a week to allow time for reconsideration. Then, the LBO staff drafts the appropriations acts containing the amounts set by the committee, and they are sent out on the floor of the House and Senate.

The appropriation for each agency (or group of several small agencies) is placed in a separate appropriations bill, and JFAC members generally stand together to support the appropriations of smaller, less controversial agencies. As a result, debate on the appropriations bills of smaller agencies is generally short (often less than five minutes), and these bills are quickly passed without amendment. The bills of larger agencies may be debated for an hour or two, and attempts may be made to amend them on the floor. Usually, however, the attempts at amendment are beaten back, and the bill is passed with the amounts recommended by JFAC. Major factors in the increases in appropriations received by state agencies, according to agency budget officials and budget analysts, are not only legislative influences, but also public attitudes and pressures, agency credibility, reputation and relationships, interest groups, and the influence of the governor and executive budget staff.[8]

Gubernatorial Veto

As provided in the state constitution, the governor has a line-item veto dealing with appropriations bills. When the veto is used during the legislative session, the governor has five days to inform the house from which the bill originated. To override the veto, a two-thirds majority of the legislators present in each house is required.

Recent Idaho governors have used the veto sparingly and with mixed success, as illustrated in the following two examples. During the 1983 legislative session, Democratic Governor John Evans vetoed the appropriations bills for several programs, including public schools and higher education, because he believed the funding levels were inadequate. The vetoes were not overridden. In some cases, the Republican-controlled legislature approved higher amounts before adjournment, which became law with or without Evans' signature. For others, including the education bills, the governor convened a special session. The legislature granted minimal increases for some programs, but none for the colleges and universities, and then went home.[9]

More recently in 1988, Democratic Governor Cecil Andrus had the same experience. He vetoed the appropriations bills for the public schools and the state colleges and universities because, in his opinion, there were insufficient amounts. Although the Republican-dominated legislature sustained the vetoes, it passed new bills with the same amounts just before adjournment. Andrus allowed them to become law without signing them.[10]

Budget Execution

After the appropriations acts are passed and the legislature adjourns, state agencies revise their spending plans and prepare allotment requests. Approval of allotments by DFM analysts occurs before the beginning of the fiscal year. During the fiscal year, DFM monitors trends in agency expenditures to see whether agencies are in danger of exceeding any of their appropriations. When new situations (such as a crisis or a court mandate) require an increase in appropriations in the view of the analyst, the analyst contacts the administrator of DFM and may work with agency officials in planning to request a supplemental appropriation from the next legislature.

The most difficult budget execution problems for state agencies, the DFM, and the governor occur when budget rescissions become necessary. DFM economists monitor revenue collections on a monthly basis and contact the DFM administrator when it appears that revenues are falling sufficiently below estimates, so that the state's general fund can have a negative balance at the end of a fiscal year. Idaho has a $2 million debt limitation in its constitution, and Idaho law gives the governor the power to reduce agency allotments so that general fund expenditures do not exceed revenues and the available balance.[11]

When budget rescissions are needed, the Division of Financial Management usually has time to calculate the percentage reduction needed to rebalance the general fund budget, and agencies are asked to develop plans for making this percentage reduction. Agency officials sometimes ask for exemption or partial exemption from holdbacks, and these are reviewed by the DFM staff and acted on by the governor. Occasionally, the need for cutbacks comes with too little warning for the usual procedures. In May 1982, for example, the governor needed to reduce costs by 25 percent in the last seven weeks of the fiscal year and was forced to order "payless Fridays" to cut employees' salaries by 20 percent for the seven-week period, and take other drastic, cost-saving measures.[12]

BUDGET OUTCOMES

Another way to assess the governor's impact on budget outcomes is to examine the impact of agency acquisitiveness and gubernatorial support on agency budget success in the legislature. Table 7.1 reports the correlation coefficients for approval of agency requests and budget growth from FY1976 to 1988.[13] The notion of "acquisitiveness" is commonly used in budgeting literature to indicate the efforts of agencies to increase their budgets.[14] Gubernatorial support and legislative success are computed by dividing the executive budget recommendation or legislative appropriation by the general fund request or budget base.

Both agencies and the governor impact on legislative approval of agency requests. The more acquisitive agencies have experienced greater reductions by the governor and the legislature. The governor's support has been consistently related to legislative success. During both prosperous and lean revenue years, the governor recommended and the legislature approved greater budget growth for those agencies requesting larger increases. Furthermore, the legislature regularly appropriated larger increases when the governor supported them. For ten years in this period, legislative success was related more strongly to gubernatorial support than agency acquisitiveness, and for seven of those years the difference between the coefficients was statistically significant.[15] In sum, gubernatorial support has been an important factor affecting legislative approval of requests and budget growth.

Table 7.1
Zero-Order Correlation Coefficients, General Fund Budget Outcomes for Individual Agencies and Programs, FY 1976-1988

		Approval of Requests			Budget Growth		
		Acquisitiveness[a] with		Gubernatorial support with	Acquisitiveness[a] with		Gubernatorial support with
Fiscal Year	N	Gubernatorial Support[b]	Legislative Success[c]	Legislative Success	Gubernatorial Support[d]	Legislative Success[e]	Legislative Success
1976	54	-.12	-.24***	.20	.74*	.89*	.82*
1977	62	-.58*	-.48*	.79*	.62*	.54*	.76*
1978	62	-.36**	-.27***	.60*	.90*	.81*	.91*
1979	63	-.28***	-.37**	.69*	.45*	.65*	.71*
1980	65	-.35**	-.53**	.77*	.51*	.19	.61*
1981	62	-.33**	-.76*	.20	.62*	.15	-.07
1982	64	-.33**	-.39*	.23***	.85*	.36**	.30*
1983	59	-.44*	-.67*	.74*	.93*	.86*	.91*
1984	61	-.08	-.45*	.38**	.33**	.06	.57*
1985	58	-.37***	-.79*	.60*	.96*	.63*	.71*
1986	59	-.85*	-.90*	.89*	.52*	.43*	.76*
1987	59	-.68*	-.71*	.65*	.59*	.21***	.26***
1988	59	.19	.32***	.81*	.60*	.66*	.91*

*$p \leq .001$, **$p \leq .01$, ***$p \leq .05$

[a] The general fund amount in the request divided by the general fund amount in the budget base.

[b] The general fund amount in the governor's recommendation divided by the general fund amount in the request.

[c] The general fund amount in the legislative appropriation divided by the general fund amount in the request.

[d] The general fund amount in the governor's recommendation divided by the general fund amount in the budget base.

[e] The general fund amount in the legislative appropriation divided by the general fund amount in the budget base.

CONCLUSION

Idaho's budget is small compared to that of most states, but it has encountered serious budget problems in the past decade. Revenue and spending growth rates have been hampered by economic recession, inflation, limitations on local property taxation, and reductions in federal grant programs. In real terms, expenditures have barely kept pace with inflation.

Idaho's budget system is a hybrid with zero-base, program, and line-item features. In Idaho, legislative budget outcomes are related to revenue availability, agency efforts to increase their budgets, and executive budget recommendations. In the legislature, a key decision maker is the Joint Finance-Appropriations Committee, whose appropriations bills are nearly always enacted by the legislature without change.

We anticipate that Idaho's basic budget system will continue with occasional changes in format and procedures. We believe that budget outcomes will continue to be greatly influenced by the revenue picture, agency strategies, the interest and power of the governor, and the ideological and partisan makeup of the legislature and its powerful Joint Finance–Appropriations Committee.

8

Minnesota: Searching for Stability

JAMES E. JERNBERG

Minnesotans pay attention to state budgeting. Many believe that state government actions, reflected in the budget, have an impact on the quality of life in the state.[1] The state's citizens have long assigned a positive role to government spending to improve their collective quality of life, and have also shown a willingness to tax themselves to support that spending. Minnesota's personal income tax rates are among the highest in the nation, and spending for education, health, and human dignity services has always been above the national average. Public space has been reserved and developed for recreational use by both state and local governments. Infrastructure has been maintained and improved through the years.

This legacy, the civic culture of the state, the responsibility for which had been accepted and shared by people of nearly all political persuasions, has recently been challenged. The issue has usually been framed in terms of taxes, not unlike but less severe than the efforts to limit taxes in some other states (California or Massachusetts) over the past decade. Concern over taxes places constraints on spending. Political issues in the 1970s centered on how and where to distribute increasing revenues. The political disposition to spend—public money for public purposes by public governments—is now being tempered by proposals to spend less and/or have public purposes carried out by the private sector. The appropriate future role of government as the instrument for carrying out public policy is now a topic of debate in the budget process. The progressive tradition, long part of the environment of state budgeting, can no longer be assumed.[2]

Budgeting is not a technical exercise in Minnesota. It has become the focal point of major differences and disagreements over the role of the state in particular programs within a house, between houses, and between the governors and one or both houses, all depending on the party affiliations of the incumbents.

In recent years partisanship has been most evident in the areas of taxes, economic development, jobs and training programs, and assistance to the disadvantaged, where basic disagreements now exist over the most appropriate and effective measures to enhance the state's economy and the well-being of its people. Any discussion of state budgeting must recognize the partisan environment in which it occurs.

Finally, the state's budget and its processes have become unstable. Both the decisions and the processes in which they are made have come under criticism, serve as fodder for political debate, and have been the subject of reform efforts. Disagreements over what to do and how to do it catapulted state budgeting to center stage during most of the 1980s.

BUDGET PREPARATION

Four basic premises undergird Minnesota's budget. The state operates under a biennial budget system, with an executive budget, a constitutional requirement of a balanced budget, and a fiscal system in which the bulk of state spending (about 85 percent) takes the form of transfer payments to local governments, school districts, and postsecondary education.

The Biennial Budget

Minnesota budgets for a two-year period, as do twenty other states, with each fiscal year beginning on July 1.[3]

Planning, organizing, and managing the preparation of a biennial budget rests with the Department of Finance, a central staff agency responsible to the governor. The commissioner, who is appointed by and serves at the governor's pleasure, is expected to be an adviser to the governor, a professional manager of the state's finances, and an objective provider of accurate fiscal information to the legislature in its review and deliberation of the budget. Because of these multiple roles, the department, its leaders, and the fiscal information produced will not always enjoy the complete confidence of all participants in the process. There is an inherent institutional tension between the executive and legislative branches, and when the governor is not of the same party as one or both houses of the legislature, partisan suspicions over the credibility of forecasting estimates can abound. The legislature does not have its own revenue forecasting capability. Thus, both the executive branch and the legislature depend on the estimates provided by the Office of the State Economist, housed in the Department of Finance.

A biennial budget system is associated with a part-time citizen legislature—which is highly valued in Minnesota. In recent years, however, the biennial budget practice has come under scrutiny. It has been identified as one of the structural reasons why the state has experienced budget balancing crises, often requiring the governor either to convene special sessions to solve the imbalance or to take extraordinary unilateral measures.[4]

The Executive Budget

Under the executive budget system the Department of Finance acts as the governor's agent in relations with the spending units of the state. Governors will vary in their degree of involvement in the budget, but at the very least they will establish their broad priorities and goals at the outset (e.g., emphasis on job creation, hold the line on taxes, pursue a tax cut, improve education).

Though commonplace in most states, the fact of an executive budget system does influence decision-making behavior in Minnesota government. The governor dominates the process on the executive side, and the governor's budget figures serve as the frame of reference for the legislature as they review and approve the budget. The governor also has item-veto power over the budget and becomes a central player, with the leaders of both houses, when final negotiations begin to reconcile budget differences between the houses. Legislative leaders must take the governor into account as they draw up their compromise solutions.

Balanced Budget Requirement

The Minnesota constitution requires that the budget be in balance at the time of adoption. (There cannot be borrowing across biennia.) Budget deficits, a common phenomenon at the federal level during the past fifty years, are not permitted in Minnesota. Signs of impending imbalance, usually the result of anticipated revenue shortfalls, rather than extraordinary (beyond budget) spending, call the governor and the legislature into play to undo the imbalance, usually in the second year of the biennium.

Transfer Payments

Spending for state government operations constitutes only 15 percent of the state budget. Such a system, where most state revenues are transferred to other spending levels of government, creates dependencies and expectations by the recipient governments and institutions. The state transfer payments are built into all their regular operating budgets. They depend on these funds and expect them. Property tax levies at the local level are based on the assumption of certain levels of state assistance.

The Preparation Process

In mid-spring of the even-numbered year, usually May, knowing the governor's broad priorities, and aided by the department's Quarterly Financial Report, which updates expected revenues, the Finance Department issues budget guidelines to all spending units. The guidelines will address, in broad terms, the expected state of the economy, including expected inflation, and then place constraints on the invited budget requests. Guidelines, when sufficiently specific and in concert with early revenue forecasts, enable the Finance Department to make preliminary calculations of the prospects of a budget surplus or deficit, unaccompanied by any policy change proposals.

Although the Finance Department develops macro-budget calculations, the spending units devote the summer months preparing their budget requests for submission in early fall. Requests will incorporate both any governor's initiatives that had been communicated to the agency and agency initiatives, known as change requests. The information in the Minnesota state budget is so structured as to distinguish the cost of existing service levels for the next biennium from any new initiatives. Decision makers at all review points in the process know, because of the budget format, how much of the budget request represents the cost of carrying out existing policy at existing levels of service, and how much represents change from existing policy and service levels.

Having the budget guidelines as a frame of reference, Finance Department staff begin a review of agency requests in the fall, including executive hearings with agency representatives. Until 1984, budget hearings on the executive side were open, with some legislators, and certainly their staff, likely to attend. Executive budget hearings have been closed in preparation for the most recent budgets. Political debate increasingly centered on the budget during the 1980s, and the governor chose to protect his options from public view as long as possible. The tradition of supplying the spending committees of the legislature with copies of agency requests for the coming biennium, in the late fall, continues. This approach permits at least some preparation and anticipation by legislative staff prior to the submission of the governor's budget in late January.

December is a critical month in the preparation of the final budget. Financial analysts have been immersed in micro (program) analysis of agency budgets assigned to them. Much of the state budget is legally and politically assured of being continued from one biennium to the next, but reductions in agency requests can be made. The governor introduces his own priorities and initiatives into the budget; they must be accommodated. The governor's budget must be balanced. At the macro level, December revenue forecasts are available. The task is to craft a budget that is future oriented, that respects the developed expectations of previous budget commitments, and that takes into account the state's fiscal condition and the partisan political environment at the time. That is no small order.

The Budget

In Minnesota it cannot be said, as is sometimes attributed to the federal government when stressing the fragmented nature of Congressional budgeting, that the last time the budget is intact and unified is the moment the governor presents it to the legislature. The budget does not leave the governor in one piece. Minnesota's governors recognize the decentralized nature of legislative decision making by submitting the budget as a series of six large, thick documents that include the detail of agency requests and the governor's recommendations regarding those requests. The volumes are arranged to conform to the jurisdictional responsibilities of the various subcommittees or divisions of the legislative spending committees. Governors sometime augment their printed budget with an address to both houses of the legislature.

A few features of Minnesota's executive budget document deserve mention. The budget includes both the agency requests for each year of the biennium and the governor's recommendations. The display of agency requests reduces gubernatorial influence over budgetary information. That loss may be small when compared to the atmosphere of honesty and openness enhanced by the full disclosure practice. Only one time (1969) did a governor attempt to present a budget without the inclusion of the agency request figures. When the legislature objected strongly, the practice was abandoned after that year. Since then the Department of Finance officials have held a preliminary meeting with the legislative leadership to discuss budget format.

Having two sets of figures is an aid to legislators' calculations. They know whether the governor favors or supports an agency or program. Such a benchmark, when coupled with the request broken down into current level and change requests, makes somewhat more manageable a literally dizzying amount of information calling for decision.

The budget document is also organized and presented to facilitate various levels of detail of review. In four pages an organizational unit's budget total is broken down, first to broad program level, then to the program's activity levels, and finally to the objects of expenditure level of an activity. Spending committee members can focus on any and all these pages.

The third feature of the governor's budget document is that the governor provides nothing more than the budget documents. There is no governor's budget bill. In thirty states the executive submits a budget bill to the legislature; in only two other states (Iowa and Florida) are separate budget bills[5] prepared by each house of the legislature, as in Minnesota. What difference does it make? The current practice encourages the legislature's greater focus on detail, for the budget document, heavily detailed, is their frame of reference. With a governor's budget bill, committees could focus on reacting to proposals in the bill and not face the responsibility of developing an entire bill in the relatively short period of a legislative session. Of course, the legislature would not be barred from developing an entirely new bill. Focusing attention on the governor's bill would not only save time, but would also likely raise the level of review to broader programmatic budget issues. A budget bill need not substitute for the budget documents. The documents would continue to serve as the database for the bill. In terms of political influence, the governor would gain from an already dominant position (the legislature reacts to his numbers in the document) because his bill would become the operational frame of reference. At the same time the governor would be required to go on record very early with concrete spending and tax proposals.[6] From a legislative perspective, reacting to a governor's bill would make any attempts to add provisions that appear unrelated to budgets (commonly called "garbage bills" in Minnesota) much more obvious and visible, and have a deterrent effect on them. Although an executive budget bill is the prevalent mode among the states, Minnesota's political leaders have made no proposals to begin that practice.

LEGISLATIVE REVIEW

Critics and reformers of the budget process in Minnesota have tended to focus on the legislature rather than the executive. The governor comes to the institutional budgetary fray well equipped in resources and blessed with adequate time to prepare for the job. On almost all counts the legislature is at a major disadvantage.

The executive has over nine months to prepare the governor's budget, with supporting staff in the hundreds from agencies, departments, and Finance, whose responsibilities center on the budget. The legislature has less than four months, with a staff of slightly over twenty in both houses, ranging from one to two per spending subcommittee. The executive imposes time deadlines on itself throughout the preparation process. As a result, the budget is produced in an at least outwardly perceived atmosphere of calm. In contrast, observers see the last days and weeks of a legislative session as chaotic. The executive side appears familiar to outsiders accustomed to a hierarchical organizational model with the governor at its apex. The process seems orderly and is coordinated without noticeable disagreements. The legislature, on the other hand, seems to be fragmented, its decisions difficult to track and aggregate—all of which so often raises the question, "who's in charge?"

Legislative Organization

A key in distinguishing the process of legislative budgeting from executive budgeting is the bicameral nature of the legislature. Both houses must act on the budget. Legislatures conduct their business through the use of committees. In Minnesota the budget is divided among three major committees in each house: Appropriations, Taxes, and Education on the House side, and Finance, Taxes, and Education on the Senate side.

House Appropriations and Senate Finance, though having different title designations, perform the same spending function. Each in turn has four subcommittees (called divisions in the House), with identical jurisdiction over specified portions of the governor's budget. The subgroups cover (1) higher education, (2) health, human services, and corrections, (3) state departments (all other agencies of state government), except (4) agriculture, transportation, and semistates (those organizations that receive some state support but are not considered conventional executive branch agencies). The typical example is the State Historical Society. Spending for aid to local school districts, which accounts for almost one-fourth of the state budget, is the responsibility of the Education Aids Division of the Education

Committee. Their decisions must also be endorsed by the Appropriations (House) and Finance (Senate) committees before being brought onto the floor of either house. Finally, formula-based general revenue sharing, local government aids in Minnesota, is part of the spending jurisdiction of the tax committees, as are the various programs of property tax relief. Within each house there is structural fragmentation, leading to six separate spending bills, as well as a capital budget bill and a tax bill to generate the needed revenues.

Until the 1985 session, the budget review process was similar in each body. The governor's budget, received in late January, would be distributed to the appropriate committees and subcommittees. Hearings would be held in each house, with central finance officials and agency representatives explaining and defending their budgets. Hearings, which are open, attract interest groups, and it would not be uncommon to have committee staff from one body attend the hearings of the other—at least as long as scheduling allowed. The committee's inquiry would invariably have the governor's recommendation as the point of departure or base. With a balanced budget requirement, adjustments to increase the governor's budget for any program or activity certainly meant a reduction would have to occur elsewhere, unless revenue were to increase. The governor's budget always sets the framework for decision.

After weeks of hearings, the subcommittees begin the allocation stage of funds through a markup process. The focus of decision making can differ, depending on the traditions of a subcommittee and the experiences of its members. Decisions can be at a broad program level, accepting the objects of expenditure base on which the program is built, or decisions can focus on specific personnel titles, equipment, and other budgetary inputs. The point of departure often will be "move the Governor's figure."

Progress on reporting bills is held up until the April quarterly revenue forecasts become available from the Department of Finance. If the forecasts are favorable, the governor may reenter the process with additional initiatives or may favor restoring earlier cuts. After considering gubernatorial revisions, the subcommittees begin reporting their bills. There is no public tracking of decisions, nor is there a running scoreboard indicating how the decisions compare with the governor's proposals and/or one house with the other. The many separate bills are developed in each house without any visible conscious coordination among them apparent to public observers.

Coordination occurs when it has to, that is, after the final Department of Finance revenue forecast is available in April and as spending committees approach their final decision stage. On the House side, the speaker, as head of the majority caucus, the majority leader, and the chairs of taxes and appropriations, along with the division chairs, meet to maintain a balance between spending and revenues. In the Senate, similar monitoring and managing occur under the leadership of the majority leader. These deliberations are informal and, for the most part, inaccessible to the public, creating almost a sense of mystique around the process, to which many, who are denied access or for whom information is difficult to obtain, object.

The informal coordination does provide guidelines to the subcommittee chairs, and budget bills do get reported with recommendations for passage and are placed on the calendar for floor debate. The majority caucus is as disciplined as the size of its majority requires when budget bills are up for a vote.

Passage of separate and differing bills by each house requires the formation of conference committees to reconcile those differences. Criticism of the legislative budget process rises at this point.[7] Conference committee members are appointed by the speaker for the House and by the majority leader, in conjunction with the Senate Committee on Committees, for the Senate. The majority leadership may or may not appoint minority representation to the conference. The conference occurs very near the end of the session just as each house is acting on other measures. Conference decisions are not "open covenants openly arrived at"; rather, frequent recesses are called as the leadership from both sides withdraws to confer with the house leadership. Depending on the advanced stage of the process and the magnitude of the issue, the governor or the governor's representative may become a party to the negotiations to establish what sort of outcome will become necessary to avoid a veto.

Criticism of the conference stage is not limited to the process alone but also extends to the products of the conference process. Conference committee reports, the compromised bills, have increasingly come to include amendments, many of which are unrelated to the subject matter of the original bills (in apparent disregard of the constitutional requirement that any bill be limited to a single subject). Furthermore, the report may even include measures that neither house has ever acted on. Conference bills on the budget are usually the last to be acted on (agreement comes as dawn approaches on the constitutionally imposed day of adjournment), floor amendments are not allowed, the bill must be voted up or down in its entirety, and surprise inclusions may not be known for days. These measures have come to be known as "garbage bills." This practice is usually defended in terms of the compromises necessary to gain agreement. To the extent that the governor may have been a party to the agreements, vetoes are unlikely.

Reform

Recently, the informal, at times unscheduled, nature of the budget process has earned criticism because it removes decision making from public scrutiny and makes it difficult to establish accountability for spending decisions. The mystery surrounding the macro-budget coordination in each house has also produced calls for change. In 1985 the new Republican speaker of the House attempted to create a structure to address macro-budget issues, formally and publicly, early in the session. The House created a Budget Committee (seven Republicans and three Democrats), which was mandated to report a budget resolution to the House that would establish a ceiling on spending from the general fund. The ceiling and the resolution would be binding on the House. If the Department of Finance revenue projections prevailed, adherence to the spending limit would permit a tax cut approximating $1 billion, the amount of a campaign promise made before the 1984 election. The Republicans were elected with a four-vote majority. The resolution called for a ceiling almost $600 million less than the governor's budget, which itself was a tight budget, as the Democrats, too, sensed the political appeal of a tax cut. The enforceability of the resolution's provisions was in the hands of the speaker, who could rule any measure introduced on the House floor out of order if he judged it would "bust the budget."[8]

The resolution and the conduct surrounding its implementation created substantial acrimony between the two parties in the House throughout the session. Tensions extended to relations with the Senate (controlled by the Democrats) during conference, for the House, to stay within its ceiling, shifted some spending from the general fund (to which the resolution was limited) into special funds. The Senate, politically forced into a budget-cutting posture, matched the House in these opportunistic maneuverings. In addition, both the Senate and Finance Department claimed that the budget bills passed by the House were $180 million out of balance. The House leadership charged that the Finance Department revenue estimates were unnecessarily low.

The political turmoil in which the reform was introduced hampered an assessment of the value of a Budget Committee and resolution establishing overall spending and revenue limits. The experiment also suffered because the Senate had no counterpart process. The Democrats, back in control of the House in 1987, did not continue the Budget Committee, but instead created a yet larger Ways and Means Committee to perform essentially the same functions. Less controversy arose this time as the expectations of the leadership were more manageable—and both houses were controlled by the same party as the governor. The Senate even took some informal steps in the direction of a macro-budget committee during the 1987 session.

AFTER THE BUDGET IS PASSED

With spending and revenue bills passed by the time the legislature must adjourn in late May, Department of Finance and legislative committee staff members spend the immediate weeks following reaching agreement on legislative intent. The budget then moves into the implementation or execution stage on July 1, the beginning of the fiscal year. In consultation with the agencies, the Finance Department establishes an allotment for each agency to guide and limit its rate of spending during the biennium. Agencies can then begin to encumber funds to support the programs for which they are responsible.

State financial management mechanisms of the Department of Finance then take hold to assure that agency spending conforms to appropriations and allotments. Finance also monitors revenue receipts and continues to update revenue forecasts. If updated forecasts resemble the estimates at the time the budget was passed, the implementation stage can be smooth and uneventful. As the first fiscal year of the biennium proceeds, attention can again be turned to developing guidelines to initiate preliminary work on the budget for the succeeding biennium—the recurring nature of the budget cycle.

The serenity of this period can change if revenue forecasts change. If revenues, on which the budget was based in the spring legislative session, turn out to have been underestimated, with succeeding monthly receipts exceeding estimates by substantial amounts in the millions, pressure will mount to increase the budget or cut taxes in the second legislative session the following January. Such speculation revolves around a problem of riches.

Minnesota experienced a turnabout in its budgetary fortunes in the 1980s as revenues proved unstable on the short side. Revenue forecasting estimates in the economically turbulent 1980s were in error by up to a plus or minus 10 percent. Fiscal years 1981 to 1983 were perhaps the most difficult in Minnesota's postwar history. Continuing a high-spending policy tradition from the 1970s, while harnessing revenue growth through indexing the personal income tax in the midst of an economic recession, resulted in severe revenue shortfalls and cash-flow problems.[9] The 1980–1981 shock was absorbed by shifting some transfer payments into the next biennium, an action that can be taken only once. Matters continued into the 1982–1983 biennium, forcing Governor Al Quie to call three painful special legislative sessions, involving tax increases and spending adjustments, to solve the shortfall and cash-flow problems.

By 1983 the economy improved, with the higher sales tax rates adding to the generation of a more positive financial picture, and created a budget reserve of $250 million.[10] The reserve also serves to smooth out cash-flow peaks and valleys during a biennium. The governor asked for, and the legislature granted, an increase in the reserve to $375 million in 1984, only to cut it back to $250 million in 1985 as all parties sought ways to produce major tax cuts. Along with the reserve reduction, budgets were cut substantially below requests to create a $1 billion tax cut. Subsequent revenue estimates preceding the 1986 session suggested the possibility of revenue shortfalls exceeding the reduced budget reserve. The legislature could not reach agreement on a budget balancing bill and adjourned without a decision.[11] The governor balanced the budget with an "unallotment" rather than call a special session, which is always politically unpopular.

The governor's unallotments, which severely hurt the agencies as the new reductions were added to earlier cuts in 1985 to permit the tax cut of that year, were followed by improved revenue forecasts in subsequent months. Unallotments were not restored. Work had already begun on the 1987–1989 budget.

A biennial budget system presumably has a two-year budget execution stage; the summary of events above reveals that is not the case. The possibility of unstable revenues, as well as a scheduled second session of the legislature, virtually assures that the budget will get additional attention throughout the biennium. At least in budgeting, nothing ever ends.

CONCLUSION

Minnesotans hardly view their state budget processes and outcomes as optimal. Critics are numerous, their criticisms are constructive, and proposed solutions are not lacking.

Criticism that centers on the proper role of state government in the political economy takes the form of disagreement over the substantive content of the budget. Intense partisan debate on the size of the budget, the priorities for spending, and the mix of revenues to support the spending, constitute the dynamics of the process, and will be repeated election after election and cycle after cycle. This type of criticism only reflects the vitality of the state's politics, with the solutions chosen reflecting the political majority at the time.

The structure and processes within which substantive budget decisions are made have also come under criticism, with the legislature drawing most of the attention. The use and abuse of the conference process near the end of the session is generally regarded as a major problem. Order and predictability seem abandoned and are supplanted by apparent confusion and surprises, with much of the deliberations shielded from public scrutiny. Proposed corrective measures can range from time and procedure adjustments in the conference process[12] to calls for adoption of a unicameral system, eliminating even the possibility of conference committees.[13]

The problem of revenue uncertainty, causing second-year fiscal crises, might be better managed under an annual budget cycle. The creation of budget committees, even a joint budget committee, to forge comprehensive macro-budget resolutions in the early stages of the legislative session, is seen as giving the legislature a sense of publicly visible policy direction. A legislative budget office will increase the legislature's capacity to cope with the complexity of the budget and the informational advantage held by the executive.[14]

Critiques of structure and process come from current and former legislators, good government and interest groups, academic policy researchers, and, at times, the media. This type of criticism reflects the level and intensity of interest in the conduct of budgeting in Minnesota, and concern for its stability. Events that resulted in instability are the legacy of the 1980s. The instability of the revenue system remains with the state and conditions the course of budgeting each session. The challenge in the next decade is to create solutions to restore stability.

9

Kentucky: Transitions, Adjustments, and Innovations

MERL M. HACKBART

The Taft recommendations, the Hoover Commission report, and the budget system innovations of the Johnson, Nixon, and Carter administrations all embraced an underlying thesis that creative or innovative budgetary practices would improve the efficiency and effectiveness of governmental decisions and operations.[1] Nevertheless, the thrust of reform changed over time. Budget process revisions early in this century emphasized control, whereas the Hoover Commissions of the late 1940s and early 1950s stressed performance and management enhancement. Furthermore, the presidentially sponsored initiatives of the last three decades contained various combinations of management and planning-oriented innovations.[2]

What actually constitutes budgetary innovation remains elusive.[3] Often what appears to be an innovation due to the introduction of a new procedure may, in fact, change little in the overall budget process and have little impact on decision making. Despite procedural modifications, budget preparation and control necessarily remain the major budget process emphasis.[4] The literature typically has identified budget process *changes* as innovations, while realizing that such changes may or may not affect decision making or the efficiency or effectiveness of government operations.[5]

This chapter reflects on changes in budgeting practices and activities in Kentucky as a case study of budget process transition and innovation. An earlier study identified gubernatorially mandated or supported change in the budgetary process as the key factor influencing budgetary innovation in state government.[6] Similar patterns have been observed in the federal government, where many presidents have supported budget process changes. In essence, budget innovations have been found to be more successful if implemented concurrently with organizational adjustments. Reorganizational efforts often lead to a reassignment of responsibilities, new internal interactions, and a general environment that is more conducive to the adoption of new budget process techniques.

Kentucky has undergone significant changes in budgeting practices in the past decade and a half. As a result, it offers a unique setting in which to study the

effects of executive, organizational, and other factors influencing budgetary innovations. Its uniqueness arises from administrative changes that occur regularly
because Kentucky governors are not constitutionally allowed to succeed themselves. Consequently, they serve a single four-year term with two legislative sessions, and they have only a limited period within which to exert their influence
on state policy. Given this time constraint, recent governors have often turned
to budget and financial management innovations to enhance their ability to exert
policy leadership. At the same time, the relatively rapid turnover of administrations creates a political/organizational environment that is also conducive to budget
process change. New governors often attempt to exert policy leadership by initiating organizational and administrative changes. Therefore, two factors contribute
to the budget "innovation environment" in Kentucky: *the executive leadership
factor*, reflecting strong incentives to influence policy quickly within a single term;
and *the organizational change factor*, resulting from incentives to obtain policy
control by administrative/organizational adjustments. Both factors previously were
identified as positive environmental change variables affecting innovation in the
budgetary process and were shown to simultaneously influence budget innovation.[7]

In Kentucky, organizational changes resulting from the desire of the executive
branch leadership to influence policy have affected the budget process in a substantial way. In recent years, however, legislative budget initiatives have also im-
pacted the state's budget decision-making procedures. As the executive branch
reduced its influence on the legislature by withdrawing from the politics of selecting the legislative leadership, the legislature responded by aggressively pursuing
its independence of the executive branch. Such actions led to budgetary process
changes and innovation as well.

The period covered by this chapter extends from 1972, the midpoint of Governor Wendell Ford's administration, through 1987, the last year of Martha Layne
Collins' administration. During this period Kentucky had a total of four governors including Ford (1970–1973), Julian Carroll (1974–1979), John Y. Brown,
Jr. (1979–1983), and Martha Layne Collins (1983–1987). All are Democrats who
served during times of significant economic change, including a period of coal
boom and manufacturing growth (Ford); rising energy prices, manufacturing
growth, and increasing per capita income relative to the nation (Carroll); deep
economic recession and revenue shortfalls (Brown); and slow economic recovery,
a weak energy sector, and expanded service employment (Collins). Unable to
regain its pre-recession relative per capita income level, Kentucky has been in
a continual state of fiscal stress since 1981.[8]

In this chapter, budgetary changes and the evolution of the Kentucky budget
system are tracked across the four administrations. We consider both process and
organizational adjustments in order to reflect on the leadership as well as the
organizational factors that have influenced changes or innovations in the state's
budget process. In the case study review, three periods are identified: (1) the
organization and budget process change period, (2) the budget refinement period,
and (3) the legislative independence and fiscal stress management period.

ORGANIZATIONAL AND BUDGET PROCESS CHANGE

The "new wave" of state government organizational change hit Kentucky in 1972 during the administration of Governor Wendell Ford. In that year, Governor Ford initiated the first comprehensive reorganization of state government since the 1930s by issuing an Executive Order creating the Executive Department for Finance and Administration and the position of secretary of the governor's cabinet. Pursuing a policy of centralization and policy leadership, the Ford plan created a total of six "super cabinets" in 1973 to institutionalize the comprehensive reorganization. The cabinets included policy planning and budget units designed to aid in formulating policy direction and financial plans. A key element of the 1972–1973 reorganizational effort was the creation of the Office for Policy and Management (OPM), which contained a budget function and a planning function, and was administratively located in the Executive Department for Finance and Administration. OPM, the budget and planning arm of the governor, was created by incorporating the previous Budget Division and the Kentucky Planning and Development Office (KPDO) and took on a major policy formulation and execution role for the chief executive. Its creation was followed by several budget process innovations and changes.

At the initiative of the executive and with the support of the legislative branch, a program budgeting and evaluation system was designed and installed. Budgeting by program was mandated, and the Kentucky General Assembly passed legislation requiring that every state program be reviewed and monitored every six months by program status reports.[9] The purpose of the program status report was twofold. First, this six-month review was seen as an internal management tool that required managers and cabinets to periodically review and evaluate their program accomplishments relative to their budget plans. Second, the status reports were viewed as a means of enabling the state budgeting and planning office to monitor the overall efficiency and effectiveness of state programs. Similarly, the Legislative Research Commission, the staff arm of the legislature, could use the reports to review program progress and to become more knowledgeable about state programs during the interim period between biennial legislative sessions.

As noted, the program status report was an element of the revised program budget and management control system. Included in the budgeting system was the requirement to (1) appropriate to a "major" program, (2) budget at the program level, and (3) financially control and account for expenditures at the program level. This system change necessitated a comprehensive redesign of the accounting system to permit the retention of programmatic data as well as line-item data within the program. Efforts were also undertaken to align major programs and subprograms with organizational units, an effort facilitated by the simultaneous nature of Governor Ford's overall reorganizational effort and budget reform initiative for Kentucky state government.

Efforts were made to associate programs and subprograms with cabinets, departments, and divisions and to identify these breakdowns in the accounting system.

Under this budget structure system, the legislature appropriates to major program areas, such as a cabinet, and the OPM subsequently makes allotments to programs (i.e., a department) within major program areas. Major program alignments with cabinets were designed to be flexible, depending on the size of the agency. For example, a major program could include an entire cabinet or a division of a cabinet. Program delineations typically follow organizational structures as well. The key management concept in the overall financial/organizational structure design was that an individual manager should be identified as being in "control" of a budgeted unit. As a consequence, the manager could exercise managerial discretion and adjust line items of expenditure within the program to meet contingencies, as long as the manager conducted his or her activities within the appropriated funding level for the program. Equivalently, cabinets are responsible for single or multiple major programs where central budget and accounting control is focused. The use of the allotment process provides an additional central financial management control device that the state budget director can utilize in the event of financial contingencies, such as state revenue shortfalls or equivalent financial emergencies.

Legislative consideration of Kentucky's budget also changed significantly during the 1970s. The Kentucky Senate and House have historically had separate Appropriations and Revenue Committees with general responsibility for legislative budget review. The committees meet separately during legislative sessions and jointly between sessions to monitor the revenue and budget issues. Formal budget review by the Kentucky legislature is, however, a relatively new phenomenon. For example, although some House Appropriations and Revenue Committee budget review activity occurred in 1972, routine budget hearings were not initiated until 1974. The Senate Appropriations and Review Committee began separate formal hearings in 1982.

The House Appropriations and Revenue Committee held its first structured budget review with subcommittees in 1976. Nine program area subcommittee chairmen (now six) were named from within the House Appropriations and Revenue Committee and charged with review responsibility for specific segments of the executive budget. The budget process role of the committee was temporarily enhanced in 1976 when the staff was expanded to eight full-time staff members and the legislature began the development of a "legislative budget." Although the Legislative Research Commission later halted the preparation of the budget, the action was a precursor of the emergence of legislative independence which gained prominence in the 1980s.

BUDGET REFINEMENT PERIOD

The comprehensiveness of the 1972–1973 reorganization and budget process change required significant adjustments for Kentucky state agencies. Consequently, when Governor Carroll replaced Governor Ford, upon Ford's election to the Senate, organizational and budget change was minimized. The major efforts were directed toward fine-tuning the Ford administration adjustments to the budgeting system. For example, the program status report process was terminated because of the lack of involvement and support of the cabinets, except for the Cabinet for Human Resources, which found the review process useful in the large cabinet setting. In addition, the planning function of the Office for Policy and Management was operationally eliminated as planning was more fully merged programmatically with the program budgeting process. As a result, OPM policy analysts consider program plans and budget requests as elements of the same process.

Later in the Carroll administration, in 1976, the popularity of the Carter administration's zero-base budgeting (ZBB) approach encouraged Kentucky to adopt elements of the process. Kentucky's zero-base budgeting system adjustments involved refining certain elements of the existing program budgeting system by selectively adopting features of the ZBB approach.[10] The adjustments made to the program budgeting process involved the critical review of base levels of program support combined with detailed assessments of requests for "increments" or packages above the minimum including expansion or enhancement packages. Such requests were considered additive and independent of the minimal program level of effort or the budget base. The integrated or hybrid budgetary system that emerged utilized major programs, and minor programs as its principal focus and elements of zero-base budgeting for assessing alternative levels of activity. The Carroll administration's revised system remained essentially intact in 1987. The budget display includes output measures that encourage legislative and managerial emphasis on program outcomes rather than on line items of expenditure associated with the execution of the program.

Since 1976 the hybrid system has undergone additional change in two primary areas, namely (1) the development of a capital budget and (2) enhancements of the budget preparation process to more precisely define the budget base and to encourage agencies to utilize agency funds before requesting general fund appropriations. For example, the 1987 budget preparation guidelines included directions for making adjustments to line-item components of the program base and for enhancement requests.[11] The budget guideline refinements emerged during the Brown administration as Kentucky was faced with serious revenue constraints and budgetary shortfalls. As a result of this period of fiscal stress, the administration was forced to exert strong fiscal management leadership. Each of these more recent budgetary process changes is discussed further in the following section.

Legislative budget procedures also evolved during this period. The professionalism of the legislative budget review process was further enhanced following the 1978 session by the establishment of a separate legislative Budget Review Office. This office provides general staff support to the Appropriations and Revenue Committees during budget preparation and review.

LEGISLATIVE INDEPENDENCE AND FISCAL STRESS MANAGEMENT PERIOD

The 1980s ushered in a period of extreme fiscal stress for most states. Similarly, Kentucky experienced a deep economic recession beginning in 1981. State revenue growth fell short of projections, and the state had to take actions to prevent a fiscal year deficit, inasmuch as the state's constitution prohibits such deficits. The state's revenue condition was exacerbated by tax reduction actions mandated by a special session of the state legislature called by the lieutenant governor in 1979.

The combination of the recession and the revenue reductions precipitated by the 1979 special session resulted in Kentucky's first shortfall in over a decade in FY1981. Reacting to the shortfall, the Kentucky Finance and Administration Cabinet (previously the Executive Department for Finance and Administration), within which the budget office was located, issued a "Secretary's Order," which reduced appropriations by an amount sufficient to balance the budget. An "Order" is the legally established mechanism by which the legislature delegates authority for budget cutbacks during the interim between legislative sessions. This same process was utilized to meet the financial shortfalls experienced in the succeeding fiscal years of 1982, 1983, 1984 (two), 1987, and 1988 (one). The order was unique in that the secretary of finance initiated the budget cuts based on his statutory responsibility to insure that the state not end the fiscal year in a deficit condition. Subsequently, the legislature was asked to confirm the budget reductions during the next regular legislative session with what amounted to an ex post revised appropriation. The order was not challenged by the legislature, affected agencies, or other governmental units. However, the legislature was kept informed of the proposed actions and received full briefings about the budget cuts directed by the Secretary's Order. Such communications probably added to legislative support for the budget actions.

The move toward legislative independence gained momentum in the 1982 legislative session with the passage of House Bill 649.[12] The bill encompassed a series of legislative changes designed to strengthen the legislature's role in the budget process. The creation of a professionally staffed Budget Review Office endowed the legislature with the capability to participate in budget decision making in a more meaningful way. Included in House Bill 649 were requirements that (1) the governor submit his or her budget by the fifteenth day of legislative session (his or her first budget) or by the tenth legislative day (for a governor's second budget); (2) the budget include a budget reduction plan, thereby restricting the governor's ability to redirect resources in the event of a shortfall; (3) the Legislative Research Commission (LRC) be authorized to write the state budget instructions; (4) the legislative branch draft a budget memorandum to clarify legislative intent; and (5) the budget be in the form of a resolution rather than a bill. Other actions taken by the legislature included measures affecting the interim legislative committee process, block grants, appointments, reorganizations, and regulations.

The budget authority bill, HB 649, was eventually subjected to a court challenge along with other measures in *L.R.C.* v. *Brown* (664 S.W. 2d 907 [Ky 1984])[13] The statutory challenge involved substantive executive/legislative branch issues regarding executive branch prerogatives, legislative authority, and the separation of powers. While holding for the executive branch in the majority of the issues raised regarding appointments, regulations, and the like, the Kentucky Supreme Court, in its opinion issued in January 1984, held that the legislature through the LRC had the power to formulate budget instructions for the biennial general fund budget. Moreover, it upheld the budget reduction language requirement and budget submission date requirements of HB 649.

The court's delegation of budget instruction preparation authority to the legislature was apparently based on the court's judgment that the legislature had the right to be informed of information relevant to the legislative process. Since 1984 the Budget Review Office has issued budget instructions. This unit has also assumed the responsibility for preparing the budget memorandum that details changes made to the executive budget during the biennial legislative session. The ruling made Kentucky somewhat unique relative to other states in regard to preparing the executive budget. In most states, of course, the executive branch exercises the leadership role in the budget preparation process.

As a result of actions taken in FY1984 to meet two shortfalls within one fiscal year, a second court case emerged under the title of *Armstrong* v. *Collins* (709 S.W. 2d 437 [Ky 1986]) which was decided in 1986. Under the Secretary's Order of 1984, departmental or agency fund substitutions for general fund appropriations were ordered. Similarly, in Collins' 1984 budget recommendations, agency funds were budgeted by fund substitution and enacted into law by the appropriations bill. Technically, the restricted revenue funds and special funds were transferred to the General Fund, under a central administrative expense assessment concept, and then appropriated.[14] The court upheld the legislature's ability to transfer agency funds via an omnibus budget bill and, by inference, the executive branch's authority to utilize the Secretary's Order mechanism to perform the same function. Exceptions were noted for transfers of retirement and Kentucky Reinsurance Association or Worker's Compensation Fund monies. The decision held that the budget bill was, in essence, "superior" to other bills and effectively overrode other existing state statutes. In addition, because the court held that the budget was a "bill" rather than a resolution, the budget has now been incorporated into the Kentucky Revised Statutes as KRS Chapter 47. The section is completely revised by each legislative session with the passage of a new budget bill for the upcoming biennium. The court's ruling that the budget had to be enacted as a "bill" was, in part, predicated on the fact that the Kentucky constitution requires that the governor be permitted to veto items of the appropriations bill line by line.[15] The court also held that because of special language embedded in HB 649 regarding a budget reduction plan for financial contingencies, future Secretaries' Orders do not have to be ratified by reference in subsequent budget bills and have the force of law when issued.

CAPITAL BUDGET

Another example of legislative independence/leadership and fiscal stress interacting to bring about budget process change in Kentucky is in the area of capital budgeting. The impetus for developing a more formalized capital budgeting process emerged for three reasons. First, the budget office staff realized that the addition of a capital component to the executive budget would improve the decision-making processes regarding capital expenditures; second, the withdrawal of the federal government from the financing of infrastructure and other public facilities put greater strain on the state of Kentucky during an already fiscally stressful period; and third, the legislature began to become concerned with the issue of debt management and the increased use of debt financing for capital expenditures. In response to intensive legislative questioning regarding capital budgeting and approval procedures during the aforementioned 1979 special session, the 1980 executive budget was the first to clearly display the capital projects that would be financed in the next biennium. In essence, it represented the beginning of formalized capital budgeting in Kentucky. Prior to the 1980 budget, the executive branch managed capital acquisitions based on previous legislative authorization. Such authorizations were operationally regarded as extending beyond budget periods and tended to be silent with regard to funding source. As a result, once authorization was provided, projects could be undertaken if sufficient funds became available during a biennium. With the 1980 "capital budget" and project approval process, only legislatively approved and funded projects could be undertaken during the biennium. If authorized projects were not started, they had to be reauthorized in the budget for the subsequent biennium.

In 1984, as a result of increased fiscal stress and reduced federal government infrastructure commitment, a more sophisticated capital budget process was initiated. Agencies were required to assess capital needs, evaluate alternatives, and specify the planned funding sources and processes as part of their capital request. For example, if bond financing was sought for capital expenditures, the source of debt service and the debt service appropriation (agency funds, project revenue, or general fund appropriations) had to be specified if the project was to be financed by general fund money. This process insured that the Kentucky General Assembly was aware of the long-term obligation that the bond-financing proposal carried with it. In addition, debt service requirements had to be estimated with the assistance of the newly established Office of Investment and Debt Management (OIDM), set up within the budget office. Established by the Brown administration, the OIDM was intended, in part, to enhance the debt management procedures of the state, including debt capacity assessment, debt marketing and monitoring, and management of the state's debt position.[16] With the establishment of new capital budgeting procedures and the increased emphasis on the assessment of the state's ability to incur more debt for financing capital acquisitions, the OIDM became an integral component of the budgeting process. Moreover, the capital planning and budgeting process was fully integrated into the operating budget planning and review process already in existence.

SUMMARY

Budget process change can be temporary or permanent. The degree of permanency probably depends on the perceived utility of innovations by succeeding budget process players, including budget office staff, executive branch officials, and legislators and legislative staff officials.

The period from 1972 to 1987 brought significant budgetary process change in Kentucky. Initially fostered by state government reorganization and management reform movements of the late 1960s and early 1970s, budget preparation and assessment processes of 1973 were modified and adjusted throughout the 1970s. The 1980s brought innovations in budget execution due principally to fiscal stress management needs. At the same time, pressures fostered by the emergence of legislative independence influenced the character and approach to budget preparation and execution as well as the capital budgeting approach used in Kentucky. Also noteworthy was the increased role of the judicial branch during the period in influencing budget policies and procedures.

As noted, the emergence of the Kentucky legislature as a partner in the budget preparation and review process began in the early 1970s when the legislature enhanced its ability to deal with the budget complexities by establishing formal budget hearings, recruiting professional staff, and establishing a separate Budget Review Office. The 1980s brought greater legislative independence and further refinement of the legislative budget review process, including the establishment of a separate Senate budget review process and the legislature's more direct involvement in the budget preparation process. However, the greater legislative involvement in the budget process did not detract from the budget innovations initiated by the executive branch. The legislative branch apparently accepted the development of "hybrid" budget process procedures as positive budget innovations.

Kentucky's experience with budgetary innovation and change in the past decade and a half suggests that legislative independence, fiscal stress, and judicial interpretation should be added to the previously recognized state budget innovation inducing factors of executive leadership and reorganization. Regardless of cause, however, Kentucky's budgetary innovations have been adjusted, modified, and integrated to create a hybrid system that meets the traditional budget preparation and control needs as well as the budget planning and execution requirements of contemporary decision makers. A similar integrative fate probably awaits budget process innovations, regardless of implementation reason.

10

Florida: Miles to Go and Promises to Keep

GLORIA A. GRIZZLE

Chapter 216 of the Florida Statutes stipulates the procedures to be followed in preparing and administering the state budget. This chapter highlights those procedures and uses a few examples to suggest how the major participants in the budget process interact with each other. This budgeting process serves one of the most rapidly growing states in the nation. Florida is now the fourth most populous state and adds a quarter to a third of a million persons to its population each year. The final section of this chapter summarizes the state's fiscal condition, one of the major factors that will influence how participants in the budgeting process will in future years decide who will benefit from what programs and who will bear the burden of paying for these programs.

POLITICAL STRUCTURE

Traditionally a Democratic state, Florida has had only two Republican governors since Reconstruction. Both chambers in the legislature have consistently had Democratic majorities throughout the past century. But party affiliation may be less important than political ideology and the quest for power as indicators of how elected officials behave. Party discipline is not a hallmark of Florida politics, and party affiliation is not a good predictor of how legislators will line up on resource allocation issues.

Twice in recent years a conservative group of Democrats in the Senate has formed a coalition with the Republicans to form a working majority. During the Democratic primary in 1986, the more liberal of the two front runners won the nomination.

Subsequently, a conservative Democratic leader in the Senate openly supported the Republican candidate for governor, and the more conservative loser of the Democratic primary switched to the Republican party after the election and then became the chief of staff for the newly elected Republican governor. Formerly elected as a Democrat to the cabinet post of attorney general, this new chief of staff then returned to the cabinet as a Republican secretary of state less than a year later. This opportunity arose when the elected incumbent secretary of state resigned in midterm to take a job with a national investment firm (where they make money the old-fashioned way). The governor capitalized on the secretary of state's departure to appoint his chief of staff to serve as secretary of state, making the former Democrat the first Republican to serve on the cabinet.

The House is normally less conservative than the Senate and more supportive of the governor's program. In 1987, however, the governor was Republican, (having previously been a Democrat and mayor of Tampa), and conservative Senate Democrats combined with Republicans to form a majority, elect the president of the Senate, and support the governor's program. The governor, having campaigned to cut $800 million of "waste" out of the state budget, introduced a budget in which increases were to be funded by extending the sales tax to cover services and by implementing a state lottery. This legislation passed both houses and was signed, except for various line-item vetoes, into law by the governor. The governor then changed his position on the services tax and called the legislature into special session to repeal it. After three special sessions, the legislature repealed the tax on services and raised the sales tax on the previous tax base one cent.

Participants in Budget Formulation

As is the case with other states, the legislature, governor, the agencies, and interest groups are the primary participants in Florida's budget process. Although the governor is the state's chief budget officer, the heads of about half the state's agencies are independently elected or appointed by a majority of the elected executives who collectively comprise Florida's unique Cabinet. They are, therefore, more independent of the governor than are the agency heads whom the governor appoints. The relative influence of the governor and the legislature in formulating the budget has shifted back and forth over the decades.

Legislative appropriations committees and their subcommittees review executive budget requests and prepare appropriations bills for floor consideration. Their staffs have grown substantially in size and influence during the past thirty years. Before 1959, the legislative appropriations committees had no independent staff. By 1975 the staff had grown to such an extent that at least one staff member claimed that the legislative staffs had greater capability for budgeting and program review than executive budget staff. He went on to say, "it has been found that the executive budget officers can seldom make the transition to legislative staff positions. They are accustomed to mere 'paper processing' and are less inclined to be insightful or analytical."[1]

In 1979 the governor's budget staff was transferred from the Department of Administration to the Executive Office of the Governor. Known as the Office of Planning and Budgeting, this office became responsible for policy development as well as budget development and administration. The office's positions were filled with policy-oriented analysts who are educated in a wide variety of disciplines and who could hardly be described as "paper processors."

Budget Preparation Calendar and Processes

Florida has a biennial budget process. A supplemental budget (which may contain as many pages as the biennial budget itself) is submitted for the second year in the biennium. Several features of this process distinguish Florida from most other states. First, consensus-estimating conferences, given statutory authority in Chapter 216.134 of the Florida Statutes, develop much of the data that set the context within which resource allocation takes place. These conferences produce not only the revenue forecasts that both the governor and the legislature use, but also national and state economic forecasts, state demographic forecasts, and estimates of the caseload for such programs as Medicaid, Aid to Families with Dependent Children, education enrollment, and the prison population. The conferences produce one set of estimates before the governor submits his recommendations to the legislature and a second set before the legislature appropriates funds. The purpose of these conferences is to insulate the technical aspects of budgetary forecasting from political influence, while giving specialists the opportunity to explore and challenge alternative sets of assumptions.

The revenue-estimating conference will illustrate this feature of the budget formulation process. Ground rules are contained in a memorandum of understanding signed by the state economist representing the governor and the staff directors of the House and Senate Finance Committees. The legislative and gubernatorial staffs each have their own econometric forecasting capability and subscribe to different national econometric services. The procedure first estimates economic variables for the nation, then the state's economy, and finally transportation revenues and general revenues. Meetings are public and are attended by the three principals mentioned above as well as representatives from the Department of Revenue and the legislature's Economic and Demographic Research Division; elected officials do not attend. Estimates must be arrived at by consensus, and all parties agree to use them as the "official estimates."[2] The accuracy of forecasts that these conferences produce has increased over the last several years, with errors in four of the last five years being less than 1 percent.

A second feature of the budget formulation process is the treble nature of budget guidance to agencies and review of the agency budget requests. The agency requests are known as the Legislative Budget Requests, and much of the content as well as the timing of these submissions is mandated in Chapter 216 of the Florida Statutes. This law requires that the Office of Planning and Budgeting staff and the legislative appropriations committees' staffs jointly develop instructions to agencies. Agency budget requests must be submitted simultaneously to both the governor and the legislature by November 1. The legislative staffs therefore review the agency requests before the governor submits his budget recommendations to the legislature in February, forty-five days before the beginning of the legislative session in April. The governor submits his budget recommendations during the period that the appropriations committees are holding budget hearings, typically from January through March before the legislative session begins.

As is typical for state legislatures, the two chambers review the agency budget requests and governor's recommendations separately. Both the Senate and House appropriations committees divide themselves into subcommittees along functional lines—for example, education, transportation, and highway safety; law enforcement, corrections, health, and rehabilitative services; and general government. These subcommittees begin their deliberations well before the legislature convenes on the first Tuesday in April, and they present their reports to the full committees in April. By law these meetings are open to the public.[3]

Although citizens may attend these meetings, few can follow much of what is going on in them after the budget hearings are over and negotiations begin in earnest. Legislators work from computer printouts that identify the issues being discussed by codes such as 2A or 3B. Citizens attending the meetings do not have these computer printouts. The legislators may turn off their microphones and mumble and whisper as they discuss tradeoffs in order to reach compromises. If a citizen could hear what was being said, the discussion might sound like this: "How about if we go with you on 2A and all of 3, if you will go with us on everything else?"[4]

Each full committee prepares an appropriations bill that it submits for floor debate. After the House and Senate each debate their respective appropriations bills and pass them, the two chambers must negotiate their differences so that both the House and Senate can pass a single appropriations bill.

Another feature important to understanding legislative budgeting behavior is the relationship between the House and Senate. In preparing the appropriations bill, the two houses maintain an adversarial relationship. They do not take to the conference committee appropriations bills that would fund the items they think meritorious. They take appropriations bills that they believe put them in the best bargaining posture. As a result, the House bill may exclude items that it wants but believes the Senate leadership also wants. This tactic provides leverage for the House to bargain with the Senate to include some items in the conference bill that the House wants but the Senate has excluded. The Senate may do the same.

The speaker of the House and the president of the Senate each appoint about seven of their appropriations committee members to serve on the conference committee. During the negotiations, House and Senate leadership meet separately to work out their strategies for getting the conferees in the opposite chamber to agree to include the items they want. These meetings have traditionally been held in private and are not open to the press. As former House Speaker Ralph Haben maintained to the press, "We [the House] cannot negotiate education, transportation or criminal justice if the Senate knows what our bottom line is before we get started. The negotiation [in conference committee] would be useless."[5]

The conference committee's report, reflecting the agreed upon compromises, is transmitted to each chamber to be voted up or down. Amendments to this report are not permitted, and the report typically is not ready until the end of the session. House and Senate members have little choice but to approve the report, thereby conferring the real decision making to a small minority of the legislature. Objecting to this procedure a few years ago, former Senator Buddy McKay complained that the trend toward voting for the leadership position, regardless of one's personal preferences, was "a deterioration in the process. . . . It's an undue centralization of power in the system."[6]

Decision Rules

Appropriations are made to budget entities, which are generally the division level in an agency. Information in the budget request and the governor's recommended budget is presented by budget entity. Within each budget entity the data are classified by appropriations category. Appropriations categories are summary objects of expenditure, such as salaries and benefits, other personal services, expenses, data processing, and operating capital outlay. These categories are the level at which decisions are usually made.

Because of the way the budget is built up from the budget-entity level by individual agencies and because the legislative appropriations committee recommendations are basically a compilation of subcommittee recommendations, one might think of the budget as little more than an aggregation of individual, unrelated decisions modified by bargaining over individual items in the conference committee.

In fact, the budget entity requests are guided by parameters set by the legislature, the governor's and legislative staffs acting jointly, and the consensus-estimating conferences. The estimating conferences provide the revenue forecast, thereby setting the ceiling within which the total budget must conform. They also provide caseload estimates, which are a primary determinant of the size of many requests for education, social service, and corrections programs. Although the budget is split up among subcommittees for legislative review, the appropriations chairpersons typically give each committee a target allocation that limits their overall recommendation, if not the subcommittee's allocation of that total among budget entities. Finally, much of the budget is determined by allocation formula, either contained in statutes or by agreement between the governor's and legislative staffs.

The allocation formula that controls the largest block of funds, 38 percent of all general revenues in fiscal year 1987–1988,[7] is for supporting local school districts, the Florida Education Finance Program. According to this formula, the state's share of school support varies among the school districts, depending on each district's capacity to tax itself. The number of students is determined by weighting full-time equivalent students by cost factors to reflect the differences in resources required to educate the physically handicapped, emotionally disturbed, and so on. The basic student allocation is modified to reflect differential costs in the various school districts. Although the formula sets the criteria that the legislature will use to determine the total allocation and its distribution among the school districts, it leaves the task of estimating the numbers for each term in the equation.[8]

In addition to shaping the budget by these factors, the guidelines given each agency specify what information is to be used to justify the budget request and how that information is to be classified. Budget requests are justified according to three basic categories: funds necessary to continue current programs, to improve programs, and to implement new programs.

The Budgeting Approach

Like most state budgets, Florida's budget is a hybrid incorporating remnants of past budget reforms. Budget entities are also broken down by summary objects of expenditure (not detailed line items). Section 216.163 of the Florida Statutes now requires that the governor's recommended budget express explanations and justifications in terms of "program-effectiveness measures, program-efficiency measures, workload, productivity adjustments, staffing standards, and any other criteria needed to evaluate the delivery of governmental agencies." Within this format, decisions focus primarily on the issues presented for each budget entity.[9] The budget contains two sections: operations and fixed capital outlay.

Paradoxically, a former governor who advocated program budgeting while a member of the state legislature[10] misjudged the legislature's reaction to a program budget. In the second year of his term, he submitted a supplemental budget that was short on the customary budget detail (including the agency's budget requests) but long on arithmetic errors. The unexpected effect of this thrust toward program budgeting, which the budget reform literature tells us should strengthen the power of the chief executive, was to weaken further the governor's power in the budget process. The legislature's reaction to this changed budget format was to change Chapter 216 in 1983 to mandate the budget's content and format in more specific detail, to require that the governor's staff and the legislative staff jointly develop the budget instructions sent to the agencies, and to direct agencies to submit their independent judgment of their needs to the legislature.[11]

During subsequent years, the administration emphasized improved performance measurement and established performance agreements between the governor and the appointed heads of agencies. The latest evolution, initiated toward the end of Robert Graham's administration, is state planning, with agency functional plans linked to budgets through extensive crosswalking from approved plans to agency budget requests. Also noteworthy is the extensive automation of budget preparation, legislative appropriation, and budget execution systems. Agencies input their budget requests on-line to a common database used by the governor, the House, and the Senate, but the system assures security to guard each organization's need for privacy.[12]

Budget Execution

In budget execution, continual tension exists between (1) the need to control agencies to ensure that spending is legal, economical, and in conformance with legislative intent and (2) the need to give agencies the flexibility necessary to achieve their purposes. The appropriations act stipulates how much an agency may spend for each purpose. In addition to the appropriations act, many other tools serve to hold the executive branch accountable as it spends the public's funds. Included among them are a quarterly release system for apportioning spending over the fiscal year, restrictions limiting the transfer of funds across appropriations categories, procedures regulating the procurement of goods and services, and procedures regulating the accounting for financial transactions and personnel actions. The Florida Fiscal Accounting Management Information System seeks to integrate all these controls into a total system that can provide timely and accurate information for budget administrators. In addition, the auditor general, appointed by the legislature, conducts financial and performance postaudits. The legislature now requires the auditor general to complete a performance evaluation of each state program at least once every ten years. Until about five years ago, the primary participants in budget administration were the agencies who spend the funds, the Governor's Office of Planning and Budgeting, and the Administration Commission. The Administration Commission consists of the governor and the cabinet. The cabinet includes the following independently elected officials: the attorney general, secretary of state, comptroller, treasurer and insurance commissioner, commissioner of agriculture, and commissioner of education.

Prior to 1983, agencies had the authority to make transfers between appropriations categories within a budget entity not to exceed 5 percent and transfers between budget entities within identical categories of appropriations not to exceed 5 percent. The Administration Commission had the authority to amend the operating budget to effect budget amendments in amounts that exceeded agency authority, except that transfers could not be made across state agencies.

During the first term of the Graham administration, the legislature grew increasingly dissatisfied with executive branch actions that it believed ignored legislative intent. In three of those four years, the legislature and executive branch took their disagreements to court. To quote one legislative proponent of passing a law to limit the executive branch's authority, "We believe there's a design on his [the governor's] part to erode the constitutional responsibility of the Legislature by abusing the authority we've given him."[13]

As a result, the legislature amended Chapter 216 of the Florida Statutes, strengthening the legislature's oversight role. The legislative appropriations committees must now receive notices of the following actions: all actions to eliminate a deficit caused by a revenue shortfall; all actions releasing emergency and deficiency funds appropriated to the Executive Office of the Governor; Administration Commission approval of new programs or changes in current programs that require additional financing; agency application for authorized positions to

exceed the total provided in the appropriations acts; agency transfers within the
5 percent ceiling as well as agency requests for transfers above the 5 percent
ceiling.

The following quote from Chapter 216.181(2) of the Florida Statutes conveys
the tone of these amendments:

If the chairmen of the legislative appropriations committees object in writing to the Executive Office of the Governor that the General Appropriations Act has been violated or
is proposed to be violated, then the Governor shall instruct the affected state agency to
immediately change its spending actions or proposal to conform with legislative intent
if the Governor concurs with the chairman's objections. If in the judgment of the Governor, the General Appropriations Act has not been violated or proposed to be violated,
then the Administration Commission shall review the spending action or proposal. Such
spending action or proposal may be affirmed by a two-thirds majority affirmative vote
of the members present with the Governor voting in the affirmative. In the absence of
an affirmative vote of two-thirds of the members of the commission present and with the
Governor voting in the affirmative, the commission shall instruct the affected state agency
to cease such spending action or modify its proposal.

Additional requirements that executive budget analysts consult with legislative
analysts before taking action may be attached to specific appropriations categories
by means of provisos. Taken together, all these requirements permit legislative
analysts to be heavily involved in day-to-day budget administration.

FINANCIAL CONDITION

Florida might best be described as an underachiever. While its resource base
is about average for the states as a whole, the tax burden that its citizens carry
is among the lowest in the country.

Since 1967, the Advisory Commission on Intergovernmental Relations (ACIR)
has reported two indices for state governments—one measuring capacity to tax
based on the state's wealth and the other measuring the state's actual tax collections. The tax capacity measure represents the amount of revenue "that each state
would raise if it applied a nationally uniform set of tax rates to a common set
of tax bases."[14] During the sixteen-year period from 1967 to 1982, Florida's
tax capacity has ranged from 1 to 4 percent above the national average.[15] As
Table 10.1 indicates, per capita income for the state is also about the national
average.

Florida is well below average in terms of tax burden (Table 10.1). ACIR's
tax effort index, calculated by dividing actual state and local tax collections by
estimated tax capacity, reflects a general downward trend from 84 percent in 1967
to 72 percent in 1982.[16] Similarly, the number of state employees per one thousand state population and total state spending per resident fall into the bottom
quartile of state governments.

Table 10.1
Florida Financial Condition Indicators

Resource Base	Florida Data	Florida's Rank*	States' Average	Data Year
ACIR Tax Capacity Index[a]	104	18	100	1982
Per capita income[c]	$13,742	19	$13,150	1986
Economic Vitality				
Unemployment Rate[c]	4.6%	42	6.7%	1986
Per capita income growth[b]	30%	16	35%	1980–84
Job growth[c]	32.5%	2	12.8%	1980–86
Population growth[c]	19.8%	4	6.4%	1980–86
Tax Burden				
ACIR tax effort index[a]	72	48	100	1982
State employees per 1000 pop.[c]	8.5	39	11.5	1986
Per capita state expenditures[b]	$1,048	41/47	$1,588	1985
Financial Management Practices				
Bond rating (Standard and Poor's)[c]	AA		AA	1987
Outstanding general obligation debt per capital[b]	$257	20	$290	1986
Unfunded pension liability[d]	46%			
General fund expenditures as a % of revenues[c]	99.48%	32	99.72%	1986

*Rankings are from highest (=1) to lowest (=50).
Sources: a. Advisory Commission on Intergovernmental Relation, 1982
Tax Capacity of the Fifty States (Washington, D.C., 1985).
b. "The 50 States," City & State, 3:5 (May 1986), pp. 14–42.
c. "The 50 States," City & State, 4:4 (April 1987), pp. 14–47.
d. Florida Comprehensive annual Financial Report, Fiscal Year
Ended June 30, 1986, p. 132.

Low-tax burden in Florida translates into a backlog of unmet needs. The state's tradition of underinvestment has created sizable infrastructure needs that far outstrip its current revenues. As an example, an advisory group to the speaker of the House of Representatives recently reported that $16.2 billion were needed for expressway and arterial construction for additional highway system capacity, $5.3 billion for wastewater treatment, and $17 billion for stormwater treatment.[17] As an example of needs unmet by social programs, the same report noted that 30 percent of the state's children live in poverty, 50 percent have no safe child care, 62 percent receive no preventive health care, and 90 percent of school-aged mothers are not in school.[18]

Coupled with this record of underachievement is a picture of considerable economic vitality. In a state where immigration greatly exceeds outmigration, Florida was in the past six years fourth in population growth and second in job growth rates among the states. While its unemployment rate is relatively low, it is primarily a service-based economy, and its growth in per capita income does not match its growth in jobs.

Indicators of financial management practices paint an uneven picture of the state's fiscal condition. The combined pension liability and outstanding general obligation debt of $887 per resident in 1985 amount to more than a year's general revenue collections. The state has a large unfunded pension liability of more than $7 billion. Contribution rates are currently adjusted to amortize the unfunded actuarial accrued liabilities over a thirty-year period.[19] This amortization rate is similar to the mean of twenty-nine years reported in a recent survey of public pension funding.[20] Of the pension systems reporting in this survey, 72 percent have an unfunded actuarial liability. Annual pension fund receipts in Florida are currently over four times as much as disbursements (Table 10.1).

Florida's general obligation debt outstanding is close to the average for all the states. The state's bond ratings, an indicator of its credit worthiness, are currently investment grade. Standard and Poor's bond rating for Florida is AA and Moody's is Aa. Seventeen states have higher AAA or AA+ bond ratings, and ten have lower ratings.

Revenue collections have grown at a healthy rate of 10 percent a year over the last decade. General fund revenues are slightly greater than expenditures (Table 10.1), and the state has a small rainy-day fund.

In some other respects, the state's financial management practices are noteworthy. In accordance with generally accepted accounting principles, the state uses the modified accrual basis of accounting for revenues and expenditures. All state agencies use the State Automated Management Accounting Subsystem of the Florida Fiscal Accounting Management Information System. Florida is the first state to conform to the guidelines for the comprehensive annual financial report.[21]

In sum, Florida is not a state under fiscal stress due to declining revenues, erosion of its economic base, and a high tax burden. Its tradition of low taxation and underinvestment coupled with a rapidly growing population, however, has created a huge unfunded need for public services. If Florida fails to cope with this problem, the next decade will witness a significant decline in its quality of life.

11

Utah: Legislative Budgeting in an Executive Budget State

F. TED HEBERT

Among the American states, Utah is unique. Not only does it have an unusual history as the Mormons' place of settlement and headquarters of the Church of Jesus Christ of Latter-day Saints (LDS), but it is culturally and demographically distinct from its neighbors. The state's present political climate—even matters of fiscal and budgetary affairs—are affected by this history and by cultural phenomena that set Utah apart.

Mormon teachings place a very high value on conceiving and bearing children. As a result, Utah has an extraordinarily young population (median age 25.5), thanks to its having the second highest birth rate in the United States (second to Alaska). Although the number of births per one thousand population dropped during the 1980s from 28.6 in 1980 to 21.4, it remains substantially above the national rate of 15.7 (1987). Utah's population has grown rapidly, and continues to do so, having expanded 38 percent between 1970 and 1980 and another 15 percent between 1980 and 1987. During this most recent period, only seven states exceeded Utah's rate of growth. But unlike these other fast-growing states, Utah's growth resulted entirely from natural increase rather than from excesses of in-migration over outmigration.

Utah's large families place an extraordinary burden on public education institutions. Between 1975 and 1985, the school-age population grew by 97,000, a 30 percent increase, while across the United States the number of schoolchildren dropped by 6 million, a decrease of 12 percent.[1] The size of the state's student population produces a strong anomaly: although Utah has historically given strong support to education (having the second highest percentage of high school graduates among persons twenty-five years old and over in 1980); although a large portion of total state and local spending goes for elementary and secondary education (Utah ranks thirteenth in the nation); and although only four states spend more than Utah per $1,000 personal income for education, Utah spends *less* per child in public schools than any other state ($2,297 compared to the national figure of $3,723 in 1986).[2]

Eighty-four percent of Utah's population lives in urban places, making it the seventh most urban state in the country, immediately following New York. In its early history, arriving Mormon settlers were systematically dispersed around the state into settlements that grew into small communities. In its more recent history, Utah's population has become highly concentrated in the state's two metropolitan areas—Salt Lake City-Ogden and Provo-Orem. These two areas contain 77 percent of the people, with Salt Lake County alone home for more than 700,000 of the state's 1,665,000 people.

Not only Utah's population but also the state's public institutions are extraordinarily concentrated. Unlike many states in the West, where state institutions were systematically and competitively distributed to various areas of the state (one getting the university, one the capitol, one the prison, and perhaps another the state hospital), most of Utah's major state facilities were established and have remained in Salt Lake City or the immediate area.

The converse of Utah's status as an urban state is its status as a public land state, with 61 percent of all property in the state owned by the federal government. This position puts it fourth behind Alaska, Nevada, and Idaho. The state is home of five national parks (Arches, Bryce, Canyonlands, Capitol Reef, and Zion), has 8,046 thousand acres of national forest land, and 22,076 thousand acres of land administered by the Bureau of Land Management, as well as smaller amounts under control of the Department of Defense and other agencies.[3]

UTAH'S SLUGGISH ECONOMY

Utah's economy has climbed back from the depression of the early 1980s only with great difficulty. In 1983 average unemployment in the state stood at 9.2 percent, somewhat below the national figure of 9.6 percent, but until quite recently it had not fallen much below the 6 percent rate—averaging 6.6 percent, 5.9 percent, and 6.0 percent in 1984, 1985, and 1986, respectively. In July 1987 it stood at 6.5 percent, one-half percentage point above the national figure. This is an unusual position for Utah, since in recent decades the state has usually managed an unemployment rate about one percentage point *below* that of the nation as a whole.[4] Fortunately for the state, 1988 and early 1989 brought substantial improvement.

Along with much of the country, Utah's job structure is moving rather quickly to be clearly dominated by service-producing rather than goods-producing industries. In Utah, this means a shift away from some rather high-paying jobs in the mining, metals, and petroleum industries. In 1986 alone, the state lost 7,136 jobs in the goods-producing sector. Although the service-producing sector grew by 16,887, many skilled workers found themselves accepting reduced pay for the jobs they could find.[5]

Although Utah does not quickly come to mind when one thinks of the petroleum-producing states, it does rank tenth in oil production. Consequently, it along with other states has suffered the shock of falling oil prices, as exploration and development were curtailed and the value of production dropped.

Finally, the federal government has a substantial presence in Utah. Already mentioned is its large role as a landowner. Because much of this land is subject to leasing for mineral exploration and production and for development as recreation areas, federal decisions can have a dramatic impact on the state. (In 1986 the state received $36 million as its portion of mineral lease funds from the federal government.) In addition, the location of several major defense contractors in the state has brought substantial federal contracts to Utah in recent years (1985 estimate for total federal procurement contracts, $1.2 billion). Direct federal salaries and wages in the state totaled $1.1 billion.[6]

UTAH'S FINANCIAL STATUS

Utah's appropriation of funds from all sources for 1988 (including federal funds, income from bonded debt, and locally levied property tax for schools) totals approximately $2.8 billion. The principal categories of state spending are public education (36.4 percent), higher education (12.3 percent), transportation (11.9 percent), social services (9.9 percent), and health (9.5 percent).

State tax revenue is derived mainly from the sales and use tax ($607 million estimated for 1988), the individual income tax ($533 million), and the motor fuels tax ($95 million). The most important story about these revenue sources has been the very slow growth they have shown in recent years. Sales tax revenue grew only 0.58 percent in 1986 over 1985 and only 0.30 percent in 1987; the income tax grew 4.35 percent and 7.50 percent; while the motor fuels tax grew 3.16 percent and 3.60 percent. Thus, there has been little growth revenue to support increased service demands, most notably in the field of education. In fiscal year 1987, the governor and the legislature were compelled to make midyear reductions. Although the governor has authority to make across-the-board cuts, the practice followed is to rely principally on the legislature to adopt changes. This occurred in both a special session held in November 1986 and in the 1987 regular session. The regular session also faced a set of tax increase proposals submitted by the governor, and acted to increase three major taxes (income, sales, and motor fuels) along with several minor ones, adding an estimated $163 million to state revenue.

In comparison to other states, Utah is about ''average'' in the extent to which fiscal activity is concentrated at the state level. Of total own source state and local revenue, 54.5 percent is state generated—roughly comparable to the national figure for all states of 56.0 percent.

BUDGET PREPARATION IN UTAH

In most respects, Utah's executive budget preparation process would be familiar to anyone who has examined that of the federal government or most other states. As in all states except South Carolina, Texas, and Mississippi, primary responsibility is placed on the governor.[7] Utah statutes provide that ''The governor shall within three days after convening of the Legislature in annual session, submit a budget for the ensuing year."[8]

The budget calendar begins with distribution of budget forms and instructions by the Office of Planning and Budget (OPB) in June. Requests are prepared for each line item in object of expenditure format, giving detail to the subobject level (i.e., breaking office expenses down to requests for office supplies, printing and binding, books and subscriptions, photocopy expenses, small office equipment, and office furnishings, and presenting similar detail for other objects). Actual expenditures are presented for the last completed fiscal year (July 1 to June 30 constituting Utah's fiscal year), as well as authorized expenditures for the current year and the requested amounts for the coming year.

Although Utah does not use the current services base approach that some other states have adopted, agency requests for additional resources to support initiation of new programs or expansion in the scope of existing programs are presented separately from other requested amounts. Each of these proposals must be supported with a problem statement and a statement of objectives, as well as a presentation of two major alternatives considered and a justification for the one chosen.

Typically, these agency submissions are received in September or early October, after which OPB briefs the governor. Budget hearings (in which the governor participates) are held during October and November. A tentative budget is assembled by mid-November. Final recommendations are completed by early December in order to meet the statutory requirement that a draft copy be delivered to the state's legislative fiscal analyst "on a confidential basis" thirty days before it is due for presentation to the legislature.[9]

Executive budgeting in Utah in its present form is relatively new, having been adopted in 1979. Previously, the Budget Office had been a unit subordinate to the Department of Finance, while the state planning coordinator had been within the governor's office. Governor Calvin Rampton (1965–1977) was in most respects his own budget officer. By the end of his long tenure, he had little need for an elaborate budget staff. His successor, Governor Scott Matheson, moved quickly to create a stronger executive budget office, securing legislation to establish it as a separate unit responsible to the governor. This legislation gave the governor authority to combine the Office of the State Planning Coordinator with the budget office. Matheson took this step in 1983, creating the present Office of Planning and Budget. Today, the director of OPB is the budget officer, and the deputy director is the state planning coordinator, with all analysts serving as both planning analysts and budget analysts.

THE LEGISLATURE'S ROLE IN UTAH BUDGETING

Students of budgeting in the federal government have had a great deal to say about the importance of agency efforts to prepare themselves for legislative responses to the executive budget.[10] Internal hearings become rehearsals for later hearings before congressional appropriations subcommittees; interest group support is carefully cultivated; plans are formulated to appeal House decisions to the Senate. Although changes that began with passage of the Congressional Budget and Impoundment Control Act of 1974 are slowly modifying the process, the focus of attention remains on the appropriations committees and their subcommittees. LeLoup's comment of a few years ago remains accurate: "Within the executive branch, the annual appropriations hearings are still one of the most important events in an agency's life."[11] Budget committees, superimposed on the previously existing system, have left the detailed examination of specific proposals largely to the appropriations subcommittees. The same is true of the Congressional Budget Office; its staff has not undertaken to prepare congressional budgets that include agency and program-level detail.

The major exception to these generalizations about the congressional budget process has appeared in the last few years, as Congress has struggled with efforts to curtail the deficit. Beginning in 1980 with use of the reconciliation process as a method for the parent body to instruct its committees (including the appropriations committees), greater attention has been given to detail. Still, for most agencies at most times, annual appropriations are the province of appropriations subcommittees and their staffs. It is principally through them that Congress has continued to play an important role in budgetary decision making.

At the state level, the emergence and spread of executive budgeting may have been accompanied by a general decline in legislative influence over fiscal matters. Alan Balutis and Daron Butler note the widespread acceptance of the view that state legislative performance in the budgeting process is inadequate.[12] They add, however, that far too little is known about the role of legislative fiscal staffs in the states. Their book, *The Political Pursestrings*, provided a set of important and useful accounts written by several members of fiscal staff units and also presented more systematic analyses of the staffs in three states. Based on these studies, Balutis and Butler conclude that the influence which fiscal staffs exercise rests on their abilities to help legislators by providing intelligence (both technical and political), assisting with integration (minimizing conflict), and increasing the legislature's ability to innovate. They admit, however, that we need to know much more about the influence and role of legislative staffs, both fiscal and general.[13] Their call for more research with this focus is echoed by Lee and Johnson who lament the lack of knowledge about executive agency–legislature fiscal relations at the state level, comparable to what we know about the process at the federal level. They call for "in depth comparative analyses, particularly focusing upon budget processes in state legislatures."[14]

The remainder of this chapter is devoted to this end. While it is not explicitly comparative in nature, it provides a look at one state in which the legislature has adopted several particularly innovative approaches.

The Formal Structure and Process of Legislative Review

Because relationships between executive agencies and the legislature are conditioned by the formally established review process, that process is the place to begin. In Utah it is an interesting place, because in some respects Utah's procedures are perhaps unique among the states.

Like a number of other states, Utah has a legislative staff office with specific responsibility for assisting the legislature in fiscal matters, the Office of the Legislative Fiscal Analyst. It was created in 1966, at the recommendation of a Legislative Study Commission, to replace a one-person fiscal assistant associated with the Legislative Council. Today there are three legislative service units: the Office of Legislative Research and General Counsel; the Office of Legislative Auditor General; and the Office of Legislative Fiscal Analyst. Each reports to a subcommittee of the joint Legislative Management committee. In the case of the fiscal analyst, this subcommittee's major role is to recommend to the management committee the person to be appointed as fiscal analyst. In practice, the fiscal analyst's office is much more closely related to the committees of the appropriations process, in a manner to be described below. Statutes provide for the major duties of the Fiscal Analyst's Office to analyze in detail the executive budget before the convening of the legislative session and to make recommendations to the legislature on each item or program that appears in the executive budget; to prepare cost estimates on all proposed bills that anticipate government expenditures; and to prepare a review and analysis of revenue estimates for existing and proposed revenue acts.[15] In addition, the Fiscal Analyst's Office has authority to conduct studies during the interim period between legislative sessions, to inform the legislature of instances of the administration failing to carry out legislative intent, and to publish at the end of each session a summary of legislative actions affecting the state's financial condition.

The Utah legislature is not alone in relying on some kind of staff review of the executive budget. *The Book of the States, 1986–87* identifies thirty-five states as doing so, along with nine that rely on a joint committee and six that depend on separate committees in each legislative chamber.[16] (Counted in the thirty-five are all states in which a staff agency takes part, even along with one or more committees.) Among the states, however, the nature of these review offices varies widely and includes legislative councils, controllers general, legislative auditors, fiscal analysts responsible to single chambers, and committee staffs.

Utah's Office of Legislative Fiscal Analyst remained quite small until 1970, having only three or four professional employees during its first four years. It has expanded to the point that it now has a professional staff of thirteen. This expansion resulted indirectly from the state's adopting a constitutional amendment shifting from biennial to annual legislative sessions, with alternate sessions restricted to budget matters (unless opened to other matters by a two-thirds vote). During these budget sessions, only the appropriations committees were to be highly active, raising the question of just what tasks could be assigned to legislators on other committees. Utah's solution was a unique one. *All legislators* were assigned to the appropriations committees. Joint appropriations subcommittees were created, with each legislator assigned to serve on one. Each subcommittee is staffed by at least one professional from the Fiscal Analyst's Office. (Two persons staff the subcommittees on Higher Education and on Social Services and Health.)

Requiring that the nine subcommittees report to the full Joint Appropriations Committee (the entire legislature) could prove unwieldy, to say the least, when the time came to make the tradeoffs necessary to balance the budget. To avoid this difficulty, the legislature has created an Executive Appropriations committee of sixteen members: the majority leadership of the Senate (3); the majority leadership of the House (4); the minority leadership of the Senate (2); the minority leadership of the House (3); the chairs of the House and Senate Appropriations Committees (2); and one additional member of the minority party from each chamber (2). Under this scheme, regardless of its margin in the chambers, the maximum advantage which either party can have in the Executive Appropriations Committee is two votes (nine to seven). The committee is co-chaired by the House and Senate Appropriations Committee chairs.

The job of reconciling the total appropriations recommended by the subcommittees with anticipated revenue falls to the Executive Appropriations Committee. It must adhere to the constitutional provision that, "no appropriation shall be made or any expenditure authorized by the Legislature whereby the expenditure of the State during any fiscal year, shall exceed the total tax then provided by law . . . unless the Legislature making such appropriation, shall provide for levying a sufficient tax . . . to pay such appropriation or expenditure within such fiscal year."[17]

If the Executive Appropriations Committee finds it necessary to alter appropriation items sent to it by the subcommittees, legislative rules direct it to return the items to the subcommittees with guidelines or directives. However, the committee has authority to make any further changes it finds necessary to balance the budget and complete the appropriations bill. Utah employs an omnibus appropriations bill covering most agencies, an additional bill covering state aid to public education, in some years a capital spending bill, a supplemental bill for the current year, and a "bill bill" covering costs of legislation enacted during the session.

Utah's governor has item veto authority but rarely uses it. For reasons to be described shortly, appropriations bills seldom reach the governor's desk until the very end of the session. Thus, although the veto can be used to totally prevent the funding of an item, it is not a useful tool to secure a reduction in amount—unless the governor is willing to call a special session for further consideration. In practice, although the threat of veto no doubt carries some weight, it is rarely used.

Legislative Review in Practice

The importance and power of the legislative fiscal analyst is well understood in Utah. The governor's recommendation through the Office of Planning and

Budget is only a starting point for the agency seeking support for its budget request.

As a matter of practice (although it is not statutorily required), OPB sends copies of departmental requests to the fiscal analyst even before the governor's budget hearings are held. These go forward in late September, as soon as OPB considers the requests complete. In fact, OPB may have little choice but to do so, since the fiscal analyst has statutory authority to "obtain access to all records, documents, and reports of the departments, agencies, and other units of state government, necessary to the scope of his duties, including the power to sub-poena records and agency officials when necessary for this purpose."[18]

The Fiscal Analyst's Office thus begins the examination and review process without knowing the governor's recommendation. Fiscal analysts most likely have been in touch with agency budget staff well before this time and have begun preliminary analysis of agency requests. Each individual analyst in the Fiscal Analyst's Office is given considerable discretion on just how to approach the analysis task. Although some maintain close and frequent contact with personnel at both the department and bureau levels, regularly meeting with agency person-nel and attending meetings of governing boards, others keep a more distant rela-tionship. Rather than there being a "standard" description of the analyst's job, the approach varies with the individual analyst, with the nature of the agency being analyzed and with the choices of the individuals involved.

As a result of several practices of the Fiscal Analyst's Office, the analysts' recommendations for agencies are usually below those made by OPB. First, the fiscal analyst refuses to recommend tax increases. If the governor's budget has been brought into balance by anticipated revenue from a proposed tax increase (or, as was recently the case, by revenue anticipated from increased tax auditing), expenditure recommendations must be brought down if balance is to be maintained—and the fiscal analyst adheres to a requirement that his or her recom-mendations will be in balance. Second, the fiscal analyst uses independent revenue estimates. These are often below those of OPB. For the 1988 budget, the legislature's final estimates of revenue from continuing sources in the state's ma-jor funds (the fiscal analyst's original estimates are not available) were 14 per-cent below the governor's. Finally, as standard practice the fiscal analyst removes all salary increases from the individual agency recommendations, encouraging the legislature to treat salary increases separately, which are to be added back just before passage of the appropriations bills.

The fiscal analyst does not conduct formal hearings before preparing recom-mendations for the legislature, although informal discussions with agency leaders are held, either at the agency's office or at the fiscal analyst's. Some of the in-dividual analysts keep agencies well informed of the recommendations they are going to make to the legislature, whereas others prefer to let the agency find out when the report is presented to the appropriations subcommittee.

Thus, although Utah is in form an executive budget state, the joint appropria-tions subcommittees are actually presented two budgets—the governor's and the legislative fiscal analyst's. The fiscal analyst's, however, is not assembled into a single document. Only members of the legislative leadership receive copies of the full set of recommendations, placed in ring binders. Each appropriations subcommittee receives only the recommendations concerning the agencies for which it is responsible.

Beyond conducting their analyses of agency budgets and presenting their own recommendations, each individual fiscal analyst staffs the appropriations subcommittee responsible for his or her agencies. This includes arranging meetings and briefing the subcommittee on the fiscal analyst's revenue estimates and why these differ from the governor's, responding to legislators' requests for specific data, and presenting the fiscal analyst's recommendations.

Under normal procedures, once the analyst has presented the recommendation, agency personnel testify. Some of the subcommittees cast votes on individual items as they are considered (i.e., appropriations for programs or bureaus), whereas others hold all votes until the agency's entire appropriation has been considered. Subcommittee members take the analyst's recommendations quite seriously. In fact, some believe that the governor's recommendation may not get as much attention as it deserves. Even though analysts often point out the reasons why their recommendations differ from the governor's and alternatives to the particular one they recommend (sometimes noting that if revenue is greater than anticipated particular agency needs should be considered), some legislators tend to focus immediately on the analyst's recommendations. Frequently, a legislator will move that the subcommittee accept the analyst's recommended amount. One story is told of a legislator who felt so frustrated by his colleagues' refusal to consider alternatives that he moved that the "entire book" (the analyst's report) be accepted. The motion passed; the subcommittee completed its work early. In short, the legislature gives the legislative fiscal analyst's recommendations very serious consideration, often giving them more weight than the governor's budget itself.

Some agency personnel see the legislators' reliance on the fiscal analysts as a difficult problem. They approach the appropriations subcommittee ready to "take on" the analyst. Although such an aggressive attitude may work in some instances, it probably would not in most. With the analyst's position as a legislative staff member, legislators would likely be ready to jump to the defense of the analyst's recommendation and to give little attention to what the agency director really has to say.

The legislative fiscal analyst sometimes places the OPB staff in an uncomfortable position. Although OPB furnishes agency requests to the fiscal analyst and must, by law, forward a preliminary budget a month before the session, the fiscal analyst's recommendations are often kept secret until they are delivered to the appropriations subcommittee. In some instances, neither OPB nor individual agencies have much opportunity to prepare responses.

In many respects, then, the staff of the Fiscal Analyst's Office plays a critical role in Utah budgetary decision making. The legislature takes the analyst's independent revenue estimates quite seriously and often use them in its deliberations.

Appropriations subcommittee decisions (some with fiscal analyst's numbers) are forwarded to the Executive Appropriations Committee. Here they are assembled into the major appropriations bills and forwarded to the two chambers. But this is far more than a simple "assembly" process. The Executive Committee is quite powerful—especially when it considers issues regarding major appropriations items. Normally, it sends its bills to the floor on the last day of the session, often *very late* on the last day. Consequently, the Executive Committee must take into account all major controversies and make the compromises necessary to secure final passage. It accomplishes this so well that floor amendments are rare. The last-minute portion of the process is smoothed by the committee's practice of grant- ing its co-chairs authority to make technical adjustments without calling the full committee into session. This is usually done in consultation with the fiscal analyst. An example of this process is the adjusting of appropriations for all departments to reflect legislative actions on salary increases.

Utah's unusual appropriations committee structure makes all legislators a part of the appropriations process (a system continued, even though the state now holds annual general sessions). Although most legislators have been able to affect deci- sions regarding only one or a few agencies, they have at least participated. As described by the fiscal analyst:

Participation in the subcommittee budget hearings process enables legislators to become thoroughly familiar with a functional area of state government, and also tends to foster trust in the total appropriations process because the legislators are aware that all aspects of the budget are examined by their peers in the same way that they examine the budgets they are assigned to hear. This is not to say that all legislators approve of the recommen- dations of the subcommittee—it does ensure, however, a complete understanding of the various elements of the budget.[19]

To this should be added the qualification that a legislator might be quite dissatisfied with the numbers that come out of the Executive Appropriations Committee. Rarely do legislators attend meetings of appropriations subcommittees other than the ones on which they serve. Doing so is made logistically difficult by the subcom- mittees all meeting at the same time. Legislators who have concerns about pro- grams or agencies that are not under their own subcommittee's jurisdiction generally seek to influence the Executive Appropriations Committee. They try to identify one of its members who will "carry their cause" and instruct the rele- vant subcommittee to make the desired change.

CONCLUSION

Utah's unique process for legislative budget consideration faces a difficult challenge in the immediate future. The enormous pressure placed on the state to increase funding for public education (presently at the elementary and secon- dary levels, later for higher education) would strain any system.

Presently, the legislature is assuming an especially large portion of responsibility for the critical decisions that must be made. For 1988 Governor Norman Bangerter had agencies prepare their budgets at a level of 94 percent of the then current year and to suggest "building blocks" above that amount. Even so, he found it necessary to propose the substantial tax package described above. As the 1989 budget was prepared, the governor committed himself to proposing no further tax increases—and the previous increases were the subject of an initiative petition to secure their "rollback" in the 1988 election. The rollback effort failed.

Nevertheless, at best, the tax increases of 1987 were only an interim step. Without improved revenue growth, Utah will continue to face enormous problems simply attempting to keep up with pressures for meeting increased service demands.

Especially important, as the legislature attempts to confront these problems, is the division of responsibility between the appropriations subcommittees, on the one hand, and the Executive Appropriations Committee on the other. Because all legislators serve on one of the subcommittees, many develop strong commitments to "their" agencies. This feeling may be accentuated by a newly adopted procedure of having the subcommittees meet during the interim between legislative sessions, as standing committees have done for some years. Legislators' sense of loyalty to particular agencies, should it increase, would further strengthen the role of the Executive Appropriations Committee, as the legislative institution that must take a broader view and—during the coming difficult times—reduce appropriations requests that the subcommittees are reluctant to cut.

In several respects, then, Utah's unique procedures for legislative fiscal action are still evolving. The role of the Legislative Fiscal Analyst's Office as provider of critical analysis of the governor's budget is well established. But activities of the appropriations subcommittees continue to develop, as do those of the Executive Appropriations Committee. As the system presently functions, it provides a broad opportunity for involvement by many legislators—a feature praised by individual members as well as by the fiscal analyst. This is accomplished without complete loss of focus in the appropriations effort, thanks to the critical actions of the Executive Appropriations Committee near the end of the consideration process. It assumes the task of ironing out any final difficulties—but does so at the cost of excluding many members who were involved in earlier decision stages. Some members feel strongly that the Executive Committee goes too far when it alters the work of the "specialists" on the subcommittees, not only in making deeper cuts, but sometimes by inserting funds for projects the subcommittees have excluded.

The next few years will be a critical test of Utah's unusual system. It will very likely be under enormous pressure. Only the passage of these years will tell whether it is sufficiently institutionalized to withstand the pressures of increasingly difficult budgetary decision making and whether it is indeed an innovation worthy of consideration by other states.

12

Texas: Legislative Budgeting in a Post-Oil-Boom Economy

GLEN HAHN COPE

Budgeting in the state of Texas is a legislative process. Although the governor and the governor's budget staff do prepare an executive budget, the legislature controls the budget process and, in most cases, the fiscal decisions contained therein. Modern governors have exerted more or less influence over the state's budget depending more on their personal political influence than on the formal powers assigned to them by the Texas constitution and statutes. This chapter describes the budget process in Texas and discusses the state's current fiscal condition during a time of transition from an economy based on agriculture and natural resources, especially oil, to a more diversified, technology-based economy.

The Texas state governmental system originated in the Republic of Texas, an independent nation from 1836 to 1845, when it entered the United States as the twenty-eighth state. Its governmental structure, however, was shaped by Reconstruction and by the response of Texas politicians to the policies imposed by Union governors after the Civil War. The constitution now in effect was adopted in 1876. Although it has been amended over two hundred times, several attempts to ratify a new, more modern constitution have been rejected. As a result, Texas is one of the very few states that have not "reformed" their governmental structures in the twentieth century. The legislature's control of the budget process, and the relative lack of gubernatorial influence and power in that process, ensue from the unwillingness of the 1876 constitution writers to give the major power to any one individual, elected or appointed, in the government.

Although the governor of Texas was designated as the chief budget officer in 1931, an independent executive agency, the Board of Control, prepared budgets, managed government property, and performed state purchasing functions until 1949. In 1949 the Legislative Budget Board was created by statute to prepare budget estimates for the legislature. The Board of Control retained its other administrative functions, but budget preparation became solely a legislative function. In 1951 the governor was given the responsibility of preparing an executive budget, but control of the process remained firmly in the legislature's hands. Only one recent governor has been able to induce the legislature to consider the executive budget as the official one for legislative action. That was Governor John Connally, who managed this feat through the force of his personal political influence over legislative leaders, not by virtue of constitutional or statutory provisions.[1]

BUDGET PROCESS AND REFORMS

The Legislative Budget Board is a ten-member body composed of the lieutenant governor, who chairs the board, the speaker of the House of Representatives, the chairpersons of the House Committee on Revenue and Taxation, the House Appropriations Committee, the Senate Finance Committee, and the Senate State Affairs Committee, plus two other senators, appointed by the lieutenant governor and two other representatives, appointed by the speaker. The Legislative Budget Board (LBB) has a staff of over sixty, headed by an executive director appointed by the board. The LBB staff is nonpartisan. Although in practice both houses of the legislature have been controlled by Democrats in recent times, both Republicans and Democrats have served as committee chairs and members of the LBB.[2]

The LBB staff is divided into three sections: Budget, Estimates, and Program Evaluation. The Budget Section and the Estimates Section are essentially the state's budget office. The Estimates Section is responsible for preparing legislative fiscal notes for every bill introduced which might have economic impact for the state government. They work with the state comptroller and treasurer, both of whom are independently elected officials, to determine the revenue estimates for each biennial budget. They also conduct studies in the areas of revenue and taxation, at the request of the LBB. The Budget Section is responsible for examining and analyzing budget requests received from state agencies and preparing budget recommendations for the LBB. The Program Evaluation Section is responsible for a performance audit and program evaluation system established by statute in 1973. These evaluations do not include agency "sunset reviews," however; they are done by a separate Sunset Review Commission which evaluates every state agency on a ten-year rotating cycle.

The Governor's Office of Budget and Planning prepares the executive budget, which reflects the governor's policies and priorities. Constitutionally, Texas has a "weak governor" system, in which the governor appoints very few department heads and has few official powers. Many departments are headed by commissions whose members are appointed by the governor for fixed, staggered terms, whereas others are headed by elected commissioners. Even those departments whose commissions are appointed by the governor are not under the governor's direct control, because only at the beginning of the second term does a governor have the opportunity to appoint a majority of the commissioners of all departments, unless enough previously appointed commissioners resign early. Department executive directors, appointed by commissions, and independently elected commissioners who head departments, therefore, may not owe allegiance to the governor, as directly appointed departments heads would. This means that the governor's budget priorities may not necessarily represent those of the executive agencies as a whole, except to the extent that the governor can exert political influence over them.

Budget preparation in Texas is characterized by a higher degree of cooperation between the legislative and executive budget staffs than might be expected from the above description and than is true in many other states. The Governor's Office of Budget and Planning and the LBB staff prepare a joint budget instructions for all state agencies, which are sent to them jointly approximately one year before the biennial legislative session begins in the January of odd-numbered years. Some gubernatorial budget staffs, knowing their executive budget would have little influence over the legislative deliberations, have attempted to make their mark through requirements for inclusion of particular types of information or use of specific formats. For the most part, the LBB and its staff are less interested in the format of budget requests submitted and readily agree to revisions of the jointly issued instructions, as long as the information they value most is easily accessible.

Once state agencies have received the joint budget preparation instructions, they have about three months in which to complete their budget requests and submit them simultaneously to the Governor's Office of Budget and Planning (OBP) and the LBB. Joint budget hearings are usually held by LBB and OBP staffs from June to September prior to the beginning of the legislative session in January, so that agencies can defend their budgets prior to the development of staff recommendations. At the same time, the LBB Estimates Section prepares revenue estimates and projects the fiscal impact of major legislation and policy proposals anticipated in the coming legislative session. Estimates of state revenues are prepared by the state comptroller, who is constitutionally required to deliver revenue estimates to the legislature prior to the beginning of each biennial legislative session and to certify that funds are available to pay for the state's budget after it is passed by the legislature, before it can be sent to the governor for his signature. This is the so-called pay-as-you-go provision of the Texas constitution, which requires that the state have a balanced budget.

The LBB usually meets during the summer and establishes general guidelines for the LBB staff examiners, based on preliminary revenue estimates. Based on these guidelines, the staff prepares recommendations to the LBB for each agency; the recommendations undergo an internal staff review before being submitted to the Legislative Budget Board members. Staff presentations to the LBB are made in open meetings in October and November, at which LBB members question staff and agency representatives on budget requirements and make agency-by-agency decisions on their recommendations for the biennium. The LBB budget traditionally has been a "current services" budget, which funds existing programs and policy changes already included in state laws. It includes new programs or initiatives only when there is a strong consensus that the new programs will actually be adopted in the legislative session. The LBB budget, therefore, is a very conservative document, which is used as the base for final budget development, rather than as a policy statement reflecting a legislative agenda.

It is at this point in the budget process that the governor's executive budget development process diverges from the LBB process. After the joint hearings, OBP staff also develop budget recommendations that are submitted to the governor in October and November, paralleling the LBB process. The governor's budget, however, does reflect gubernatorial policies and initiatives, including both reductions and increases to agency budgets and new programs or policy changes the governor intends to propose to the legislature. For comparison purposes, the governor's budget usually includes a current services level, as well as recommendations wherever these differ. The composition of the governor's budget has varied considerably among governors and, except in the Connally administration, as noted above, is not used as the basis for legislative budget development.

The format of the Texas budget, used by both LBB and OBP staffs, is the zero-base budget (ZBB). In September 1973 the Legislative Budget Board and the governor agreed to adopt ZBB as the basis of budget preparation for the next biennium (1976–1977), which would begin September 1, 1975. They directed their staffs to develop a ZBB system, which they did after consultations by staff, LBB members, and the governor with Governor Jimmy Carter of Georgia and his staff. The resulting system was an adaptation of ZBB suitable for Texas' legislatively controlled budget process. When first implemented, ZBB required agencies to submit their budget request in decision packages at potentially four levels of funding: a minimum level at which programs could operate, which was defined as not to exceed 75 percent of the previous year's current services base; level two, defined as the base level; level three, an increase of not more than 19 percent; and level four, an increase of 20 percent or more.[3] Agencies were only required to submit a level-three or level-four request if they could justify increases in that range, and many did not. Very few level-four requests were made, and fewer were approved. After the first experience with ZBB, the levels were modified somewhat, especially level one. For the 1984–1985 biennium beginning September 1, 1983, for example, level one was defined as not to exceed 90 percent of the 1983 budgeted funding level. Level two remained at the 100 percent level, but level three was set at 110 percent of the previous biennium. Level four remained at 120 percent. Agency priority tables ranking all agency decision packages in order of importance and performance indicators justifying the requests were also required.[4]

After the Legislative Budget Board completes its fall meetings with agencies and its own staff members, it adopts budget recommendations and revenue estimates for submittal to the full legislature for consideration. These decisions are usually made by mid-December, leaving several weeks for the LBB staff to draft the actual budget bill based on those recommendations and for the budget document and bill to be printed prior to the beginning of the legislative session in January. The governor's office follows a similar timetable and presents the executive budget, but not a budget bill, with the governor's biennial budget message to the legislature in January. The governor's budget is often less detailed than LBB's, except in those program areas in which the chief executive is proposing new initiatives or significant changes. The Texas legislature then has before it two budgets for consideration. The House Appropriations and Senate Finance Committees use the LBB version as their working document, while they consult the governor's for guidance on new policy directions or, in the case of the 1988–1989 biennium, targets for cutbacks.

The state's overall fiscal condition has considerable influence over the way the budget process proceeds in Texas. Not only do the ZBB levels change with revenue projections, as might be expected, but some aspects of the process itself have been modified to accommodate problems caused by fiscal difficulties. This was most evident in the budget development process for the 1988–1989 biennium, when declining state tax revenues resulted in projections of deficits in FY1987, as well as the next biennium.

Two special sessions of the legislature were held in August and September 1986 to try to resolve the immediate and longer term revenue problems. The results of these sessions were twofold. First, sales taxes and taxes on gasoline, diesel fuel, and liquid petroleum gas were raised temporarily and state spending was reduced, to solve the FY1987 revenue shortfall. Second, because the two sessions were called in August and September 1986, they interfered with the normal LBB schedule for budget review with agencies. This was further exacerbated because 1986 was an election year for statewide offices, including governor and lieutenant governor, and state legislators. When the special sessions were over, LBB members went home to campaign, leaving the staff to prepare budget recommendations. Two LBB meetings were held, but members did not have enough time to resolve the serious fiscal problems and balance the budget for the biennium. The estimates were published and submitted to the legislature by their staff, but without LBB approval and recommendation. This left serious unresolved problems, requiring future tax increases and expenditure reductions, for the legislative committees during the regular legislative session. The legislature eventually balanced and passed the 1988–1989 biennial budget in a special session during the summer of 1987.

Although Texas' budgeting system is based on a structure adopted in 1949 and a constitution ratified in 1876, the staffs' budgetary techniques are quite modern. As described above, Texas uses ZBB as the basis for developing both the governor's and LBB's estimates. The flexibility of ZBB is reflected in the ease with which the decision package request levels can be modified to reflect changing revenue forecasts. For the 1988–1989 biennium, for example, the four levels were: level one, 80 percent or less of the FY1987 budgeted amount; level two, not to exceed 90 percent of FY1987; level three, the FY1987 base, or less; and level four, above 100 percent of FY1987, which was allowed only for cases in which there was a demonstrable need for an increase, such as requirements of court orders affecting the Mental Health and Mental Retardation and Corrections departments.[5] The LBB staff uses a fairly sophisticated computer system to calculate funding formulas, to aggregate budget data, and to track agency budgets through the LBB, governor's OBP, and committee versions. (In the regular 1987 session of the legislature, not including the subsequent special session, there were twelve versions of the appropriations bill.) The computer system was first implemented in the late 1970s, but the most sophisticated applications were not implemented until 1987. More improvements are planned for implementation in the next several years, including the ability to download data to microcomputers in legislators' and staff members' offices for individual analysis.[6]

The Automated Budget and Evaluation System for Texas (ABEST) was developed specifically for the LBB staff by in-house computer systems analysts. A separate system had previously been developed for higher education budgeting, to incorporate the complex funding formulas used. Eventually, integration of the two systems may be possible, but the sheer size of the education budget and the complexity of the formulas (it takes three days for that budget to be produced, even on the computer) makes system consolidation a lower priority than implementation of other system capabilities now being planned. These include integration of the separate word processing system for bill production with ABEST and development of more sophisticated system security measures. The objective is to enable the governor's OBP staff, which has recently requested access to the system, to use it without either the legislature or the governor giving away political strategies through information stored on the computer. Although other states may have similar dual-access security problems, the nature of Texas' dual budget production system and the legislative rather than executive control of the process make computer security both more difficult and more desirable. To the politicians' and staffs' credit, they have provided access to LBB's system for OBP staff while these problems are still being resolved. This action shows more political cooperation than might be expected of a Democratically controlled legislature and the state's first Republican governor since Reconstruction.

Because of the conservatism of the LBB budget development process, the governor can exert considerable influence in the budget process by proposing specific programs and policies in the executive budget. When the governor and the legislative majority are from the same party, the governor is seen as the head of the party, and his or her initiatives are usually followed by the legislature, albeit often with modifications. During his first term in office (1979–1982), Republican Governor Bill Clements asserted himself more through his line-item veto and other legislative initiatives than through the budget process. When he took office again in 1987 (he had been defeated by Democrat Mark White in 1982), however, he had made a campaign issue of state spending reductions and a ''no new taxes'' platform. As a result, he needed to exert strong leadership on budget issues. To do so, instead of a traditional executive budget, his staff prepared an Executive Policy Budget, a compact document showing total appropriations levels and funding sources by major program, with policy proposals indicating how those totals would be reached, mostly by cutbacks.[7] The legislature responded by asking where his line-item budget was. The concept of a policy budget from the governor is sound, inasmuch as it is only his policy initiatives that the legislature really considers under Texas' legislative budgeting system. Whether the idea continues and is used in subsequent biennial budgeting cycles will depend on the political climate and the willingness of Governor Clements and his successors to educate the legislature and especially the LBB on its merits.[8]

TEXAS BUDGETING IN FISCAL CRISIS

Neither the governor nor the LBB, however, was the major influence over the budget process in the 1980s. The revenue difficulties experienced by the state, which previously had enjoyed large budget surpluses, have dominated budgetary politics. This is evidenced (1) by the incumbent Democratic governor's need to call two special sessions of the legislature in 1986 on the budget, which resulted in tax increases in an election year; and (2) by the Republican governor's inability to get a budget passed in the regular 1987 session of the legislature, necessitating another called session in the summer of 1987 and further tax increases, notwithstanding his "no new taxes" campaign rhetoric.

Historically, Texas has had a boom and bust economy. Originally based on agriculture, for example, cotton, beef cattle, and lumber, the state's economy eventually was dominated by oil and gas production and related industries. The economy began to diversify in the 1970s, with more emphasis on services and high-technology industries, as well as manufacturing. Texas became an urban rather than a rural state, with 75 percent of its population living in cities. It also experienced rapid population growth throughout the 1970s and early 1980s as a result of both immigration and high fertility levels, especially among its growing Hispanic population. Rising oil prices in the 1970s contributed to economic growth and provided a steadily growing tax base for the state. Oil production, however, was declining. Since Texas' severance taxes are based on the value rather than the volume of production, tax revenues increased; from 1972 to 1982 tax collections on oil and gas rose 700 percent, an average annual growth of 22.7 percent. When oil prices began to fall in 1982, so did severance tax revenues, which resulted in projected deficits and the need for tax increases in the mid-1980s.[9]

The fiscal difficulties of the state of Texas are caused more by its tax structure than by its economy as a whole. Although both the decline in oil prices and the devaluation of the Mexican peso have caused major economic problems, especially in certain regions of the state, the overall state economy continued to grow through the mid-1980s (though more slowly than in the early part of the decade). This growth is expected to continue through 1990. The tax structure, however, relies most heavily on two types of taxes: general sales taxes and oil and gas severance taxes. In the early 1980s these two taxes comprised about two-thirds of state tax collections, with motor fuel, corporate franchise, motor vehicle sales, and other excise taxes making up the balance of tax collections. In the 1988–1989 biennium, oil and gas tax revenues were expected to decline 21 percent, following a fall of 40 percent in the 1986–1987 biennium. As a result of this drop, their contribution to state tax collections is expected to fall to about 10 percent of total tax collections. The difference between approximately one-third of tax revenues in 1980 and 10 percent in 1989 has been a significant contributor to the state's fiscal difficulties.[10]

The other element of the Texas tax structure that added to fiscal stress in the 1980s was the sales tax. The retail sales tax is based on the value of goods purchased. Therefore, collections tend to increase with both population and inflation. A growing part of the Texas economy, however, is service-oriented, and services were not included in the sales tax base. The state levies neither a personal nor a corporate income tax, and political sentiment regards both quite unfavorably. Texas does have a corporate franchise tax, which is based on net worth rather than income. The state thereby receives proportionally more revenue from manufacturing than service industries, a growing part of the state's economy. Corporate franchise tax collections are expected to grow only 0.3 percent in the 1988–1989 biennium over 1986–1987, accounting for about 8 percent of state tax revenues. Thus, the sales tax is the major source of tax revenue within the current structure.

A third element in the state's fiscal structure is the use of dedicated funds to finance many state activities. In FY1986 taxes made up 55.6 percent of total state revenue, with the remainder composed of federal funds, state lands income, interest, and fees. Most of the nontax revenue, as well as a significant portion of tax revenues, are dedicated to specific uses. About 30 percent of total revenues in the 1988–1989 biennium are dedicated for particular purposes and thus are unavailable for support of general programs.[11] These include federal funds for highways, social services, and education, licensing and other fees supporting specific agencies, college and university tuition funds, and earnings from the Permanent School Fund and the Permanent University Fund, which are comprised of oil and gas royalties from land owned by the two major state university systems and school districts. Those funds were created when oil was found on school and university land; the beneficiaries can use the earnings from the funds, but not the principal.

Although the state can borrow from some of the dedicated funds, at market rates, actual use of those revenues is restricted. Many of these funds are dedicated constitutionally, but some could be released by legislative action. Politically, however, the largest ones, the school and university funds, have sufficient support that any alteration to their dedicated nature would probably be impossible. Use of smaller funds, now dedicated, that could be made available would give lawmakers increased flexibility but would not solve the state's fiscal problems.

The state's economic problems resulted in a $231 million fiscal year-end deficit in 1986 and a projected $2.9 billion deficit in FY1986–1987. Because of the FY1987 problems, the governor called a special session of the legislature in August 1986 to solve the budget crisis. Through various bookkeeping measures, cancellation of a scheduled employee pay raise, and assignment of interest earned on local sales tax trust accounts to the state rather than local governments, the projected deficit was lowered only to $2.3 billion, which required the governor to call another thirty-day session in September 1986. In that session, the state sales tax was increased from 4 1/4 percent to 5 1/4 percent from January 1, 1987, through August 31, 1987, and taxes on gasoline, diesel fuel, and liquid petroleum gas were raised temporarily from 10 to 15 cents per gallon. Additional spending reductions brought the projected deficit to less than $1 billion.[12]

During the regular legislative session in 1987, the appropriations and taxation committees attempted through the normal legislative process to balance the budget.[13] Without benefit of a Legislative Budget Board recommendation that was balanced and under the governor's threat to veto any bill that raised taxes more than the temporary increase did in 1986, the legislature failed to pass an appropriations bill by the time the regular 140-day session ended. The projected deficit for FY1988–1989 was $5 to $6 billion, which included the $1 billion shortfall from FY1987, depending on the level of appropriations finally passed. In another thirty-day special session called in July 1987, the legislature finally resolved the budget crisis by making both the sales and motor fuels tax increases passed in 1986 permanent, further increasing the state sales tax to 6 cents and extending it to cover some previously untaxed services. Other measures included passage of a $110 per year occupation tax on professionals, such as physicians, lawyers, accountants, and architects.[14] The governor signed the measures into law after the legislature also passed a bill that gives the governor more authority over the budget when the legislature is not in session.

These actions by the legislature in 1987 increased taxes by $5.7 billion for the 1988–1989 biennium and put the state on sound financial footing, based on revenue projections made in 1987. Texas still does not have a personal or corporate income tax, although sales taxes are now 8 percent in many large cities; the state share is 6 cents, the local share is 1 cent, and large cities have the option of adding up to 1 cent for transit systems. Further state financial problems, if they occur, may prove more difficult to solve without taxes on personal or corporate income. Most observers believe that will be the next fiscal requirement, but income taxes are still so politically unpopular that constitutional amendments banning them are introduced in every session of the legislature. As the demographics of the state change, however, from immigration and growth in ethnic minority populations, income taxes could become more acceptable. Historically, the sales tax has been an efficient revenue producer for the state, and its expansion to include some services will enhance that role. Whether an income tax is passed in the near future in Texas may depend more on the performance of the enhanced sales tax than on political or demographic changes in the electorate or the legislature.

Overall, the fiscal outlook for the state of Texas appears to be good, barring further catastrophic drops in either the price of oil or the value of the peso. The state has a good revenue base, although it may be more dependent on sales taxes than is ideal. Its economy is diversifying from an agricultural and natural resource base to include computers and biotechnology. The state's budgeting system, though controlled by the legislature in contrast to most other states with executive budgets, is automated and professionally staffed. Revenue estimates are also quite professionally done by the staff of the elected state comptroller. Texas politics, long controlled by Democrats, are also becoming more diverse, including ethnic minorities and even Republicans in the corridors of power. The state's optimistic spirit, though overly taxed by the oil crisis and recession of the mid-1980s, seems to continue to dominate the Texas economy and, with a dose of caution thrown in, the state's fiscal picture as well.

13

Mississippi: Does the Governor Really Count?

EDWARD J. CLYNCH

Most public policies in Mississippi emerge from an ongoing tug of war between change agents pulling the state into the mainstream of American life and status quo forces resisting a restructuring of the traditional order. Budgeting holds center stage in this struggle. Rules of the budget game control which actors participate in allocating state resources. Ironically, traditionalists and modernists do not disagree about the consequences of a gubernatorially dominated budget process. Status quo supporters suspect that enhancing executive power over spending decisions, particularly at the expense of the legislature, threatens the traditional order. Change advocates agree. They believe that a strong governor could successfully improve government services that are so critical to social advancement, even if additional taxes proved necessary. Moving Mississippi into the American mainstream requires services that allow all citizens, including the state's 36 percent black population, to function in a modern society.

During this century the struggle between reform advocates and supporters of the traditional order have periodically focused on the rules of the game governing budget decision making. In 1955 the legislature created a legislatively dominated Commission on Budget and Accounting. The statute designated the governor as nonvoting chairperson and key legislative leaders from each chamber as members of the five- and later eleven-member Budget Commission. The eleven-member commission included the lieutenant governor, as presiding officer in the State Senate. The Budget Commission hired a director, who served at their pleasure, to oversee the operations of the professional staff. The state constitution limited governors to a single four-year term, whereas the lieutenant governor and other legislative leaders could serve an unlimited number of terms. Most governors, who lacked the budgetary expertise of seasoned legislative leaders, failed to overcome the lack of formal gubernatorial authority. The legislative leaders, who controlled the Budget Commission, made the major budget decisions during the budget preparation, legislative approval, and budget execution phases.[1]

Mississippi government edged toward a more executive-centered system with the "separation of powers" when the state Supreme Court in November 1983 declared unconstitutional the long-standing practice of legislators serving on boards and commissions with executive responsibilities.[2] The case, initiated by then Attorney General and later Governor Bill Allain, altered the procedures affecting budget decision making. It forbade legislative involvement in budget execution, but it did not prevent the legislative leadership from developing a budget for submission to the legislature. In adopting new rules, the legislature narrowly interpreted the court decision so as to maintain as much legislative control as possible. Senate Bill 3050, which passed in May 1984, established the Joint Legislative Budget Committee (JLBC) consisting of the same ten legislative leaders who served on the old Budget Commission. The law established the Legislative Budget Office, with a director and six analysts, to serve as the staff arm of the JLBC.

The legislature realized that it needed to create an executive branch agency to monitor and control the spending of state money. Governor Allain's veto threat enabled him to influence the content of Senate Bill 3050 and force the legislature to take his desires into consideration. The legislature agreed to set up the Fiscal Management Board (FMB), composed of the governor and two gubernatorial appointees.[3] In 1989 the legislature abolished the FMB and created the Department of Finance and Administration which includes a budget division with a political appointee as director.[4] Consequently, the Mississippi legislature, like its Texas counterpart, receives two budget proposals—one from the governor and one from the legislative leadership.[5]

THE PREPARATORY PHASE

Revenue Estimates

Mississippi, like most states, must finish each fiscal year in the black, which ties the amount of money appropriated directly to expected dollars.[6] If the gubernatorial and JLBC budgets project different levels of anticipated receipts, the way is open for executive/legislative conflict. Budget actors in Mississippi escape from this box in a couple of ways. First, a 1985 law specifies that the legislature's sine die estimate is the official state estimate.[7] The governor possesses the authority to cut budgets if revenue estimates fail to meet projections, but the chief executive cannot point to a lower gubernatorial projection as justification for making reductions.

Second, and more importantly, routines exist to establish a joint executive/legislative revenue estimate. The responsibility for revenue estimation in Mississippi rests with two entities, the Mississippi Center for Policy Research and Planning, an agency responsible for forecasting changes in the Mississippi economy, and the State Tax Commission, the office responsible for collecting revenues and implementing the state tax code.[8] In addition, both the Department of Finance and Administration and the Legislative Budget Office employ staff persons with forecasting expertise. These persons review projections and raise questions about the reasoning behind the numbers.

Setting the revenue estimate for Mississippi is an informal process followed by formal ratification. Technical forecasters from each of the four units exchange information, reconcile any differences, reach a consensus on the amount of revenue available for spending, and then make presentations to a joint meeting of the governor and the JLBC. The Governor and the JLBC adopt the same estimate. This "sacred" number caps the level of recommended spending by the governor and the JLBC. As one participant in the informal consensus-setting process puts it, "budget decision makers want to know: what is the best estimate of what Mississippi will have to spend, not how much money will be raised from revenue sources." Because Mississippi has experienced budget rescissions in four of the last eight years, persons adopting an estimate prefer a built-in cushion to guard against future cuts.

Budget Guidelines

With prodding from the governor, Mississippi's budget format is edging toward program budgeting. The state's budget decisions still emanate from agency requests organized into five general object classifications: personal services, contractual services, commodities, capital outlay/equipment and subsidies, loans and grants. Agencies submit most information on joint Finance and Administration/LBO forms. In addition to last year's spending, the forms include a continuation or a "current services category" which reflects the cost of continuing current activities. It is usually higher than last year's spending because of uncontrollable price increases. The expansion category details the cost of increasing the level of existing activities. The new activity category delineates the dollars necessary to begin a new service.

In addition to submitting a request for their total agency budget, spending units must submit program narratives and a dollar figure for each major program element. Budget analysts believe in the accuracy of data for total budgets, but they admit that many agencies lack cost information for programs. Governor Ray Mabus successfully advocated the establishment of a pilot program budget for FY1990. The Governor's Office of Finance and Administration and LBO selected twelve agencies to participate in the process. To a large degree the pilot effort resembles performance budgeting. Agencies must identify workload costs for major activities. The governor hopes that a framework for program budgeting will evolve. At this point most agencies lack the data necessary to measure the cost per item of service. Pilot agencies must also provide "effectiveness" data, but the guidelines recommend the reporting outputs and not measurable results (e.g., cost of public water supplies tested rather than measures that gauge the impact of testing).

Decision rules governing budget submissions by agencies are set in part by the guidelines, in part by informal understandings, and in part by Mississippi's tight budget situation. Informal understandings include an expectation that agency continuation requests cover known or solidly anticipated cost increases for non-salary items, particularly for big ticket items like utilities. In addition, agencies are expected to include program escalations and even new programs that will bring substantial federal money into Mississippi, especially if the state match is minimal. Since 1981, financial realities have tempered requests for additional spending, especially for new programs. Agencies realize that the state lacks substantial new money. In the last few years Mississippi has allocated its modest increments for salary increases, the funding of programs mandated by the federal courts, especially correctional facilities, and for public kindergartens and other educational programs mandated by the Educational Reform Act of 1982.

Initial Review of Agency Submissions

Larger agencies usually initiate separate meetings with their analysts at the time of submission to explain their proposal and to answer any initial questions. At this point budget reviews focus only on the technical aspects, with the analysts making sure all needed information is present. Analysts have not yet received instructions through which they can judge the content of agency budget requests. Occasionally, agencies will omit funding for new programs mandated during the last legislative session, and the analyst will tell them to rework their budget to include a funding request. Neither Finance and Administration nor LBO analysts make recommendations until after review hearings are completed.

Joint Legislative Budget Committee Hearings. The Governor's Department of Financial and Administration dropped budget hearings in 1988. Instead, their analysts now attend legislative hearings. JLBC hearings resemble carbon copies of what took place before the Budget Commission. Any agency may testify. The comprehensive approach results from the need to give everyone a "chance" to influence the budget which serves as a legislative working document. LBO analysts prepare summaries of agency requests for committee members, but no briefing occurs. Occasionally, committee members request additional information which the staff then obtains from the agency. The agency director normally makes the presentation, and key department heads attend. The hearings provide most agencies with an opportunity to present their song and dance and receive the thanks of the chairperson. Committee members rarely ask questions of minor agencies. Larger agencies receive more time for the presentation and must usually field questions. When questions occur, they rarely become contentious. The informal rules of the game are, "don't go after people—don't pursue persons on the spot."

The hearings receive mixed reviews from legislators. Many recognize that the hearings serve a useful purpose in allowing everyone a few minutes, even if it takes weeks to complete the process. At the same time, some lawmakers desire more focus on larger agencies. As one legislative leader puts it, "the hearings should be a time to dig into top agencies. The JLBC does not really care, and in 90 percent of the time the small agencies do not object to LBO recommendations."

Budget Review and Staff Markup. Once the hearings are complete, Finance and Administration and LBO analysts complete their markup. The procedures and operating rules do not vary to any great extent for the two units. If revenue estimates project additional money, each organization's financial analyst indicates the percentage increase for the contractual and commodity categories considered reasonable for continuation budgets, given inflation and other known increases. Analysts use the guidelines as benchmarks. If the request is less than the guidelines, the amount asked for is put in the recommendation. If the request exceeds the guidelines with a good justification, the analyst may recommend a little more than the benchmark. As one person familiar with the process noted: "It all depends on the analyst." Some just check the numbers and go by the guidelines. Others will recommend a little more if there is a good justification. The dollar figure plugged in for salaries is based on a state personnel board projection of current-year costs and is not subject to change by analysts.

The LBO analysts seem less likely to raise critical questions than their Finance and Administration counterparts. For the most part, they just review each budget with the idea of providing enough money to cover continuing services. As one observer put it: "The LBO only does what it is required to do by the JLBC. The Staff takes no initiative and does not go one step further than requested." As a general rule, the staff will identify items mandated by federal law or regulation, state or federal court orders or prior legislative mandates. For instance, the FY1987 JLBC budget recommended funding the kindergarten program and a $1,000 across-the-board teacher pay raise. Both were mandated by previous legislative action.[9]

The Governor's Budget Recommendation. The governor is required to issue a budget by November 15.[10] However, Governor Allain, as a lame duck, did not release a budget in mid-November 1987. The governor's budget format has nudged the process in the direction of program budgeting. This document now includes program narratives, even for subunits of major agencies. However, these general narratives only contain information already known to legislators and others involved in the budget process.[11]

Governor Allain was not very interested in the newly acquired gubernatorial budget-making authority. As governor he did not even set major spending priorities. The Governor's budget staff determined how much money remained once ongoing programs were covered. The staff then developed a plan for spending unallocated resources based on the governor's public statements. They took the plan to Allain and told him: "Governor, we believe these are your priorities." He generally accepted them with little comment. Ironically, Governor Allain as attorney general brought the suit that toppled legislative budget hegemony. Nevertheless, he knew that only limited new money existed, and perhaps he also believed that the legislature would put his budget in the wastebasket anyway, so why bother.

He did use the his budget document for FY1987, however, to advocate shifting resources from special fund to general fund agencies.[12] Highlighting the highway department budget as a focal point, he specifically recommended ending the diversion of $50 million of general sales tax receipts to the highway department, replacing the $50 million with a general fund appropriation of $27 million. He suggested distributing the remaining $23 million among agencies supported by the general fund.[13]

The JLBC Budget Recommendation. The Joint Legislative Budget Committee is required to issue a budget by December 15.[14] The JLBC document remains the budget scrutinized in detail by the legislature, and the committee completes budget preparation with this in mind. The LBO director and assistant director examine budget analyst recommendations and make adjustments to fit spending within expected available revenues and to include known preferences of JLBC members. When the committee cycles through agency budgets and satisfies itself that current services costs are covered, it may ask the staff to identify critical needs. The JLBC either accepts or rejects these recommendations. In addition, committee members will ask for additional money for particular items of interest to them. Questions assume the line of "is this included?" rather than questioning the wisdom of including particular items. Generally, the rule of mutual reciprocity applies. Items that committee members ask for are added to the budget unless there are strong objections from the LBO analyst, which is rarely the case. Agencies often work with committee members to request items that are not likely to be part of the LBO recommendations such as capital improvements, new positions, or anything over and above inflation increases for nonsalary items.

The JLBC recommends salary realignments and general increases if money remains once the items discussed above are placed in the budget.[15] The amount designated to realign salary competitiveness is based on projections by the State Personnel Board. When the JLBC recommends a general salary increase, it follows a procedure used by the old Budget Commission. That is, the JLBC budget indicates the cost of a 1 percent raise for various categories of persons who are compensated from the state budget—individuals affiliated with public schools, junior colleges, universities, and the remaining state employees. Raises are then set by the legislature, often at the end of the session, when later revenue estimates are available.

The decision rules used by the LBO and JLBC reflect the determinism of the system. Budget decision making in Mississippi is arranged in a way that limits the flexibility of budget reviewers, particularly in a tight money situation. Clearly, the JLBC views the "base" as sacred. The committee makes no meaningful effort to review existing spending. Budget decisions reflect a subtraction system. Starting with an updated general fund revenue estimate, items are then subtracted until all anticipated revenue is committed: (1) the amount needed to fund the continuation budget is deducted; (2) items added by the JLBC during the markup system are then subtracted; (3) money needed for the salary realignments to keep positions competitive with the private sector and, in some cases, with similar public positions in the Southeast, is then deducted. After all these items are covered, the remaining resources are available for program expansions, new programs, and salary increases.

The JLBC budget, like Budget Commission documents, does not include narrative statements. Spending breakdowns are included for subunits of larger agencies that are very similar to governor's divisions. Clearly, the JLBC budget is not a policy statement. Rather, it reflects compromises resulting from bargaining and accommodation among the ten legislative members.

LEGISLATIVE APPROVAL

The legislature receives two proposals—one from the governor and one from the Joint Legislative Budget Committee. With the exception of Governor Mabus's first legislative session in 1988, the legislature, not surprisingly, ignores the governor's budget recommendations and reacts to the JLBC proposal. The governor's budget has occasionally provided rhetorical ammunition for appropriations subcommittee chairs who disliked one of the agencies under their jurisdiction. Even in these instances the effect was more rhetorical than substantial. The governor's lower recommendation was used to question the JLBC spending request, but the final appropriation closely resembled the JLBC submission.

Political parties do not affect budget decisions in Mississippi. The Democrats have elected all governors in this century, and the legislature includes only a few Republicans. Neither party organizes in the legislature. In fact, a few Republicans even serve as committee chairpersons.

The legislature considers and passes 250 appropriations bills each session. There is no omnibus appropriations process in Mississippi as in some other states. The legislature divides appropriations bills between the House and Senate, with each chamber having first consideration of about half the bills. There is no real pattern or reason for the division; it just evolved over time.

Each chamber divides its appropriations committees into subcommittees, ten in the House and five in the Senate. The committee chairs are appointed at the beginning of each four-year legislative term by the House speaker and the lieutenant governor, the presiding officer in the Senate. Subcommittee chairs and members are appointed by the committee chairs in consultation with the speaker and the lieutenant governor.

Key work is done in subcommittees; these units make decisions during a markup session with only the committee and LBO analysts present. The JLBC recommendation serves as the starting point of committee deliberations. Discussion centers on changes in the JLBC numbers being advocated by agencies. Because agencies realize that any deviations from the JLBC budget are likely to result from subcommittee action, they often generate options for subcommittees, hoping for additional support. When the subcommittee is undecided about an item, the LBO analyst may be asked for an opinion in an effort to ascertain whether the agency really needs it or whether it can get along without it. Subcommittees are expected to operate within the rules of the game, meaning that salary adjustments owing to realignment and reclassifications for particular positions must follow personnel board recommendations, and amounts for nonsalary items must be close to Joint Legislative Budget Committee recommendations.

Full appropriations committees generally accept what subcommittees have done, although there are exceptions. Full committees act as a check and cut major increases, which exceed the original JLBC recommendation. The subcommittee report identifies and gives reasons for deviations from the JLBC budget.

Floor consideration seems anticlimactic with little debate or change to bills. The floor handler indicates whether or not the bill reflects the JLBC recommendation. If it falls below or exceeds, the floor manager states the reasons for the deviation. Cuts or increases often result from LBO staff recommendations given during markup, although changes take place because of a committee chair's desire. The only floor battles involve visible and controversial items such as a subsidy for the international ballet competition held in Jackson and the Mississippi Pavilion at the New Orleans World's Fair. Almost always, lopsided votes occur in favor of the committee position.

Almost all appropriations bills end up in conference. Most reach there, not because of disagreements, but because of a desire to postpone passage until the last minute. This approach permits the legislature to take advantage of the most up-to-date revenue estimates. In reality six-person conference committees write appropriations bills during the last forty-eight to seventy-two hours of the session with input from other legislatures. Conference committees consists of the two chairs of the full appropriations committee, the two chairs of the subcommittees that originally considered the bill, and one other member from each side. There is a tendency to split the difference when dollars are the issue. It may be more difficult to reach agreement when the disagreement concerns conditions placed on spending. The conference process allows legislative leaders responsible for submitting the JLBC budget proposal at the beginning of the session to review and alter appropriations bills at the end of the session, ensuring the outcomes will reflect their preferences. The leadership assesses the most recent revenue estimate, makes adjustments in agency budgets, and, when money permits, sets the level of salary increases.

GOVERNOR MABUS: A NEW ERA?

The initial two years of Governor Ray Mabus's administration saw increasing executive influence over budget decisions. The JLBC proposed a standstill budget for the fiscal year beginning July 1, 1988, but an updated revenue estimate at the beginning of the 1988 session suggested that an additional $200 million was available. Using the legislative budget as a starting point, newly elected Governor Mabus suggested minor cuts of $8 million from the $1.6 billion total. He then seized the initiative and proposed raising elementary and secondary teachers' salaries to the southeastern average over a two-year period. In addition, he advocated a significant increase in support for higher education. He suggested using the $200 million fiscal dividend to cover education support during the upcoming fiscal year, and he argued that natural revenue growth would provide enough additional money to cover the second year of the public school teacher pay raise. Given the lower priority that Governor Mabus gave to most noneducational state government activities, his budget did not include raises for regular state employees. However, the legislature provided a small pool to adjust professional salaries which no longer were competitive in the job market.[16]

In 1989 the legislature funded the second year of the teacher pay raise. In addition, Governor Mabus used the veto to shape public health expenditures. At the beginning of the 1989 session, the governor sought to close the state's three substandard and obsolete charity hospitals. He proposed diverting the $6.3 million used to fund these facilities into the state Medicaid program. The legislature passed an appropriation for these facilities after intense lobbying from hospital employees and supporters. The governor vetoed the bill, and the Senate sustained the veto. The legislature then voted to increase state Medicaid funding from $103 to $122.6 million. Since the federal government provides a 4–1 match, Mississippi's Medicaid total budget grew from $494 to $597 million. Mississippi was expected to add 90,000 persons to the Medicaid rolls over the next two years.[17]

Another fiscal victory for Governor Mabus in 1989 was legislative enactment of his capital improvements bond package. Reflecting the state's conservative preference for paying cash for long-term state needs rather than issuing bonds, the governor's bond package died during the regular legislative session when legislators could not reconcile differences in the Senate and House versions. The governor promptly called a special session that focused public attention on the legislature's alleged "failure" to "complete its work." The legislature enacted a $78.5 million compromise package to finance school improvements, prisons, and office buildings with borrowed money, representing the first installment of a projected five-year capital budget request.[18.]

Does the outcome of this session indicate a shift in budget decision making in the governor's direction? Clearly, more legislative sessions need to take place before we learn the definitive answer. In future years the legislature may not respond favorably to a governor's ideas, but Governor Mabus set the spending agenda for legislative consideration during his initial two years in office.

GUBERNATORIAL VETO

The Mississippi constitution gives the governor the item veto, but the legislature may override with a two-thirds vote in each chamber.[19] However, Mississippi agencies receive lump-sum object appropriations. A governor using the item veto must strike out all of an agency's commodities, contractual services, and so on. Unless a governor intends to close an agency (such as when Governor Mabus sought to close the charity hospitals), the line-item veto lacks practicality. If Mississippi moves to a program budget format *and* appropriates by program, the governor can eliminate particular programs instead of object expenditures for the entire agency. Governor Allain took advantage of instances where the legislature passed a separate appropriations bill for particular programs that did not meet with his approval. When the Mississippi Ballet Competition received funding through a separate appropriation, the governor eliminated this program without touching funds for other Department of Economic Development activities. Legislators understand the nature of the item veto. One suspects that lawmakers appropriate by program for activities which are more popular with a segment of the public than with the legislature and governor. The program appropriation invites the governor to exercise the item veto and take any of the ensuing heat.

BUDGET EXECUTION

Governors now control budget execution, since the separation of powers decision places this authority squarely in the hands of the executive. The legislature limits the governor's execution powers, however, by increasing the authority of the spenders. Agencies can shift up to 10 percent of nonsalary money from one object classification to another without anyone's permission. Previously, transfers required approval of the Budget Commission.

Budget execution shapes budget policy during revenue shortfalls more than at other times. The responsibility to keep revenues in line with expenditures falls to the governor. Mississippi governors can selectively reduce any general fund agency budget up to 5 percent. However, once the governor cuts all general fund agencies by 5 percent, any additional reductions must be uniform and across the board.

Another potentially important side effect emerged from the governor's attack on special funds in 1986. Governor Allain successfully proposed tapping special fund money in times of economic distress. Since July of that year, Mississippi law has subjected most state-generated special fund money to budget rescissions in the same manner as general fund appropriations. The money cut from special funds moves to the general fund. The shift reduces the size of cuts in general fund agency budgets, since the special fund money replaces a portion of the shortfall in regular general fund revenue sources.

Changes in Mississippi's budget procedures cannot be traced directly to changes in economic conditions. The separation of powers suit, however, changed the role of budget players. During the fiscal stress of the mid-1980s, control over rescissions shifted from the legislative leadership to the governor. During better economic times, Governor Mabus heavily influenced legislative debate over how to spend money that was not needed for ongoing programs. Mabus's executive budget forced the legislature to make his budget priorities the basis of their discussion.

MISSISSIPPI'S ECONOMY AND BUDGET REVENUES

Economic conditions in many ways shape the struggle between status quo supporters and change advocates for control of Mississippi's destiny. Sustained economic growth often provides adequate public resources to increase services without raising taxes. Sluggish economic conditions coupled with popular demands for more services force public officials to cut existing programs or take a bigger share of the private economy.

In the late 1970s Mississippi's economy expanded significantly beyond the national average, but in the early 1980s the state's growth was static while the country's growth surged ahead. Mississippi's economy zoomed out of the 1973–1975 recession. Between 1976 and 1980 the state's gross state product, in 1982 dollars, increased by 18.8 percent compared to a 12.7 percent climb in the gross national product.[20] Its per capita income moved from 54 percent of the national average in 1960 to 71 percent in 1979. Only South Carolina, with an 18 percent gain, closed the gap with the national average at a rate greater than Mississippi's 17 percent. Yet Mississippi still entered the 1980s with the nation's lowest per capita income.[21]

After decades of real economic growth, world conditions in the early 1980s, including declines in agricultural prices, falling energy prices, and the movement of low-skilled manufacturing jobs out of the country, buffeted the state's economy. Mississippi's 1985 per capita income slipped to 67 percent of the national average. In 1982 dollars the state's gross product between 1980 and 1985 grew only 2.6 percent while the GNP increased by 12.5 percent.[22]

Mississippi's economy dropped off in the 1980s. Does the economic downturn affect the state's revenue capacity in a meaningful way? State revenue growth kept pace and even exceeded inflation for most the 1980s, but only because policymakers in Mississippi, like many states, chose tax increases to maintain the revenue base.[23] In 1983 the state increased the general sales tax from 5 to 6 percent and raised the income tax on more affluent citizens by increasing the rate on taxable income over $10,000 from 4 to 5 percent. Although Mississippi experienced budget rescissions in four years during the 1980s and reduced many agency appropriations in 1987 when revenue fell, the tax increases permitted public kindergartens to start and elementary and secondary teacher salaries to double after 1981. When faced with no alternative because of poor economic conditions, policymakers opted for higher taxes to enhance support for education.

CONCLUSION

The struggle in Mississippi between reformers who want to bring the state into the mainstream of American life and the backers of the traditional order has spilled over into budgeting. The new budget process gives the governor more leverage than before, but the legislative leadership still retains considerable clout. Like Texas, Mississippi remains a long way from an executive-centered system. The governor develops a budget proposal, but the JLBC budget serves as the basis for legislative action. The legislature may well continue to use the JLBC budget as its working document. The legislative budget, in effect, gives the legislative leadership a chance to write the budget before legislative consideration. Not surprisingly, legislators take cues from the leadership during the session. Moreover, the leadership heavily influences the outcome of conference reports, which occur at the end of the session. As a result, the leadership controls adjustments to the JLBC document introduced at the beginning of the session.

Governor Mabus used his first budget to focus legislative attention on his spending priorities. More sessions need to elapse before a definitive judgment can be made about budget decision-making power shifting to the governor in a meaningful way. At the same time the governor now handles all budget execution matters.

State revenues received a boost in the 1980s which offset stagnant economic growth. As a result, Mississippi maintained its revenue base with tax increases and embarked on a major commitment to education.

14

South Carolina: The Demise of Legislative Dominance?

MARCIA LYNN WHICKER

Until recently, the legislature has both reigned and ruled in South Carolina. Legislative dominance is firmly rooted in the state constitution and is reflected in the formal structure of state government as well as in informal patterns of influence. The historical origin of legislative dominance is as old as the nation itself, since all thirteen original states adopted legislative-centered forms of government, reflecting the distrust of the former colonies for executive authority.[1]

Historically, legislative dominance provided a mechanism by which states in the Deep South suppressed black political participation. Reform-minded governors were checked in their ability to implement innovative state policies. Control of county government and much of local politics rested with the state legislative delegation. The heavy focus on state spending as opposed to local spending to fund education and social services assured that whites, a majority at the state level but not in many counties with majority black populations, would have the final say over the type and level of services provided. Until recent years, blacks were rarely elected to the state legislature, even from majority black counties. Legislative dominance reflected the attitudes of white political elites, particularly those from rural areas. The idea was to maintain traditional authority patterns, especially those pertaining to race relations, even at the expense of state economic development.[2]

Part of the reason why blacks are absent from Southern state legislatures, including South Carolina (which ranks only behind Mississippi in the percentage of black population), may be attributed to the greater costs of running for state office in comparison to local office. In South Carolina, prior to 1967, electing one state senator from each of the forty-six counties was a method impeding black participation.

The mixture of single-member and multi-member senatorial districts used between 1967 and the early 1980s did not result in an increased number of black senators. Running electorally in a multicounty area was often even more cost-prohibitive than running in a single county. Furthermore, multicounty districts typically have white majorities. In the early 1980s, challenged again under the Voting Rights Act provisions, state Senate selection was changed to single-member districts. Extended efforts produced politically palatable district lines, which were also free from racially discriminatory impacts.

In addition to electoral districts, government structure also promotes legislative dominance in South Carolina, which traditionally means white dominance through the use of commission directed agencies. Over 90 percent of the administrative agencies are dependent on a commission, averaging nine members in size, for their policy guidance.[3] Furthermore, out of sixty-nine agencies, the governor retains sole appointment powers in only ten. The governor must obtain the advice and consent of the Senate for commission appointments for an additional twenty-eight agencies, and approval of the legislative delegations of the General Assembly in an additional eight.

The South Carolina governor is very weak. Graham and Aiesi[4] have rated the powers of the office in five areas—tenure potential, appointive powers, budget-making power, organization power, and veto power—and have assessed those powers as very weak in three of the five areas. The governor's formal powers are strong only in tenure potential, where the term of office is four years and one reelection is permitted.

The South Carolina governor has moderately strong veto powers, which include an item veto on money bills as well as a general veto. Legislative overrides must occur with a two-thirds rather than a simple majority vote, adding muscle to this power. In the three remaining areas, however, gubernatorial powers are very weak. Ten statewide offices in addition to the governor are elected independently, and the governor appoints few alone. The legislature exerts major reorganizational power through the creation and abolition of offices and in the assignment and reassignment of duties. Furthermore, the governor shares the initiative for reorganizing state government with a legislative reorganization commission. The governor even shares budget-making power, traditionally an executive prerogative at the state level, with four other officials. These officials have separate power bases and jointly, along with the governor, compose the Budget and Control Board.

Legislative control extends to the judicial branch through the judicial selection process. South Carolina is one of only six states in which state judges are elected by the legislature.[5] In issues surrounding budgetary politics, such as the constitutionality of South Carolina's budget process, the state Supreme Court has favored positions advocated by the General Assembly.

THE SOUTH CAROLINA BUDGET AND CONTROL BOARD

Nowhere has the dominance of South Carolina's state legislature been more apparent than in the development of the state budget. If the power of the purse and the determination of "who gets what, when and why" are the guts of politics, then the legislature is where the action is. In contrast to executive preparation of the budget in most other states or preparation by some type of budget panel in a few states, South Carolina relies on a hybrid legislative-executive commission called the Budget and Control Board (BCB) to formulate the state budget. The current BCB was created in 1950 and evolved from a budget commission established in 1933.

The Budget and Control Board has strengthened the role of the legislature in state budgeting. Two of the five members of the Budget and Control Board are prominent members of the state legislature: the chairperson of the House Ways and Means Committee and the Senate Finance Committee. The governor is only one of the five members of the BCB; he chairs the BCB. The remaining two BCB members, the state treasurer and the comptroller general, are independently elected to their respective offices in statewide elections. They rarely owe the governor many political chits, since they must build their own statewide power base to secure election. The structure of the BCB then significantly weakens the governor's role in budget development and relegates the governor to a weakened position as one of four other "equals" on the BCB. In addition to the five voting members, the state auditor serves as the ex-officio secretary to the board.

The Budget and Control Board operates through six divisions. The two divisions most heavily involved in the budget process are the Finance Division, directed by the state auditor, and the Division of Research and Statistical Services, which provides economic forecasts and revenue estimates to the board.

Critics of the Budget and Control Board have charged that its mixture of legislative and executive officials violates the constitutional principle of separation of powers. In a 1977 court test of this principle, despite a South Carolina constitutional provision that specifies that the three branches of state government "shall be forever separate and distinct from each other, and no person exercising the functions of one said department shall assume or discharge the duties of the other," the South Carolina Supreme Court upheld the constitutionality of the BCB.

Budget and Control Board boosters point to the continuity which the BCB provides across different gubernatorial administrations. This continuity was particularly valued prior to the constitutional amendment in the early 1980s which allowed governors to succeed themselves. Critics have remained unconvinced, however, that a permanent executive staff serving under a gubernatorially appointed budget director could not provide the same continuity, although BCB supporters argue that staff continuity is no substitute for continuity in top decision makers.

As a function of happenstance and the noncompetitive party system at the state level where Democrats outnumbered Republicans significantly, turnover in the nongubernatorial positions on the BCB has indeed been low. Nothing, however, indicates that such continuity would persist in a competitive situation where both Democrats and Republicans contested most statewide and state legislative offices.

In addition to developing the initial budget, the BCB has considerable authority to approve the transfer of funds across categories. All transfers across major categories must receive unanimous BCB approval, giving the legislative members virtually iron-clad veto power over any transfers with which they disagree. But this transfer authority extends the budget decision process into implementation authority. This logical sequel in efficient organization pleases BCB supporters.

Supporters also argue that the BCB generally elicits healthy cooperation between the two branches of government, both increasing the likelihood that the state budget will get a fair hearing in the General Assembly and, by merging executive and legislative powers, more closely approximating a parliamentary structure whose efficiency is often extolled by U.S. political scientists.[6]

BCB critics contend that the cooperation between branches of government is more mythical than real. Some professional rivalry exists between the Budget Division of the BCB and the staff of the House Ways and Means Committee. This is the main point of intense legislative scrutiny, as well as the point where legislative examination of agency budgets is least politicized and most professional. Once preeminent in budget examination of detailed agency requests, the BCB must now share the field with a House Ways and Means Committee staff developed only as recently as the 1970s and expanded in the 1980s. As yet, the Senate Finance Committee staff includes only one budget expert and offers little threat to BCB power. The Senate Research Office, which is as much a function of personalities involved as any specific legislative mandate, has also begun to look at some budget issues. In 1987, however, it had not yet coordinated its budget examination efforts with the Senate Finance staff or other staff, even within the Senate.

Critics of the current process contend that, although agencies must typically receive BCB approval for new programs, an area where BCB action is particularly crucial, the state legislature often throws out the appropriations figures in the BCB-approved budget and starts all over again "from scratch." The state Senate reports a similar disregard for earlier decisions. Hence, the budgets passed by the two houses often differ considerably from the BCB budget, as well as from each other. Such decentralized decision making increases the importance of the legislative conference committee established to resolve the differences between the two versions of the budget passed by the two different houses. Appointees to the legislative conference are typically more senior legislators from each house, a fact that further increases the strength of legislative leadership.

Several political factors weigh heavily on the side of those who favor retaining this unusual structure for budget development. Currently, abolishing the Budget and Control Board is hardly a burning issue in South Carolina. Major budget actors, even those who point out its weaknesses, take it for granted. More importantly, short of a Supreme Court decision declaring the BCB unconstitutional, any reforms in budget structure must first be passed by the state legislature, which has generally supported retaining the BCB and its own role in budget formulation. The branch of government that must initiate reform in the budget structure is the branch of government that favors the current structure most.

THE BOARD OF ECONOMIC ADVISORS

The Board of Economic Advisors (BEA) produces the official revenue estimates for the state. It is partially staffed by the Research and Statistical Services Division of the Budget and Control Board, and it consists of four members. Two BEA members hold full-time positions in the Research and Statistical Services Division: the director of that division, and the chief economist for the state. The two additional BEA members are the chairman of the Tax Commission and the chairman, a nonpublic employee member appointed by the BCB who is not a full-time employee. The only member of the BEA who is not directly supervised by the BCB is the chairman of the Tax Commission.

Only the Board of Economic Advisors can issue official forecasts for the state. Today, if the BEA were being graded on its performance in this area, it would receive low marks. In 1987 the BEA estimates had been sufficiently overoptimistic in five of the preceding seven years that midyear cuts were necessary. This poor record in forecasting has prevailed, despite the BEA's access to elaborate and sophisticated econometric models.

Given such high-powered potential for forecasting, why has the BEA been off so much, and so consistently, in the direction of overestimation of revenues? Inside observers to the South Carolina Budget process lay the blame on the pressures of politics, especially those generated by legislative dominance. In 1987 the chairman of the BEA had served almost two decades in that capacity and had strong supporters in the state Senate. Some observers noted the long-standing personal ties between the BEA chair and the Senate which made the BEA particularly sensitive to legislative needs.

The legislature has traditionally exerted considerable influence on the BEA to produce revenue estimates to their liking. The BEA habitually revises official revenue estimates upward after the BCB has drawn up the initial budget and before the House of Representatives acts on it. This revision provides the House with additional monies to appropriate for pet projects. The same phenomenon of upward revisions has frequently occurred a second time in any budget cycle, after the House has completed its budget work and before the Senate has begun its own. Again, the upward revisions allow the Senate the freedom to appropriate monies that were not initially allocated by the House. Revenue estimates had become so rosy that by the 1986–1987 budget, official estimates exceeded anticipated actual collections by over $100 million.

One mechanism which the BEA employs to raise revenue estimates when the legislature pressures it to do so has been an upward revision of estimates of new tax dollars as a result of policy changes in the year in which the policy changes were enacted. In the 1987 budget, the legislature allocated $1.5 million to advertise for tourism. The BEA obligingly estimated that this expenditure would generate an additional $1.5 million in tax revenues *in the same year*. Similarly, the Tax Commission introduced a package to upgrade collections procedures, prompting the BEA to project $7 to $8 million additional tax dollars, with no experience concerning the effectiveness of the new collections program.

Other observers lay at least part of the blame for revenue overestimation on sluggish economic growth as well as subtle and, as yet, not fully recognized shifts in the state's economy. Traditionally dominated by textiles, that portion of the state's economy has been in decline for some years, as textile plants have fled to Third World developing countries in search of cheap labor and lower production costs.

Revenue overestimation has made midyear cuts typical rather than extraordinary. A climate of constant midyear cuts has made planning difficult, if not impossible, in many state agencies. In any given budget year when a midyear cut is anticipated, the Bureau of Economic Advisors will put agencies on notice of the likely revenue shortfall. Agencies then hold off hiring new employees.

This, however, places agencies in a catch-22 situation, for if they leave a position open for more than nine months, they lose its authorization. Should the anticipated shortfall fail to materialize, or be of lesser magnitude than expected, the agency may find itself with the appropriations for a position but no authorization for it. Midyear cuts also thwart the planning process in other ways, causing hasty spending for activities administrators are anxious to fund before anticipated cuts are announced, as well as hasty spending toward the end of the fiscal year if cuts do not occur.

CONSTITUTIONAL BUDGET CONSTRAINTS

The state is already limited to a balanced budget, and two recent constitutional amendments constrain state budgetmakers even further. First put into effect in FY1978–1979 was the constitutional requirement for a state reserve fund. The amendment prohibited the Budget and Control Board from recommending expenditures above 95 percent of the official revenue estimate. Nor could the General Assembly approve a general fund budget in excess of the same limit. Surplus funds at the end of the fiscal year accrued to a state reserve fund until the accumulated total reserve reached a designated amount of the general fund of the latest fiscal year. If the reserve fund is used to cover unanticipated deficits, it must be replenished according to a specified timetable. During Governor Riley's administration in the early 1980s, and at his urging, the state constitution was again amended to lower the required percentage from 5 to 4, with authority granted to the legislature to lower the amount yet another percent.

A second recent constitutional amendment requires that state spending be limited to a fixed percentage (approximately 7 percent) of total state personal income. The number of state employees is limited to a fixed percentage of total state population. Emergency clauses allow the legislature to override the spending limitation should extraordinary events occur. The limitation may be suspended for any single fiscal year upon a two-thirds vote of legislators present, to be not less than three-fifths of the total membership of each house. Nor can such an override be amended or repealed, except by an equivalent special vote.

Both amendments reflect the general conservative orientation of political elites in the state toward small government and a reduced role in government regulation and provision of services, a condition supporters find desirable. Critics contend that demand for government services is income elastic, expanding as fast or faster than personal income, and that the amendments are unnecessarily restrictive.

THE PRELEGISLATIVE BUDGET TIMETABLE

South Carolina essentially has a line-item object-of-expenditure budget, which includes over 130 separate classifications. Efforts in the late 1970s to overlay a program budget on the line-item format throughout all state agencies have not been successful. Some agencies have attempted to develop program budgets, but no consistent definition of administration was employed in those program budgets. Nor is the current computer accounting system readily amenable to adopting a statewide program budget. As of 1987, executive officials, as well as BCB staff, had found it impossible to derive program costs in some agencies.

State law requires a unified budget, which incorporates federal funds into the budget process, a practice begun in the early 1980s. Both the governor's office and the Joint Appropriations Review Committee (JARC) evaluate large federal grants.

The South Carolina budget process is an annual one. Unlike some states which have moved their fiscal calendars to coincide with the post–1974 federal calendar, beginning the federal fiscal year on October 1, South Carolina continues to use fiscal years that run from July 1 to June 30. The budget process begins in June, when the Board of Economic Advisors submits its preliminary unofficial revenue estimate for the year to the BCB. The BCB subsequently holds a meeting of executive department heads and agency budget officials to discuss revenue projections and technical instructions for preparing their budgets.

Agencies must submit their budget requests to the BCB for review and analysis by August 15. Department heads, members of department boards and commissions, and agency budget officials appear in open hearings before the BCB shortly following their request submissions. Although by law the BCB may complete budget hearings as late as November, in practice, to accommodate the time constraints of the budget process, hearings begin in mid-August and are completed in September.

Until Carroll Campbell, a Republican, was elected governor in 1986, the South Carolina governor played a limited role in the budget process. In addition to functioning as chairman of the BCB, the governor also issued guidelines to the agencies for their first estimates. The governor's weakness was highlighted by the fact that even in this prelegislative state, the governor could only strongly recommend adherence to his guidelines, not require it.

Despite the advocate role typically played by the agencies and the guardian role typically played by the BCB, relationships between the two are unusually cordial. The BCB staff is sufficiently small (fewer than fifteen budget examiners in the mid-1980s to review a $5 billion budget) that BCB examiners rarely have time to engage in any in-depth analysis. They often rely on agency analysts to provide input and to play a supportive role.

The BCB deliberates at the close of budget hearings over the amount of allocations to the agencies. By October, the BCB receives the official revenue estimate from the BEA. The BEA also completes a review of the current year's estimate. Agencies receive their BCB allocations in October and have until the first of November to submit detailed itemized budgets to the BCB. After reviewing the detailed agency budgets for accuracy in November, the BCB sends them to the publisher by the first of December.

The late 1970s, a time of turmoil in state fiscal affairs which produced a wave of tax and expenditure limitation proposals throughout the nation as well as in South Carolina, also proved to be a time of budget reforms. The South Carolina Budget and Control Board began operating on a more stringent "allocation basis," which has greater overtones of tradeoffs and priority setting than did the traditional budget system, under which agencies requested whatever they felt was necessary to provide adequate services.

Copies of the BCB-prepared budget are sent to the president of the state Senate and the speaker of the House within five days after the beginning of the regular session of the General Assembly on the second Tuesday in January. The state code calls for a joint open hearing of the House Ways and Means Committee and the Senate Finance Committee to consider the budget five days after the legislature receives it. This provision is largely bypassed, however, and the House and Senate develop different versions of the appropriations bills independently. Typically, the House considers the budget prior to the Senate, although in some years simultaneous consideration may occur.

THE LEGISLATIVE BUDGET TIMETABLE

The House Ways and Means Committee and the Senate Finance Committee are charged with the responsibility for reviewing both appropriations and revenue bills. The House Ways and Means Committee begins the legislative appropriations process by considering the House version of the appropriations bill. Capital expenditures are considered in a separate bond bill. The House version of the budget bill may differ from the BCB version as the House adds additional monies to pet projects and preferred functions.

After Ways and Means Committee approval, the appropriations bill is sent to the entire House for passage. State law requires that the committee present its version of the budget bill to the House for a second reading on or before the third Tuesday in February. The bill then goes to the Senate where it is submitted to the Senate Finance Committee. The committee can debate the bill for thirty-five days and, typically, increases funding again in preferred areas.

Following passage by the entire Senate, the appropriations bill is returned to the House. In most instances, there is disagreement between the House and Senate versions of the appropriations bill. The House notifies the Senate of this outcome and typically refuses to accept the Senate version. Should informal agreement not occur, members of both chambers are appointed to a conference committee. The speaker of the House appoints three members, one of whom is always the chairman of the House Ways and Means Committee, a second who is usually the second ranking member of Ways and Means, and a third member at large, typically from the minority party. The president pro tem of the Senate also appoints three conferees, always including the chairman of the Senate Finance Committee.

The conference committee is constrained by a legislative statute that restricts conferees to the House or the Senate version of any particular line item. If the initial conference committee with its limited jurisdiction is unable to resolve the differences between the two versions of the appropriations bill, it is replaced by a free conference committee with broader decision-making authority. Unlike the initial conference committee, the free conference committee does have the authority to insert new figures into the appropriations bill that lie between estimates of the two houses in order to achieve a compromise. A two-thirds vote of the entire membership of each house, taken separately, is required to elect the members of the free conference committee. Any compromise achieved by the free conference committee must subsequently receive majority approval in both houses before it is forwarded to the governor for signature. Typically, the conference report is passed on the last day of the legislative session, a date specified by law.

The commission form of agency administration in South Carolina has weakened agency ties with the governor, further reducing the chief executive's independent role and making it possible for politically strong agencies to lobby directly with the legislature. Among the stronger agencies that have achieved considerable legislative success are higher education, the technical college system, and the state alcohol and drug abuse program.

Weaker agencies that historically experienced less success include the Department of Education and the Department of Corrections. Despite passage of an innovative Education Improvement Act, sluggish revenues allowed the legislature in the mid-1980s to fund education at less than full-formula funding levels. Similarly, significant additional revenues for corrections were allocated, mostly as a result of federal court suits and threats of suits, rather than from the perception that increased funding levels were necessary or desirable.

CONFLICT OVER EXPANDED GUBERNATORIAL USE OF THE ITEM VETO

State law requires that the governor sign the appropriations bill by the first Thursday after the first Monday in June. The governor has considerable item veto power, which the state's governors have historically used sparingly. More frequent use of the item veto began during the late 1970s and the early 1980s to insure that state expenditures were balanced with estimated revenues. When subsequent revenue estimates indicated that tax collections would be less than previously expected in the official October revenue estimate, governors were required to use their veto power to make budget cuts to balance planned outlays with revenues.

Drawing on survey data from the fifty states, Abney and Lauth[7] have found that the gubernatorial item veto is as often used as an instrument of partisanship as an instrument of fiscal restraint, although the two goals are not always incompatible. In South Carolina, Democratic governor Dick Riley used the item veto extensively on the 1986 budget (over one hundred item vetoes), and Republican Governor Carroll Campbell used it repeatedly on the 1987 budget (276 line-item vetoes). The justification which both provided was an overall reduction in spending, to counter initially overoptimistic revenue estimates and to avoid midyear spending cuts. Because of the partisan conflict between the Democratic majority in the state legislature and the Republican party of the governor, the Campbell vetoes in particular also developed partisan overtones.

Item veto is the only method available to the governor to induce overall spending cuts once the budget has passed both houses of the legislature. According to Campbell aides,[8] Campbell's item vetoes were selected by the absolute dollar amount and, in particular, the degree to which the total line item approximated the desired percentage cut for any particular agency rather than their particular substantive content. Campbell publicized to agency heads that his intent was not to abolish particular line items, but rather to implement across-the-board percentage cuts, totaling 1 percent for most agencies, but two-thirds of 1 percent for corrections and one-half of 1 percent for education agencies. Youth Services received no cut. Accordingly, Campbell encouraged agency heads to request transfer authority from the BCB to move monies from other line items back into those that were vetoed.

Traditionally, state legislators are anxious to prove to their constituents that they are not prolonging the legislative session and are not drawing legislative expenses and pay needlessly. They therefore set aside only one day after the formal close of the legislative session to return to the state capitol to consider gubernatorial vetoes. On the appointed day, by close of business, the legislature had considered few of Campbell's item vetoes, and only two were overturned.

Campbell claimed victory, and by legislative inaction on the appointed day, the vetoes were sustained. The House leadership argued that the legislative session had been extended for two years, giving the House the right to reconsider the vetoes when the legislature was reconvened in January 1988. The legislature persisted in maintaining this stance for several months, leading to much game-playing (refusal to print a final budget, BCB refusal to grant transfer authority), although subsequently, the governor's vetoes were sustained.

FURTHER EXPANSION OF THE GOVERNOR'S ROLE

In 1988 Campbell introduced an executive budget to the Budget and Control Board, simultaneously dispersing copies of the governor's budget to all members of the state legislature. Any gubernatorial budget must overcome four hurdles: the Budget and Control Board, the House, the Senate, and the conference committee. All are formidable obstacles. Previously, the legislative staff reported that the legislature would not be receptive to such executive initiatives.

In 1988 two versions of the budget emerged before the Budget and Control Board, an unprecedented occurrence. In addition to the governor's "executive" budget, a second version reflected the preferences of the chairperson of the House Ways and Means Committee. A key component of the governor's budget was a reduction in the amount of monies allocated to the general reserve fund from 4 to 3 percent, resulting in an increase of $34 million that the governor requested be allocated to education. Although BCB and legislative members complained that the governor had little authority both to request a change in the law controlling the reserve fund allocation and to designate how the monies should be allocated, the budget finally adopted closely paralleled the provisions included in the governor's budget. Campbell aides expected that the introduction of an executive budget to the BCB in subsequent years would become the rule rather than the exception.

Until recently, the characterization of South Carolina's state budgeting by incrementalism and business as usual has reflected the state's political conservatism and the bias of elites toward limited government. The use of a line-item object-of-expenditure budget format has undercut priority setting and program planning. Reforms adopted in the late 1970s instructed the BCB to integrate agency plans with the annual budget. The FY1981–1982 was the first in which agency five-year plans were combined with their budgets. By and large, however, attempts to develop full-blown program budgets have failed. By the mid-1980s the abortion of attempts to develop effective program budgets, the continually overoptimistic revenue estimates, the frequency of midyear cuts, and the increase in gubernatorial item vetoes all indicated the need for significant and possibly sweeping reforms in South Carolina's budget process. Both the South Carolina Reorganization Commission and legislatively appointed commissions began to study reform options in the late 1980s.

As governor, Campbell proposed various reforms in addition to an executive budget: the development of comprehensive program budgets, agency submission of three budgets with programs ranked by priority, each at a different spending level (shades of zero-based budgeting), and funding at only 98 percent of the official revenue estimate. Clearly, any reforms that address the current problems must depoliticize the development of official revenue estimates and alleviate legislative pressure on the body that produces the estimates to raise them to unrealistically optimistic levels.

If the federal experience in the mid-1970s when severe conflict between President Nixon and a Democratically controlled Congress prompted significant federal budget reform proves to be a parallel, political conditions in South Carolina in the late 1980s, with growing conflict between a Republican governor and a Democratically controlled state legislature, are ripe for further change. The development of a meaningful program budget and more realistic revenue estimates may become the next budgetary battleground.

15

Conclusion: Budgeting in the American States—Conflict and Diversity

EDWARD J. CLYNCH AND THOMAS P. LAUTH

This volume provides the contextual information that allows us to assess the distribution of executive-legislative influence over budget decisions. It also helps us understand the nature of state fiscal conditions in the 1980s and to discern the impact of this dimension on gubernatorial and legislative budgetary power. Finally, the assortment of patterns reported here allows us to develop general classifications of states operating within the diversity of a federal system.

EXECUTIVE-LEGISLATIVE POWER EBB AND FLOW

The executive-centered "movement" implies unidirectional change, with the governor acquiring more power at the expense of the legislature. In reality, the sharing of authority not only keeps one branch from dominating the other, but also allows power to flow in both directions. At the same time, the built-in advantages of ongoing programs negate dramatic budget changes resulting from shifts of power between the governor and lawmakers. Over the last fifty years, budget scholars have reminded us that this year's budget closely resembles last year's budget. The current service base serves as a strong incremental force in most states. Inflation eats into any fiscal dividend and reduces the funds available for new spending initiatives since inflation escalates the cost of existing activities.

Despite the short-term bias toward incrementalism, changes in budget procedures that reconfigure the power of governors and legislatures carry long-term implications for budget decision making. Many states increased the governor's leverage over budget decisions by giving the chief executive the role of budget assembler and forcing the legislature into the role of budget reactor. The progression from legislative dominance to gubernatorial primacy outlined in the Illinois chapter has occurred in many other states. Many governors occupy the central place among budgeting players. This fulfills the majoritarian democracy objective described by Willoughby and others: An official chosen by the entire electorate possesses the tools to shape budget decisions. Recent trends in the direction of a gubernatorial authority have manifested themselves in Mississippi and South Carolina. The legislature still maintains a strong power base in both states, but the governor's point of view carries more weight than previously.

At the same time, evidence of movement toward increased legislative influence over budget decisions also surfaces. In states with strong gubernatorial control and accompanying legislative impotence, lawmakers took advantage of the formal separation of powers and obtained a more meaningful role. As a result, persons wishing to influence budget decision making in these states acquired more points of access. In the 1960s and 1970s Georgia's legislature moved from budget spectator to budget player. In Kentucky the legislature took control of writing budget instructions and limited the governor's free hand over budget rescissions. Many chapters mention the growth and professionalization of legislative staffs, which has enhanced the ability of lawmakers to critically review the governor's proposals.

Many legislatures use their power in the revenue-estimation process to leverage budget outcomes. Lawmakers retain a hand in determining available revenue even in most states with strong governors. By refusing to let governors unilaterally dictate the amount of money available to fund services, legislators retain a voice in making revenue adjustments, either to accommodate more spending or to put a lid on gubernatorial disbursement desires.

Partisan divisions also fuel conflict between the governor and the legislature. When the opposing party controls one or both of the legislative chambers, the governor's adversaries take advantage of the legislature's independent budget authority and try to place their stamp on the budget product. In Connecticut, Idaho, Minnesota, and Ohio, partisanship heightened conflict between the governor and legislature over budget issues. In Connecticut, conflict between the governor and legislature lessened when one party dominated both branches. In Florida, Democratic and Republican conservatives in the state Senate formed a coalition when the state elected a Republican governor in 1987. The coalition proved instrumental in getting the governor's spending and taxing proposals through the legislature.

Partisan divisions also elevate conflict in one-party states where a governor of the emerging party is elected. In South Carolina, the Republicans have moved budget conflict into the open with their own budget proposal. In Texas, the legislature has viewed Democratic governors as the head of their party and followed gubernatorial leads on spending initiatives. Bill Clements, the current Republican governor, finds the legislature less receptive to his ideas. He used the line-item veto during his first term and is attempting to influence legislative action with a "policy budget" during his current term. Clearly, partisan divisions upset the behind-the-scenes consensus building that occurs in many one-party states.

FISCAL CONDITION

A corollary focus of this book concerns the impact of a state's fiscal condition on the distribution of executive and legislative influence over budget decisions. During the 1980s, fiscal conditions varied across the states discussed in this volume.

A few states experienced steady revenue growth. However, the economies in many states underwent structural changes that led to tight revenues for at least a portion of the decade. Most states struggled through the decade with static or declining revenue.

States facing revenue scarcity resorted to a variety of techniques to meet the challenge. Their experience confirms Wildavsky's observation that many states with revenue problems look for solutions on the revenue side of the budget.[1] For instance, in the 1980s sales tax rates escalated in Minnesota, Mississippi, Utah, and Texas. Mississippi and Utah also raised income taxes, while Texas and Utah increased motor fuel taxes.

In addition, several states used "smoke and mirrors" to enhance revenues. Under legislative pressure, Connecticut and South Carolina's revenue estimators increased the amount of expected dollars to accommodate spending. California moved incoming revenues from the next fiscal year to the current one by altering withholding schedules to speed up collections. Illinois takes the prize, however, for the most innovative scheme. This state creates the illusion that the fiscal year finishes in the black by not deducting outstanding bills from the ending cash balance.

Many states also attacked revenue problems from the expenditure side as well. A majority of the states discussed here carried out budget rescissions to make ends meet. In several states, including Kentucky and Mississippi, the midyear rescission became the norm rather than the exception. Smoke and mirrors also found their way to the expenditure side of the budget. For instance, Minnesota moved transfer payments forward to the next biennium to reduce expenditures.

During the 1980s, Florida and Georgia experienced strong revenue streams. Connecticut experienced similar success until very recently. Economic booms in Florida and Georgia allowed these states to expand services from normal revenue growth, although both states raised their sales tax rate in the late 1980s. Connecticut's suburban overflow from New York gives the state the highest per capita income in the nation. Both Connecticut and Florida remain among the dwindling number of states without a general income tax. Several states moved from revenue surplus to revenue scarcity during the decade. For instance, declining energy prices sent Kentucky on a downward spiral, with the boom of the 1970s replaced by the bust of the 1980s.

DOES FISCAL CONDITION AFFECT EXECUTIVE-LEGISLATIVE BUDGET POWER?

The experiences of the states discussed here demonstrate that fiscal condition affects the outcome of the constant budget tug-of-war between the executive and the legislature. By and large, tight revenues favor the governor at the expense of the legislature, although in Kentucky legislators used cutbacks to enhance their influence. In most states, governors increase their leverage in several ways. On the revenue side, they usually take the lead when new taxes are proposed. Even in states with weak governors, such as Texas, the legislature lets the governor propose revenue solutions. Although the governor bears the onus of proposing new taxes, this situation provides the opportunity to shape the configuration of state taxes. Cutting programs also remains a job most legislators would just as soon let the governor carry out. Not surprisingly, budget rescissions usually fall to the governor, even in weak governor states like Mississippi. Governors may need to make unpopular cuts, but rescission authority provides the state chief executives with the opportunity to cut some agencies more than others and, as a result, to rework the distribution of resources. At the federal level, Congress refused to give the president unbridled authority to rearrange spending with Gramm-Rudman-Hollings cuts. The series of legislative court challenges to the governor's rescission authority in Ohio demonstrates that lawmakers understand the impact of this weapon on budget decisions.

Surpluses also carry power implications. In many states, the governor traditionally includes a plan to expend the fiscal dividend in the budget proposal. Even in Mississippi and Texas the legislature shows a propensity to follow the governor's lead when new revenue is available for disbursement, although the Democratically controlled Texas legislature shows less inclination to follow the current Republican governor. At the same time, legislatures demonstrate their desires to participate in the action. In Georgia, legislators use the second budget as a way of exercising some control over disbursing new funds.

EXECUTIVE-LEGISLATIVE BUDGET POWER: DIFFERENT PATTERNS

A precise classification of states in terms of gubernatorial and legislative budget power carries risks. The information in this book, however, suggests that states fall into the following general categories: (1) strong executive states with gubernatorial domination approaching the executive-centered process envisioned by reformers; (2) mixed states in which legislatures retain the ability to challenge executive assumptions in a meaningful way; (3) strong legislative states in which legislative leaders prepare the budget document to which legislatures react; and (4) South Carolina's fused system in which the governor, two other statewide elected officials, and two legislative leaders assemble the budget document sent to the legislature.

EXECUTIVE-DOMINANT STATES

Governors in the strong executive states of California, Illinois, and Ohio develop budget instructions, unilaterally receive and sift through spending requests submitted by agencies, and formulate the only unified budget submitted to the legislature. The lawmakers who lack access to the original agency requests use the governor's budget as a working document during the approval process. Furthermore, the veto also gives the governor leverage over budget decisions.

Illinois governors possess extremely strong veto authority with the amendatory veto, which allows them to rewrite laws rather than veto the entire bill. Even in these states, however, executive hegemony is less than complete. With the exception of California, legislatures in these states maintain a role in projecting revenue.

LEGISLATIVE ABILITY TO CHALLENGE EXECUTIVE ASSUMPTIONS

In Connecticut, Georgia, Idaho, and Minnesota the legislature and its staff receive agency requests, but the governor's executive budget still serves as the legislative working document. Nevertheless, the raw data give them the potential to make independent judgments and to challenge executive assumptions more effectively.

The extent to which legislators take advantage of the information varies among these states. In Connecticut and Minnesota, for example, legislative control remains more a potential than a reality. The governors of these states occupy the central position of governors in dominant states, with the exception that the legislature receives the agency requests. The Minnesota legislature reacts to the governor's proposal, and that state's chief executive uses the veto to configure spending patterns. In recent years, Connecticut's governors have failed to exercise line-item veto authority. Nevertheless, in 1989 the governor successfully threatened to veto the budget bill if it included an income tax on earned income.

In Georgia, the Legislative Budget Office analyzes the previous budget and agency requests to develop a current service figure for each agency. In 1975 the legislature also required a budget format that mandated numerous additional line items to increase legislative control.

In Idaho, the Legislative Budget Office receives agency requests at the same time they reach the governor. Although the legislature works with the governor's budget, the LBO provides legislators with informal evaluations of spending requests. The legislature also controls the revenue estimation process via a committee that sets the amount of revenue available for spending. The governor's veto lacks major punch as well. Paradoxically, recent governors vetoed appropriation's bills that were viewed as too low. Their subsequent requests for more money met with mixed results.

Kentucky is an example of a state experiencing legislative resurgence. The governor controls most aspects of budget formulation, and the legislature uses the governor's budget as a working document. However, in 1982 the legislature passed a statute giving the Legislative Research Office the authority to write budget instructions. The legislature used its authority to require the governor to provide a reduction plan. Kentucky implements the plan if revenues fail to meet estimated levels. In effect, the law transfers budget rescission authority from the governor to the legislature. The legislature also increased its capacity to impact budget decisions through more committee budget oversight and the establishment of the professionally run Legislative Reference Service.

LEGISLATIVE-DOMINANT STATES

In Utah, Florida, Mississippi, and Texas the legislature maintains substantial influence over budget formulation. In Utah and Florida, the process leads to substantial legislative influence without a formal leadership budget. In Mississippi and Texas, the lawmakers receive budget proposals from both the governor and the legislative leadership.

In Utah, the legislative fiscal analyst receives copies of agency requests early in the process. Although no official single-budget document is submitted to the legislature, the fiscal analyst reviews agency requests and makes budget recommendations. In addition, both the fiscal analyst and the governor's staff develop independent revenue estimates. The legislature uses the fiscal analyst's budget recommendations as a working document. Clearly, this person assumes a key role in the process. Although informal contacts occur with key legislators before the session begins, no formal mechanism exists for the leadership to put its stamp of approval on the recommendation before it reaches the legislature.

In Florida, the legislature and governor jointly develop budget instructions. The legislative staff receives agency requests simultaneously with the governor's office. The staff reviews agency requests before gubernatorial recommendations are submitted to the legislature. Although appropriations committees do not receive a separate legislative budget, these committees review agency requests independently of the gubernatorial recommendations. The legislature also works with the governor to develop consensus revenue estimates and a common understanding on the amount of money needed to cover entitlement programs.

In Mississippi and Texas, the legislative leadership uses its budget formulation powers to institutionalize legislative domination. In both states the executive shares the responsibility for writing budget instructions with the legislature. Furthermore, legislative staffs receive agency requests at the same time these items reach the governor's office. Unlike Florida and Utah, however, the legislative leadership prepares a consolidated budget recommendation and submits it to the legislature. In both states, the legislature uses the leadership budget as its working document, but in Texas lawmakers depend on gubernatorial guidance when spending any fiscal dividend and/or targeting programs for necessary cutbacks. Mississippi's dual budget system remains relatively new. Time will tell if the governor becomes the director of new spending and cuts. The initial year of Governor Ray Mabus suggests this trend may emerge in Mississippi as well.

FUSED GOVERNMENT

In South Carolina, much of the conflict between the governor and legislative leadership occurs within the confines of Budget Control Board (BCB) deliberations. The BCB produces a document representing the compromises between board members, which include the governor, two other statewide elected officials, and two legislative leader members. However, the system seems to be breaking down with the introduction of partisan politics. The current Republican governor, Carroll Campbell, uses the line-item veto more aggressively than his Democratic predecessor. Governor Campbell also submitted his own budget to the BCB and the legislature simultaneously. The legislature adopted a budget that included most of the governor's recommendations. Observers believe that governors will continue to submit an executive budget that provides the legislature with an alternative to the BCB recommendation.

GUBERNATORIAL AND LEGISLATIVE BUDGET INFLUENCE: CONCLUDING THOUGHTS

Executive and legislative influence over budget decisions varies across the United States. Naomi Caiden's assessment of federal budgeting clearly applies to all states.[2] Legislative and executive autonomy make power sharing a fact of life. The executive-centered budget movement affects some states more than others, but in no state can the governor completely monopolize legislative budget actions. Furthermore, the authority wielded by legislators in many states keeps them a long way from the executive-centered model envisioned by its champions. Clearly, budgeting in the American states reflects the variation that comes with a federal system. It also reflects the tug of war between the executive and the legislature which comes with separation of powers.

The power equation between the executive and the legislature changes over time and moves in different directions. The executive budget movement added leverage to many state governors. Conversely, power in some states moved to the legislature, with the development of more rigorous budget review procedures and additional professional budget staff who report to the legislature. Changes in partisan divisions alter power distributions in many states. "Divided government" often produces conflict over budget decisions that subside when one party regains control of both legislative chambers and the governor's office. Changes in revenue condition also modify the executive-legislative balance. Often the governor benefits, but the legislatures in some states also become more involved when more or less money is available.

The patterns in the states discussed here suggest that changes in the power equation often enhance the influence of the least engaged budget actor. Americans hold ambivalent views about concentrating political power. This indecision surfaces in regard to state budget decisions, which determine whose social values prevail. The desire for strong leadership responsive to the majority pushes legislatively dominated systems in the direction of more gubernatorial leverage. At the same time, the desire for pluralistic access opens up executive-dominated systems, which leads to more legislative influence over spending choices. As long as the American states operate with a governor and legislature independent of each other, power over budget decisions will ebb and flow between them.

Notes

CHAPTER 1

1. Anton, Thomas J., "Roles and Symbols in the Determination of State Expenditures," in Ira Sharkansky, *Political Analysis in Political Science* (Chicago: Markham Publishing Co., 1970), 209–224; Cleveland, Frederick A., "Evolution of the Budget Idea in the United States," *The Annals of the American Academy of Political and Social Science* (November 1915), 15–35; Pitsvada, Bernard T., "The Executive Budget—An Idea Whose Time Has Passed," *Public Budgeting & Finance* (Spring 1988), 85–94, along with comments on the Pitsvada article; Caiden, Naomi, "Comments," in Pitsvada, "The Executive Budget," 95–99; Fisher, Louis, "Comments," in Pitsvada, "The Executive Budget," 101–103; and LeLoup, Lance T., "Comments," in Pitsvada, "The Executive Budget," 104–107.

2. Ford, Henry Jones, "Budget Making and the Work of Government," *The Annals of the American Academy of Political and Social Science* 62 (November 1915), 1–14; Lowrie, S. Gale, "The Budget and the Legislatures," *The Annals of the American Academy of Political and Social Science* 62 (November 1915), 36–46; Miles, Rufus, E., "The Proper Function of the State Budget," *The Annals of the American Academy of Political and Social Science* 62 (November 1915), 47–63; Willoughby, William Franklin, *The Movement for Budgetary Reform in the States* (New York: D. Appleton & Co., 1918), ch. 1.

3. Schick, Allen, *Budget Innovation in the States* (Washington, D.C.: Brookings Institution, 1971), 15.

4. Hatton, A. R., "Forward," *The Annals of the American Academy of Political and Social Science* (November 1915), VII–VIII; Schick, *Budget Innovation in the States*; and Willoughby, *Movement for Budgetary Reform in the States*, 4–8.

5. Pitsvada, "The Executive Budget," 85–94.

6. Schick, *Budget Innovation in the States*, 14–19.

7. Wildavsky, Aaron, *Budgeting: A Comparative Theory of Budgeting Processes* (Boston: Little, Brown & Co., 1975), 128.

8. Schick, *Budget Innovation in the States*, 14–19; and Sokolow, Alvin D., and Beth Walter Honadle, "How Rural Local Governments Budget: The Alternatives to Executive Preparation," *Public Administration Review* (September/October 1984), 373–383.

9. Schick, *Budget Innovation in the States*, 23–24.

10. Friedman, Lewis B., *Budgeting Municipal Expenditures: A Study in Comparative Policy Making* (New York: Praeger Publishers, 1975).

11. Pitsvada, "The Executive Budget," 85–94.

12. Willoughby, *Movement for Budgetary Reform in the States*, ch. 1.

13. Schick, *Budget Innovation in the States*, 14–43.

14. Sharkansky, Ira, "Agency Requests, Gubernatorial Support, and Budget Success in State Legislatures," *The American Political Science Review* 62 (December 1968), 1220–1231 and Sharkansky, Ira, and Augustus B. Turnbull III, "Budget-Making in Georgia and Wisconsin: A Test of a Model," in Sharkansky, *Political Analysis in Political Science*, 225–238.

15. Anton, Thomas J., *Budgeting in Three Illinois Cities* (Urbana: Institute of Government and Public Affairs, University of Illinois, 1964).

16. Wildavsky, Aaron, *A Comparative Theory of Budgeting Processes*, 2nd ed. (Boston: Little, Brown & Co., 1986), p. 231.

17. Abney, Glenn, and Thomas P. Lauth, "The Line-Item Veto in the States: An Instrument for Fiscal Restraint or an Instrument of Partisanship?" *Public Administration Review* (May/June 1985), 372–377.

18. Clynch, Edward J., "Zero-Base Budgeting in Practice: An Assessment," *International Journal of Public Administration* 1 (Spring 1979), 43–64; Gosling, James J., "The State Budget Office and Policy Making," *Public Budgeting and Finance* (Spring 1987), 52–65, Lauth, Thomas P., "Zero-Base Budgeting in Georgia State Government: Myth and Reality," *Public Administration Review* (September/October 1978), 420–430; and Schick, *Budget Innovation in the States*.

19. Schick, Allen, "Micro-Budgetary Adaptations to Fiscal Stress in Industrialized Democracies," *Public Administration Review* (January/February 1988), 523–533.

20. Wildavsky, *A Comparative Theory of Budgeting Processes*.

CHAPTER 2

1. "Glossary of Budget Terms," *California State Budget 1985–86*, 83–87. Other official documents used in this chapter include the annual Budget Perspectives and Issues published yearly by the legislative analyst and the annual Summary of Legislative Action on the Budget Bill, especially FY1985, 1986.

2. Chapter 503, Statutes of 1979 as amended by chapter 323, Statutes of 1983, State of California.

3. "Program Base Analysis Attachment VII, Supplemental Instructions," Budget Letter No. 84–9 (Sacramento, Calif.: Department of Finance, August 2, 1984).

4. Budget Letter No. 84–9, 2.

5. Speech, William Hamm, Legislative Analyst to LBJ School of Public Affairs, April 4, 1984.

6. *General Fund Cost of Living Adjustments Summary 1984–85*, 20; *Total Expenditures Summary*, 9.

7. *Price Adjustment Factor Summary, 1985–86*, Summary Attachment II.

8. Interview, May 1986. Hamm was director of the Office of Legislative Analyst of the state of California for almost nine years, resigning in the spring of 1986.

9. McCaffery, Jerry, Interview with William Hamm. *Newsletter Section on Budgeting and Finance, 1986*, 3.

10. Hamm, interview.

11. Ibid.

12. The author had the opportunity to observe several subcommittee hearings in the spring of 1986 as well as conduct interviews with the Department of Finance, the Office of Legislative Analyst, the fiscal committee staff, and several agencies.

13. Legislative Analyst, Summary of Legislative Action on the Budget Bill, FY1984–1985, Table 3, *The Budget Act* (Sacramento, Calif.), 10.

14. Summary, 1984–1985, 10.

15. For an excellent description of this period, see Caiden, Naomi, and Jeffrey Chapman, "Budgeting in California," *Public Budgeting and Finance* (Winter 1982). Quote from p. 128.

16. Paddock, Richard C., "Governor Signs Budget, Vetoes 663 Million," *Los Angeles Times* (Wednesday, July 8, 1987), p. 1.

CHAPTER 3

1. Anton, Thomas, *The Politics of Expenditures in Illinois* (Urbana: University of Illinois Press, 1966).

2. Cornelius, Janet, *Constitution Making in Illinois, 1818–1970* (Urbana: University of Illinois, 1972), 33.

3. Ibid., 68.

4. Hutchinson, William T., *Lowden of Illinois* 1 (Chicago: University of Chicago Press, 1957), 295.

5. Crane, Edgar, "The Office of the Governor," in Edgar Crane, ed., *Illinois Political Process and Governmental Performance* (Dubuque, Iowa: Kendall Hunt Publishing Company, 1980), 74.

6. Ibid., 78.

7. Ibid., 77.

8. Jurgens, Nova Neuman, "Governor Lowers Budget Line by 3%," *Illinois Issues* (October 1986), 4–7.

9. Ibid.

10. Interview with the director of the Illinois Public Health Association, June 1987.

11. Bazzani, Craig S., "The Executive Budget Process," in James Nowlan, ed., *Inside State Government* (Urbana: University of Illinois Press, 1982), 41.

12. Jurgens, "Governor Lowers Budget Line by 3%."

13. Illinois Constitution, Article IV 9 (e).

14. Walters, John Nelson, "Comment: The Illinois Amendatory Veto," *The John Marshall Journal of Practices and Procedures* 11, no. 2 (Winter 1977–1978), 417–440.

15. Sevener, Don, "The Amendatory Veto: To Be or Not to Be So Powerful," *Illinois Issues* (February 1985).

16. Ibid.

17. Ibid.

18. Van Der Slik, Jack, and Ken Redfield, *Lawmaking in Illinois: Legislative Politics, People and Processes* (Springfield, Ill.: Sangamon State University, 1986).

19. Gonet, Phillip, and James Nowlan, "The Legislature," in James Nowlan, ed., *Inside State Government: A Primer for Illinois Managers* (Urbana: University of Illinois Press, 1982).

20. Van Der Slik and Redfield, *Lawmaking in Illinois*.

21. Gove, Samuel, Richard W. Carlson, and Richard J. Carlson, *The Illinois Legislature: Structure and Process* (Urbana: University of Illinois Press, 1976).

22. Gonet and Nowlan, "The Legislature."

23. Van Der Slik and Redfield, *Lawmaking in Illinois*.

24. Ibid.

25. In Illinois, the general fund is used for all monies that are not specifically allocated to other funds. Despite its residual definition, the general fund is usually considered the state's "checkbook account" and "the single most important indicator of the fiscal health of the state." Comptroller, State of Illinois, *The Dynamics of Illinois State Finance: A Fiscal Barometer* (1975), 2.

26. Bureau of the Budget, State of Illinois, *Quarterly Finance Report* (October 1984).

27. Anthony, Robert, "Games Government Accountants Play," *Harvard Business Review* 63 (September-October 1985), 161–170.

28. Illinois Economic and Fiscal Commission, *Revenue Estimate and Economic Outlook for FY 1978* (June 1977), 17.

CHAPTER 4

1. A longer, more descriptive version of this chapter may be obtained from the College of Urban Affairs, Cleveland State University, Cleveland, Ohio 44115. At the time the study was originally completed, the author was director of the Ph.D. program in urban studies at Cleveland State University.

2. Sheridan, Richard, Michael Sobul, Mark Hoffman, and Wilbur Thompson, "Ohio's Changing Economy," *Ohio Economic Trends Review* (Summer 1985), 25–30; Premus, Robert, "Long-Run Growth and Cyclical Behavior of Ohio's Economy," *Ohio Economic Trends Review* (Winter 1986), 6–13.

3. Celeste, Richard F., *Fighting Back/Rebuilding Together: A Summary of the Celeste Administration's Action Plan and Budget Submission for the Biennium, July 1, 1985 to June 30, 1987* (Columbus: State of Ohio, January 1985).

4. Patterson, Samuel C., and Gregory A. Caldeira, "The Etiology of Partisan Competition," *American Political Science Review* (September 1984), 691–707; Bibby, John F., Cornelius P. Cotter, James L. Gibson, and Robert J. Huckshorn, "Parties in State Politics," *Politics in the American States* (Boston: Little, Brown & Co., 1983), 59–96; Sabato, Larry, *Goodbye to Good-Time Charlie* (Washington, D.C.: Congressional Quarterly Press, 1983).

5. Sheridan, Richard G., *State Budgeting in Ohio* (Cleveland, Ohio: College of Urban Affairs, Cleveland State University, 1983).

6. Beyle, Thad L., "The Governor's Formal Powers: A View from the Governor's Chair," *Public Administration Review* 28 (Nov./Dec. 1968), 540–545.

7. Shkurti, William J., *Memorandum to Department Heads: Issue Analysis* (Columbus: State of Ohio, Office of Budget and Management, January 29, 1986), 1.

8. A national study by Lee and Staffeldt of state budget office personnel reported that 75 percent of Ohio's budget office staff had master's degrees or more, compared with the national average of only 35 percent. Lee, Robert D., Jr., and Raymond J. Staffeldt, "Educational Characteristics of State Budget Office Personnel," *Public Administration Review* 36 (July/August 1976), 424–428. Ohio was also identified as one of six states that

reduced the proportion of staff with business backgrounds by 50 percent or more and increased the percentage of their staffs with social science backgrounds. The authors conclude that states with large percentages of social science personnel like Ohio are "more committed to conducting program effectiveness analysis" (Lee and Staffeldt, 428), which is at the heart of rationalistic approaches to budgeting.

9. Kerker, Robert P., "Budgeting in the 1980s," *Book of the States, 1984–85* (Lexington, Ky.: Council of State Governments, 1984), 242–249.

10. Actually, Ohio's OBM budget analysts are not as involved in policy analysis, especially the establishment of alternatives, as are budget analysts in other states. However, most analysts interviewed want to be more involved and have predicted that this role will be facilitated by computerization and the revamping of the state's accounting system to get it into conformity with GAAP standards.

11. Sheridan, *State Budgeting in Ohio*, 99.

12. Balutis, Alan P., and Daron K. Butler, *The Political Pursestrings: The Role of the Legislature in the Budgeting Process* (New York: John Wiley, Halsted Press Division, 1975); Kerker, "Budgeting in the 1980s," 242–249; Pound, William T., "The State Legislatures," *Book of the States, 1984–85* (Lexington, Ky.: Council of State Governments, 1984), 79–83; Gosling, James J., "Patterns of Influence and Choice in the Wisconsin Budgetary Process," *Legislative Studies Quarterly* (November 1985), 457–482.

13. Pound, "The State Legislatures," 80.

14. Sheridan, *State Budgeting in Ohio*, 25–31.

15. Ibid., 29.

16. Ibid., 115–116.

17. Sheridan, Richard, "Budget Bytes," *Urban Fiscal Ledger* (May/June 1986), 8–10.

18. Sheridan, "State Budgeting in Ohio."

19. Ibid., 257.

20. Celeste, *Fighting Back/Rebuilding Together*; State of Ohio, *The State of Ohio Executive Budget for the Biennium July 1, 1985 to June 30, 1987* (Columbus, Ohio: Office of Budget and Management and Richard F. Celeste, Governor, 1985).

21. MacManus, Susan A., and Barbara P. Grothe, "The Fiscal Outlook for Ohio Municipalities Under Gramm-Rudman-Hollings," *Urban Fiscal Ledger* (March/April 1986), 1–8; Sobul, Michael, "How Federal Cuts May Affect State and Local Finances," *Urban Fiscal Ledger* (January/February 1986), 6–10.

CHAPTER 5

1. Governor William A. O'Neill, Budget Address, February 3, 1988.

2. State of Connecticut, "Recommendations of the Auditors of Public Accounts to the 1988 Session of the General Assembly" (Hartford, January 7, 1988), 2. Note that the fiscal year runs from July 1 through June 30.

3. Fink, David, "Senate Approves $6.2 Billion State Budget," *The Hartford Courant* (April 20, 1988), A1.

4. Levin, Michael, "It's Time to Curb Connecticut's Spending," *The Hartford Courant* (May 6, 1989), B9. The author is vice-president of the Connecticut Public Expenditure Council.

5. Remark of Representative Janet Polinksy in 1983. Carol W. Lewis, *Making Choices for Connecticut, A Handbook on the State Budget Process* (Storrs: University of Connecticut, Institutes of Public Service and Urban Research, 1984), 53.

6. Noel, Don, "High-handed Democrats Created Chaos." *The Hartford Courant* (May 6, 1988), B9.

7. Lewis, *Making Choices for Connecticut*, 29.

8. Governor William A. O'Neill, Budget Address, February 5, 1985.

9. Governor William A. O'Neill, Budget Address, February 9, 1983.

10. State of Connecticut, *Economic Report of the Governor, 1988–1989* (Hartford, Conn.: 1988), 66.

11. Advisory Commission on Intergovernmental Relations (ACIR), *Significant Features of Fiscal Federalism*, 1988, ed., 1 (Washington, D.C., December 1987), M–155, Table 39, 100.

12. Economic Report of the Governor, 77.

13. Governor O'Neill, Budget Address, 1988.

14. *The Hartford Courant* (March 1, 1988), A7, reporting results of ConnPoll of February 2–6, 1988, by the Institute for Social Inquiry.

15. ACIR, *Significant Features of Fiscal Federalism*, Table 37, 96–97.

16. So, too, do New Hampshire and Tennessee, while another seven states are without an individual income tax, ACIR, *Significant Features*, 96.

17. With a 7 percent effective rate, the tax is limited to taxpayers whose net capital gain exceeds $100 and/or whose adjusted gross income is $54,000 or more. State of Connecticut, Letter from Commissioner of Department of Revenue Services accompanying instructions for Filing for 1987.

18. Modifications include 1987 legislation to exclude 60 percent of long-term gains in order to offset the effects of the Federal Tax Reform Act of 1986. PA 559, effective January 1, 1987.

19. Lewis, Carol W., "Program Budgeting in Connecticut—The First Statewide Cycle" (Storrs: University of Connecticut, Institutes of Public Service and Urban Research, 1986), 4.

20. P.A. 81–466.

21. Lewis, "Program Budgeting in Connecticut," 7.

22. Management Analysis Center, Inc., "Implementing Program Budgeting in Connecticut," report to the Office of Policy and Management, April 28, 1982, 6. See also State of Connecticut, Office of Policy and Management, FY1985–1986 Program Budgeting Manual, which states four explicit objectives.

23. Letter from Governor William A. O'Neill to the author, June 8, 1985.

24. Remarks of Carole Donagher, Director, Office of Financial Management, Department of Income Maintenance, State of Connecticut, March 2, 1988. For further definition of "state priorities," see below.

25. State of Connecticut, Department of Administrative Services, Budget Office, "Program Planning & Budgeting Instructions Manual FY 1987–88" (Hartford, Conn., June 4, 1987), Appendix B.

26. Ibid.

27. Lewis, "Program Budgeting in Connecticut," 16.

28. Ibid.

29. Ibid.

30. Management Analysis Center, Inc., "Connecticut's Implementation of Program Budgeting: Assessment and Next Steps" (Washington, D.C.: December 1984), 15–16.

31. State of Connecticut, General Assembly, Office of Fiscal Analysis (OFA), "Public Budgeting and Expenditure Analysis in the State of Connecticut" (Hartford, October 15, 1980), 3.

32. Donohue, Leo V., Democratic Auditor of Public Accounts, January 1982, as quoted in Lewis, *Making Choices for Connecticut*, 10.

33. State of Connecticut Office of Policy and Management, *FY 1985-86 Program Budgeting Manual* (Hartford, Conn.: 1985).

34. *DAS Budget Manual*, Appendix B.

35. Lewis, *Making Choices for Connecticut*, 10.

36. Ibid.

37. Ibid., 38.

38. Ibid., 39.

39. Ibid., 27.

40. OFA, "Public Budgeting and Expenditure Analysis," 3.

41. State of Connecticut, General Assembly, Office of Fiscal Analysis, "1988–89 New and Expanded Programs in Excess of $1.0 Million" (Hartford, Conn.: May 26, 1988), computerized threshold sort.

42. Donohue, in Lewis, *Making Choices for Connecticut*, 42.

43. Telephone interview with Ralph Caruso, Director of Office of Fiscal Analysis, May 25, 1988.

44. Ibid.

45. Lewis, *Making Choices for Connecticut*, 29.

46. Fleming, James T., "Democrats Satisfied Craving for Spending," *The Hartford Courant* (May 7, 1988), D11.

47. OFA, "Public Budgeting and Expenditure Analysis," 3.

48. Lewis, *Making Choices for Connecticut*, 64–65, 79.

49. Kinsman, Susan E., "State House Passes Budget," *The Hartford Courant* (April 16, 1988), 1.

50. Lewis, *Making Choices for Connecticut*, 29.

51. Donohue, in Lewis, *Making Choices for Connecticut*, 4.

52. Governor O'Neill, Budget Address, 1985.

53. Donohue, Leo V., "Confessions of a Budgeteer," *The Hartford Courant* (September 9, 1980), 15. The author, currently Democratic auditor of public accounts, was describing his experiences as state finance director.

54. State of Connecticut, Bipartisan Commission on State Tax Revenue and Related Fiscal Policy, "Final Report," January 1983, 3.

55. Telephone interview with Ralph Caruso, Director of Office of Fiscal Analysis, May 25, 1988.

CHAPTER 6

1. An earlier version of this chapter appeared in *State and Local Government Review*, Carl Vinson Institute of Government, The University of Georgia, 1986.

2. Prior to that amendment, sitting governors could not seek consecutive terms in office, but former governors were eligible then, as they are now, to run for reelection four years after the end of their terms.

3. U.S. Advisory Commission on Intergovernmental Relations, *The Question of State Government Capacity* (Washington, D.C., January 1985), 129.

4. Secretary of State, Attorney General, State School Superintendent, Commissioner of Insurance, Commissioner of Agriculture, Commissioner of Labor, and five members of the Public Service Commission.

5. Lauth, Thomas P., "Impact of the Method of Agency Head Selection on Gubernatorial Influence over State Agency Appropriations," *Public Administration Quarterly* 7 (Winter 1984), 396–409.

6. Turnbull, Augustus B., III, "Politics in the Budgetary Process: The Case of Georgia," (Unpublished Ph.D. dissertation, University of Virginia, 1967), Chapters II and III.

7. Ibid., 81–118.

8. Ibid., 121–122; and Hoskins, Ronald B., "Within-Year Appropriation Changes in Georgia State Government: The Implications for Budget Theory," (Unpublished DPA dissertation, University of Georgia, 1983), 79.

9. Turnbull, Augustus B., III, "Georgia Budgeting: Development of Executive Budget," *Georgia Government Review* 1 (Fall 1968).

10. Murphy, Thomas B., *Atlanta Journal and Atlanta Constitution* (December 15, 1985), 1-C.

11. *Atlanta Constitution*, January 11, 1967, 1, and January 13, 1967, 1.

12. *Georgia Laws 1967 Session*, 722–725; *Official Code of Georgia Annotated*, 28-5-25.

13. Wildavsky, Aaron, *Budgeting: A Comparative Theory of Budgetary Processes*, (New Brunswick, N.J.: Transaction, Inc., 1986), 240.

14. Computed from data reported in: Georgia Department of Revenue, *Statistical Report*, (1989).

15. Computed from data reported in: U.S. Department of Labor, Bureau of Labor Statistics, *Employment and Earnings*, (May 1980 through May 1989), Table 1, "Annual Averages for States and Areas."

16. Computed from data reported in: U.S. Department of Labor, Bureau of Labor Statistics, *Geographic Profile of Employment and Unemployment*, (1980 through 1989), Table 12, "States . . . Annual Averages."

17. Computed from data reported in: U.S. Department of Commerce, Bureau of Economic Analysis, *News* (1980 through 1988), Table 1, "Per Capita Personal Income, by State and Regions."

18. Lauth, Thomas P., "Mid-Year Appropriations in Georgia: Allocating the Surplus," *International Journal of Public Administration* 11 (1988), 531–550.

19. The Georgia State Finance and Investment Commission consists of the governor, president of the Senate, speaker of the House of Representatives, state auditor, attorney general, commissioner of agriculture, and the director, fiscal division, Department of Administrative Services.

20. Anton, Thomas J., "Roles and Symbols in the Determination of State Expenditures," *Midwest Journal of Political Science* 11 (Fall 1967), 27–43.

21. Sharkansky, Ira, "Agency Requests, Gubernatorial Support and Budget Success in State Legislatures," *The American Political Science Review* 62 (December 1968), 1220–1231.

22. *Constitution of the State of Georgia*, Article 3, Section 6, Paragraph 2(a).

23. Lauth, Thomas P., "Exploring the Budgetary Base in Georgia," *Public Budgeting and Finance* 7 (Winter 1987), 72–82.

24. Georgia Office of Planning and Budget, *General Budget Preparation Procedures: Fiscal Year 1987*, (1986), 37.

25. Lauth, Thomas P., "The Executive Budget in Georgia," *State and Local Government Review* 18 (Spring 1986), 62–63.

26. Abney, Glenn, and Thomas P. Lauth, "The Line Item Veto in the States: An Instrument for Fiscal Restraint or an Instrument for Partisanship," *Public Administration Review* 45 (May/June 1985), 372–377.

CHAPTER 7

1. "The 50 States," *City & State* 4, no. 4 (April 1987), 24.

2. Ibid., 14.

3. State of Idaho, Legislative Budget Office, *1986 Idaho Legislative Fiscal Report for FY1987 to the Joint Senate Finance-House Appropriations Committee* (May 1986), 26; State of Idaho, *1987 Idaho Legislative Fiscal Report for FY1988 to the Joint Senate Finance-House Appropriations Committee* (May 1987), 17.

4. For a description of the adoption of the Idaho zero-base budget system and an evaluation of the system, see Duncombe, Sydney, John Andreason, and Lawrence Seale, "Zero-Base Budgeting in Idaho—An Evaluation After Five Years," *The Government Accountants' Journal* 30 (Summer 1981), 25, 26.

5. Kinney, Richard, "At the Hub of Idaho State Budgeting: A Study of the Budget Analysts in the Gem State," Paper prepared for the 47th Annual Conference of the American Society of Public Administration, Anaheim, California, April 12–16, 1986, 7, 8.

6. Duncombe, Herbert S., and Florence Heffron, "Legislative Budgeting," in Jack Rabin and Thomas Lynch, eds., *Handbook on Public Budgeting and Financial Management* (New York: Marcel Dekker, 1983), 443.

7. Kinney, "At the Hub of Idaho State Budgeting," 9.

8. For a description of the perceptions of Idaho agency budget officials, executive budget analysts, and legislative budget staff, see Duncombe, Sydney, and Richard Kinney, "The Politics of State Appropriation Increases: The Perspectives of Budget Officers in Five Western States," *The Journal of State Government* 59 (September/October 1986), 113–123.

9. State of Idaho, Legislative Budget Office, *1983 Idaho Legislative Fiscal Report to the Joint Senate Finance-House Appropriations Committee* (June 1983), 27–28; State of Idaho, Legislative Data Center, *Daily Data—Final Edition, Forty-Seventh Idaho Legislature, First Regular Session, January 10, 1983, Through April 14, 1983.*

10. State of Idaho, Legislative Budget Office, *1988 Idaho Legislative Fiscal Report for FY 1989 to the Joint Senate Finance-House Appropriations Committee* (May 10, 1988), 3; State of Idaho, Legislative Data Center, *Daily Data—Final Edition, Forty-Ninth Idaho Legislature, Second Regular Session, January 11, 1988 Through March 31, 1988.*

11. Idaho Constitution, Article VIII, Section 1, and *Idaho Code*, Section 67–3512A.

12. Duncombe, Sydney, and Richard Kinney, "Cutbacks—Idaho Style," *Public Budgeting and Finance* 4 (Summer 1984), 88.

13. Our samples are not random ones, and we are restricted from commenting on the statistical significance of our findings. However, to identify possibly "important" relationships, we indicate those coefficients with significant levels of 0.05 or better, a convention used in the state budgeting literature. For example, see Sharkansky, Ira, "Agency Requests, Gubernatorial Support and Budget Success in State Legislatures," *The American Political Science Review* 62 (December 1968), 1220–31.

14. Ibid.

15. For the test of significance we used, see Blalock, Hubert M., *Social Statistics* 2d ed. (New York: McGraw-Hill, 1972), 407.

CHAPTER 8

1. The state's largest newspaper recently gave feature front-page coverage to questions of Minnesota state budget policy and practice. See *Star Tribune*, Newspaper of the Twin Cities (January 24, 25, 26, 1988).

2. Most of the pages that follow are based on personal observations of the budget process in Minnesota over the past decade and on informal discussions with legions of executive officials, legislators, legislative staff, and representatives of organized interests. In addition, considerable reliance was placed on Blazar, William A., "Minnesota's Approach to Budgeting: Executive and Legislative Responsibilities," *Minnesota Tax Study Commission Report*, Vol. 1, edited by Robert Ebel and Theresa J. McGuire (St. Paul, Minn.: Buttersworth Publishing, 1986), and Sederberg, Charles H., *The Minnesota State Biennium Budget Cycle*, Occasional Paper Number 3 (Center for Educational Policy Studies, University of Minnesota).

3. Yondorf, Barbara, and B. J. Summers, "Legislative Budget Procedures in the 50 States," *Legislative Finance Paper #21* (Denver, Colo.: National Conference of State Legislatures, January 1983), Table A-2, 6.

4. See McCormack, Patrick J., "Annual or Biennial Budgeting?," unpublished Plan B paper (Humphrey Institute of Public Affairs, University of Minnesota, December 1986).

5. Yondorf and Summers, "Legislative Budget Procedures," Table C-3, 34.

6. I am indebted to Dean Royce Hanson, principal investigator of the project team for the Study of the Future of the Minnesota Legislature, for this insight.

7. See McCormack, Patrick J., *The Third House: The Role of Conference Committees in the Minnesota Legislature*, paper in the Future of the State Legislature series (Humphrey Institute of Public Affairs, University of Minnesota, September 1985).

8. See "Jennings (Speaker David) Urges Fast Work on House Budget," *Minneapolis Star Tribune* (January 24, 1985), 4b.

9. For an insightful analysis of the budget shortfall problem faced by the state of Minnesota in the early 1980s, see *General Fund Budget Reductions Program Fiscal Year 1981 State of Minnesota, A Case Study*, National Association of State Budget Officers, (Washington, D.C., September 1980).

10. For an in-depth study of the budget reserve issue, see Folkman Gordon, *The Budget Reserve* (Office of Legislative Auditor, October 31, 1984).

11. I am indebted to Kevin Kajer, fiscal analyst for the Minnesota House Appropriations Committee, for the insight regarding the implications of the legislature's abdicative action.

12. McCormack, *The Third House*.

13. Unicameralism is strongly advocated by former State Senator George Pillsbury, a longtime student of the legislature.

14. A Joint Budget Committee has been recommended by Kevin Kajer in "Legislative Budgeting in Minnesota," unpublished Plan B paper, Humphrey Institute of Public Affairs, University of Minnesota, January 1988. State Senator Richard Cohen has recommended a legislative budget office.

CHAPTER 9

1. Mikesell, John L., *Fiscal Administration: Analysis and Applications for the Public Sector* (Chicago: Dorsey Press, 1986), 135–167.

2. Schick, Allen, "The Road to PPB: The Stages of Budget Reform," *Public Administration Review* (December 1966), 243.

3. Schick, Allen, "The Road from ZBB," *Public Administration Review* 38 (March/April 1978), 178.

4. Ramsey, James, and Merl Hackbart, *Innovations in State Budgeting: Process and Impact* (Lexington: University of Kentucky, Center for Public Affairs, 1978), 32.

5. Ramsey and Hackbart, *Innovations in State Budgeting: Process and Impact*, 32.

6. Patton, Janet, and Merl Hackbart, *Innovation in State Government Processes: An Analysis of Selected Programs*, (Lexington: University of Kentucky, Center for Public Affairs, 1976), 31.

7. Ibid.

8. Center for Business and Economic Research, *Kentucky Annual Economic Report: 1987* (Lexington: University of Kentucky, Center for Business and Economic Research, 1987).

9. Hackbart, Merl, Levis McCullers, and James Ramsey, *Program Evaluation and Review: The Kentucky System*, (Lexington, Ky: University of Kentucky, Bureau of Government Services, 1975).

10. Ramsey and Hackbart, *Innovations in State Budgeting: Process and Impact*.

11. Governor's Office for Policy and Management, *Commonwealth of Kentucky: Executive Budget Request Manual, 1988–90* (Frankfort, Ky.: Governor's Office for Policy and Management, 1987).

12. Carson, Ronald, "The 1984–86 Kentucky State Budget," *Kentucky Economy: Review & Perspective*, Vol. 8, no. 2 (1984), 3–7.

13. Snyder, Sheryl G., and Robert M. Ireland, "The Separation of Governmental Powers Under the Constitution of Kentucky: A Legal and Historical Analysis of L.R.C. v. Brown," *Kentucky Law Journal* (1984–1985), 165.

14. Carson, "The 1984–86 Kentucky State Budget," 3–7.

15. Snyder and Ireland, "The Separation of Governmental Powers Under the Constitution of Kentucky," 230.

16. Ramsey, James, and Merl Hackbart, "State and Local Debt Capacity: An Index Measure," *Municipal Finance Journal* (Winter 1988).

CHAPTER 10

1. Kyle, Joseph, "Florida Legislative Budget Review Process," in Alan Balutis and Doron K. Butler, eds., *The Political Pursestrings: The Role of the Legislature in the Budgeting Process* (New York: John Wiley, 1975), 71.

2. Klay, William Earle, and Patricia Irvin, "Revenue," in Thomas C. Foss and Thomas D. Sutberry, eds., *State Budgeting in Florida: A Handbook for Budget Analysts* (Tallahassee: Florida State University, 1984), 32–33.

3. "Planning and Budgeting," *Florida Statutes*, Chapter 216, Section 216.172.

4. Ezell, Wayne, "Sounds of Silence Pervade Meeting on Budget Strategy," *Tallahassee Democrat* (1978), 1D, 6D.

5. "Haben Discourages Sunshine Challenge," *Tallahassee Democrat* (June 21, 1981).

6. Schultz, Dave, "Duty Often Determines How Legislators Vote," *Tallahassee Democrat* (May 19, 1980), 1–2B.

7. Martinez, Governor Bob, *Building a Better Florida: Budget Recommendations for 1988–89* (Tallahassee: State of Florida, 1988).

8. Potter, Carla, and Bill Odom, *Financing Florida's Public Schools* (Tallahassee: Florida Senate Committee on Ways and Means, 1980).

9. Turnbull, Augustus B., and Patricia Irvin, "The Florida Appropriations Process—An Overview," in Thomas C. Foss and Thomas D. Sutberry, eds. *State Budgeting in Florida: A Handbook for Budget Analysts* (Tallahassee: Florida State University, 1984).

10. Graham, D. Robert, "The Florida Budget—The Old Myth and New Reality," *Florida Planning & Development* (March-April 1969), 1–7

11. "Planning and Budgeting," *Florida Statutes*, Chapter 216, Sections 216.023 and 216.031.

12. Klay, William Earle, and Pyeong J. Yu, "Constitutional and Administrative Implications of Computers," *Public Productivity Review* (Winter 1988), 193–203.

13. DeFord, Susan, "Lawmakers, Graham Battle Over Budget," *Tallahassee Democrat* (May 1, 1983), 1B, 4B.

14. Advisory Commission on Intergovernmental Relations, *1982 Tax Capacity of the Fifty States* (Washington, D.C.: ACIR, 1985), Vol. 55.

15. Advisory Commission on Intergovernmental Relations, *1981 Tax Capacity of the Fifty States* (Washington, D.C.: ACIR, 1983), 29.

16. Ibid.

17. *The Sunrise Report* (Tallahassee: The Speaker's Advisory Committee on the Future, Florida House of Representatives, 1987), 38–39.

18. *The Sunrise Report* (Tallahassee: The Speaker's Advisory Committee on the Future, Florida House of Representatives, 1987), 12.

19. *Florida Comprehensive Annual Financial Report*. Fiscal Year Ended June 30, 1986 (Tallahassee: State Comptroller).

20. Zorn, Paul, "Public Pension Funding: Preliminary Results from a Survey of Current Practices," *Government Finance Review* (August 1987), 7–11.

21. McCall, Sam M., Deputy Auditor General, State of Florida. Reported in conversation in April 1987.

CHAPTER 11

1. Christensen, Michael, "A Look at the Utah Economy and the State Budget," *Utah Economic and Business Review* (June 1987), 6.

2. Ibid., xx; U.S. Department of Commerce, *Governmental Finance in 1984–85* (Washington, D.C.: U.S. Department of Commerce, 1986), 26, 104.

3. Fairfax, Sally K., and Carolyn E. Yale, *Federal Lands: A Guide to Planning, Management, and State Revenue* (Washington, D.C.: Island Press, 1987), 203.

4. Christensen, "A Look at the Utah Economy and the State Budget," 23.

5. Ibid., 3, 4.

6. Utah Foundation, *Statistical Review of Government in Utah, 1987* (Salt Lake City: Utah Foundation, 1987), 26.

7. Council of State Governments, *The Book of the States 1986–87* (Lexington, Ky.: Council of State Governments, 1986), 220–221.

8. *Utah Code Annotated* 63-38-2.

9. Ibid.

10. Wildavsky, Aaron, *Politics of the Budgetary Process*, 4th ed.(Boston: Little, Brown, 1984), 63–126; Lee, Robert D., Jr., and Ronald W. Johnson, *Public Budgeting Systems*, 3rd ed. (Baltimore: University Park Press, 1983), 198–211.

11. LeLoup, Lance, T., "Appropriations Politics in Congress: The House Appropriations Committee and Executive Branch Agencies," *Public Budgeting and Finance* (Winter 1984), 81.

12. Balutis, Alan P., and Daron K. Butler, eds., *The Political Pursestrings: The Role of the Legislature in the Budgetary Process* (New York: John Wiley, Halsted Press Division, 1974), 16.

13. Ibid., 201–209.

14. Lee and Johnson, *Public Budgeting Systems*, 204.

15. *Utah Code Annotated* 36-12-13.

16. *The Book of the States, 1986–87*, 223.

17. *Constitution of Utah*, Article XIII, Section 9.

18. *Utah Code Annotated* 36-12-13.

19. Office of the Legislative Fiscal Analyst, *Appropriations Report, 1987–88* (Salt Lake City: Office of the Legislative Fiscal Analyst, 1987), 9.

CHAPTER 12

1. Interview with William C. Hamilton, Governor's Office of Budget and Planning, 1982.

2. The descriptions of the Texas budget process in this chapter are based on the Texas constitution and relevant statutes, the author's experiences and observations, and Zively, Lane A., "LBB Process," Texas Public Employees Association (undated mimeo). This information was supplemented by interviews with Lieutenant Governor William P. Hobby, Homer Scace, Greta Rymal, and Robert Norris of the Legislative Budget Board, and Sheila Beckett of the Governor's Office of Budget and Planning, 1987.

3. William C. Hamilton interview, 1982.

4. Governor's Budget and Planning Office and Legislative Budget Office, "Detailed Instructions for Preparing and Submitting Requests for Legislative Appropriations for the Biennium Beginning September 1, 1983" (Austin: State of Texas, March 1982).

5. Governor's Budget Office and Legislative Budget Office, "Detailed Instructions for Preparing and Submitting Requests for Legislative Appropriations for the Biennium Beginning September 1, 1987: Executive, Administrative, Human Service and Selected Agencies of Public Education" (Austin: State of Texas, March 1986).

6. Interview with Greta Rymal, LBB, 1987.

7. William P. Clements, Jr., Governor of Texas, "Executive Policy Budget: State of Texas, 1988–89 Biennium" (Austin: State of Texas, February 1987).

8. Interview with Sheila Beckett, Governor's Office of Budget and Planning, 1987.

9. "Texas Taxes Do Not Mirror Texas Economy," *Fiscal Notes* (January 1986), Texas Comptroller of Public Accounts Newsletter, 1–4.

10. "Biennial Revenue Forecast: Lean Times Ahead," *Fiscal Notes*, (January 1987), Texas Comptroller of Public Accounts Newsletter, 1–8.

11. Ibid., 1–2.

12. "Fiscal 1986 in Review," *Fiscal Notes* (November 1986), Texas Comptroller of Public Accounts Newsletter, 1–3.

13. The discussion of Texas' current fiscal situation and future prospects are based on documents obtained from the Lieutenant Governor's Office, the Legislative Budget Board, and the Texas Association of Taxpayers, as well as interviews with Craig Pederson,

Office of the Lieutenant Governor, John Bell, Office of the State Treasurer, and William Allaway and Billy Hamilton of Texas Association of Taxpayers, Inc., 1987.

14. Howard LaFranchi, "Lone Star Revenue Bill Brings Grumbles About the 'State of Taxes'," *The Christian Science Monitor* (July 23, 1987), 4.

CHAPTER 13

1. Ogle, David B. *Strengthening the Mississippi Legislature* (New Brunswick, N.J.: Rutgers University Press, 1968), 103–119. Governor William Winter influenced the commission more than any other governor. His leverage resulted from his long-standing acquaintance with legislative members and his willingness to assert leadership. Winter, unlike other governors, actually ran the meetings and was able to have a person of his choosing made the staff director.

2. *Alexander et al.* v. *State of Mississippi By and Through Allain.* November 23, 1983. 441 So. 2D 1339.

3. Clynch, Edward J., "Budgeting in Mississippi: Are Two Budgets Better Than One?," *State and Local Government Review* (Spring 1986), 49–50. The Clynch piece describes the Mississippi budget process set up in 1984.

4. Mississippi Code, 1989 Section 27–104–1.

5. Cope, Glen Hahn, "Texas: Legislative Budgeting in a Post-Oil-Boom Economy," Chapter 12 of this volume.

6. Mississippi Code, 1985: Section 27–103–101.

7. Mississippi Code, 1985: Section 31–17–173.

8. Mississippi Code, 1985: Section 31–17–123.

9. Joint Legislative Budget Committee, *State of Mississippi Budget Fiscal Year 1987*, May 1, 1986, 9.

10. Mississippi Code, 1985: Section 27–103–139.

11. Allain, Bill, *State of Mississippi Executive Budget: 1985–1986,* November 15, 1985 and Allain, Bill, *State of Mississippi Executive Budget: 1986–1987,* November 15, 1986.

12. *Starkville Daily News*, January 17, 1986.

13. *Starkville Daily News* (b), January 17, 1986.

14. Mississippi Code, 1985, Section 27–103–113.

15. The State Personnel Board provides a projection of the amount of money necessary for realigning positions.

16. *The Clarion-Ledger*, January 21, 1988.

17. *The Sun Herald*, March 27, 1989.

18. *The Clarion-Ledger*, April 19, 1989.

19. Constitution of Mississippi, November 1, 1890: Article IV, Section 2.

20. Paul D. Warner, "Mississippi Economic Review and Outlook," Mississippi Research and Development Center, March 1987, 1.

21. U.S. Bureau of the Census, *Statistical Abstract of the United States: 1980* (100th edition), U.S. Department of Commerce, Washington, D.C.

22. Warner, "Mississippi Economic Review and Outlook," 1.

23. Ibid.

CHAPTER 14

1. Birch, Harold B. "South Carolina State Government Administrative Organization: The Orthodox Theory of Administration Revisited," *Government in the Palmetto State* (Columbus: University of South Carolina Bureau of Government Research and Service, 1983), 122.

2. Black, Earl, and Merle Black, *Politics and Society in the South* (Cambridge, Mass.: Harvard University Press, 1987).

3. Birch, "South Carolina State Government Administrative Organization."

4. Organization, Graham, C. Blease, and Donald P. Aiesi, "The Role of the Governor in South Carolina," *Government in the Palmetto State* (Columbia: University of South Carolina Bureau of Government Research and Service, 1983), 106.

5. Neubauer, D. W., *America's Courts and the Criminal Justice System* (Belmont, Calif., Wadsworth Publishing Co., 1979).

6. Putnam, Robert D., *The Comparative Study of Political Elites* (Englewood Cliffs, N.J.: Prentice–Hall, 1976); Burns, James MacGregor, *The Deadlock of Democracy: Four-Party Politics in America* (Englewood Cliffs, N.J.: Prentice–Hall, 1963).

7. Abney, Glenn, and Thomas P. Lauth, "The Line-Item Veto in the States: An Instrument for Fiscal Restraint or an Instrument for Partisanship?," *Public Administration Review* (May/June 1985), 372–377.

8. Ayres, Q. Whitfield, Senior Executive Assistant for Budget Policy, Office of the Governor, South Carolina, Personal interview (August 1987); Carter, Luther F., Senior Executive Assistant for Finance and Administration, Office of the Governor, South Carolina, Personal interview (August 1987).

CHAPTER 15

1. Wildavsky, Aaron, *A Comparative Theory of Budgeting Processes*, 2nd ed. (Boston: Little, Brown, 1986), 229.

2. Caiden, Naomi, "Comments," in Bernard T. Pitsvada "The Executive Budget— An Idea Whose Time Has Passed," *Public Budgeting & Finance* (Spring 1988), 95–99.

Selected Bibliography

Abney, Glenn, and Thomas P. Lauth, "The Line-Item Veto in the States: An Instrument for Fiscal Restraint or an Instrument of Partisanship?" *Public Administration Review* 45 (May/June 1985), 372–377.

Abney, Glenn, and Thomas P. Lauth, "The Governor as Chief Administrator." *Public Administration Review* 43 (January/February 1983), 40–49.

Albritton, Robert, and Ellen Dran, "Balanced Budgets and State Surpluses: The Politics of Budgeting in Illinois," *Public Administration Review* 47 (1987), 143–152.

Anthony, Robert, "Games Government Accountants Play." *Harvard Business Review* 63 (September/October 1985), 161–170.

Anton, Thomas J., "Roles and Symbols in the Determination of State Expenditures." In Ira Sharkansky, *Political Analysis in Political Science*, Chicago: Markham Publishing Co., 1970, 209–224.

Anton, Thomas J., *The Politics of Expenditures in Illinois*. Urbana: University of Illinois Press, 1966.

Anton, Thomas J., *Budgeting in Three Illinois Cities*. Urbana: Institute of Government and Public Affairs, University of Illinois, 1964.

Balutis, Alan P., and Daron K. Butler, eds., *The Political Pursestrings: The Role of the Legislature in the Budgeting Process*. New York: John Wiley, Halsted Press Division, 1975.

Bazzani, Craig S., "The Executive Budget Process." In James Nowlan, ed., *Inside State Government*, Urbana: University of Illinois Press, 1982.

Beckman, Ada E., "The Item Veto Power of the Executive." *Temple Law Quarterly* 31 (Fall 1957), 27–34.

Beyle, Thad L., "The Governor's Formal Powers: A View from the Governor's Chair." *Public Administration Review* 28 (November/December 1968), 540–545.

Blazar, William A., "Minnesota's Approach to Budgeting: Executive and Legislative Responsibilities." In *Minnesota Tax Study Commission Report*, Vol. 1, edited by Robert Ebel and Theresa J. McGuire. St. Paul, Minn.: Buttersworth Publishing, 1986.

Caiden, Naomi, "Comments." In Bernard T. Pitsvada, "The Executive Budget—An Idea Whose Time Has Passed." *Public Budgeting & Finance* 6 (Spring 1986), 95–99.

Caiden, Naomi, and Jeffrey Chapman, "Budgeting in California." *Public Budgeting and Finance* 2 (Winter 1982) 111–129.

Carson, Ronald, "The 1984–86 Kentucky State Budget." *Kentucky Economy: Review & Perspective* 8 no. 2 (1984).

Christensen, Michael, "A Look at the Utah Economy and the State Budget." *Utah Economic and Business Review* 47, no. 6 (June 1987), 2–9.

Cleveland, Frederick A., "Evolution of the Budget Idea in the United States." *The Annals of the American Academy of Political and Social Science* 62 (November 1915), 15–35.

Clynch, Edward J., "Getting Along with Less in Mississippi: Allocating the Cuts." *International Journal of Public Administration* 22 (1988), 551–579.

Clynch, Edward J., "Zero-Base Budgeting in Practice: An Assessment." *International Journal of Public Administration* 1, no. 1 (Spring 1979), 43–64.

Crane, Edgar, "The Office of the Governor." In Edgar Crane, ed., *Illinois Political Process and Governmental Performance,* Dubuque, Iowa: Kendall-Hunt Publishing Company, 1980.

Dometrius, Nelson C., "Some Consequences of State Reform." *State Government* 54, no. 3 (1981), 93–98.

Duncombe, Herbert S., and Florence Heffron, "Legislative Budgeting." In Jack Rabin and Thomas Lynch, eds., *Handbook on Public Budgeting and Financial Management,* New York: Marcel Dekker, 1983.

Duncombe, H. Sydney, John Andreason, and Lawrence Seale, "Zero-Base Budgeting in Idaho—An Evaluation After Five Years." *The Government Accountants' Journal* 30 (Summer 1981), 25–26.

Duncombe, H. Sydney, and Richard Kinney, "The Politics of State Appropriation Increases: The Perspectives of Budget Officers in Five Western States." *State Government* 59 (September/October 1986), 113–123.

Fisher, Louis, "Comments." In Bernard T. Pitsvada, "The Executive Budget—An Idea Whose Time Has Passed," *Public Budgeting & Finance* 6 (Spring 1986), 101–103.

Ford, Henry Jones, "Budget Making and the Work of Government," *The Annals of the American Academy of Political and Social Science* 62 (November 1915), 1–14.

Friedman, Lewis B., *Budgeting Municipal Expenditures: A Study in Comparative Policy Making.* New York: Praeger Publishers, 1975.

Gonet, Phillip, and James Nowlan, "The Legislature." In James Nowlan, ed., *Inside State Government: A Primer for Illinois Managers.* Urbana: University of Illinois Press, 1982.

Gosling, James J., "Patterns of Influence and Choice in the Wisconsin Budgetary Process." *Legislative Studies Quarterly* 10 (November 1985), 457–482.

Gosling, James J., "The State Budget Office and Policy Making." *Public Budgeting and Finance* 7 (Spring 1987), 51–65.

Gove, Samuel, Richard W. Carlson, and Richard J. Carlson, *The Illinois Legislature: Structure and Process.* Urbana: University of Illinois Press, 1976.

Graham, D. Robert, "The Florida Budget—The Old Myth and New Reality." *Florida Planning and Development* 20 (March/April 1969), 1–7.

Guhde, Robert, and Husain Mustafa, "Incremental Budgeting: A Test of the Model." *International Journal of Public Administration* 5 (1982).

Hackbart, Merl, Lewis McCullers, and James Ramsey, *Program Evaluation and Review: The Kentucky System*. Lexington: University of Kentucky, Bureau of Government Services, 1975.

Hatton, A. R., "Forward." *The Annals of the American Academy of Political and Social Science* 62 (November 1915), VII–VIII.

Jones, L. R., and Jerry L. McCaffery, *Government Response to Financial Constraints: Budgetary Control in Canada*. Westport, Conn.: Greenwood Press, 1989.

Kerker, Robert P., "Budgeting in the 1980s." *Book of the States, 1984–85*. Lexington, Ky.: Council of State Governments, 1984, 242–249.

Klay, William Earle, and Patricia Irvin, "Revenue." In Thomas C. Foss and Thomas D. Sutberry, eds., *State Budgeting in Florida: A Handbook for Budget Analysts*, Tallahassee: Florida State University, 1982.

Kyle, Joseph, "Florida Legislative Budget Review Process." In Alan Balutis, ed., *The Political Pursestrings*, New York: John Wiley, 1974, 69–79.

Lauth, Thomas P., "Mid-Year Appropriations in Georgia: Allocating the 'Surplus'." *International Journal of Public Administration* 11 (1988), 531–550.

Lauth, Thomas P., "Zero-Base Budgeting in Georgia State Government: Myth and Reality." *Public Administration Review* 38 (September/October 1978), 420–430.

Lauth, Thomas P., and Stephen C. Rieck, "Modifications in Georgia Zero-Base Budgeting Procedures: 1973–1981." *Midwest Review of Public Administration* 13 (December 1979), 225–238.

Lee, Robert D., Jr., and Raymond J. Staffeldt, "Educational Characteristics of State Budget Office Personnel." *Public Administration Review* 36 (July/August 1976), 424–428.

Lee, Robert D., Jr., and Ronald W. Johnson, *Public Budgeting Systems*, 3rd ed. Baltimore: University Park Press, 1983.

LeLoup, Lance T., "Appropriations Politics in Congress: The House Appropriations Committee and Executive Branch Agencies." *Public Budgeting and Finance* 4 (Winter 1984), 78–99.

LeLoup, Lance, T., "Comments." In Bernard T. Pitsvada, "The Executive Budget—An Idea Whose Time Has Passed." *Public Budgeting and Finance* 6 (Spring 1986), 104–107.

Lewis, Carol W., "Program Budgeting in Connecticut—The First Statewide Cycle." Storrs: University of Connecticut, Institutes of Public Service and Urban Research, 1986.

Lewis, Carol W. *Making Choices for Connecticut, A Handbook on the State Budget Process*. Storrs: University of Connecticut, Institutes of Public Service and Urban Research, 1984.

Lowrie, S. Gale, "The Budget and the Legislatures." *The Annals of the American Academy of Political and Social Science* 62 (November 1915), 36–46.

MacManus, Susan A., and Barbara P. Grothe, "The Fiscal Outlook for Ohio Municipalities Under Gramm-Rudman-Hollings." *Urban Fiscal Ledger* 3 (March/April 1986), 1–8.

Mikesell, John L., *Fiscal Administration: Analysis and Applications for the Public Sector*. Chicago: Dorsey Press, 1986.

Miles, Rufus E., "The Proper Function of the State Budget." *The Annals of the American Academy of Political and Social Science* 62 (November 1915), 47–63.

Patterson, Samuel C., and Gregory A. Caldeira, "The Etiology of Partisan Competition." *American Political Science Review* 78 (September 1984), 691–707.

Patton, Janet, and Merl Hackbart, *Innovation in State Government Processes: An Analysis of Selected Programs*. Lexington: University of Kentucky, Center for Public Affairs, 1967.

Pitsvada, Bernard T., "The Executive Budget—An Idea Whose Time Has Passed." *Public Budgeting & Finance* 6 (Spring 1988), 85–94.

Pound, William T., "The State Legislatures." In *Book of the State*, 1984–1985. Lexington, Ky.: Council of State Governments, 1984, 79–83.

Premus, Robert, "Long-Run Growth and Cyclical Behavior of Ohio's Economy." *Ohio Economic Trends Review* 2 (Winter 1986), 6–13.

Ramsey, James, and Merl Hackbart, "State and Local Debt Capacity: An Index Measure." *Municipal Finance Journal* 9, no. 1 (Winter 1988), 7–18

Ramsey, James, and Merl Hackbart, "Impacts of Budget Reform: The Budget Office Perspective." *State and Local Government Review* 14 (January 1982), 11.

Ramsey, James, and Merl Hackbart, *Innovations in State Budgeting: Process and Impact.* Lexington: University of Kentucky, Center for Public Affairs, 1978.

Sabato, Larry, *Goodbye to Good-Time Charlie* (1983) 2nd ed. Washington, D.C.: Congressional Quarterly Press.

Schick, Allen, "Micro-Budgetary Adaptations to Fiscal Stress in Industrialized Democracies." *Public Administration Review* 48 (January/February 1988), 523–533.

Schick, Allen, "The Road from ZBB." *Public Administration Review* 38 (March/April 1978), 177–180.

Schick, Allen, *Budget Innovation in the States.* Washington, D.C.: Brookings Institution, 1970.

Schick, Allen, "The Road to PPB: The Stages of Budget Reform." *Public Administration Review*, 26 (December 1966), 243–258.

Scicchitano, Michael J., "The Legislative Budget Office in Georgia: A Study of Politics and Analysis." In Carole W. Lewis and A. Grayson Walker III, eds., *Casebook in Public Budgeting and Financial Management.* Englewood Cliffs, N.J.: Prentice-Hall, 1984, 65–69.

Sharkansky, Ira, "Agency Requests, Gubernatorial Support, and Budget Success in State Legislatures." *The American Political Science Review* 62 (December 1968), 1220–1231.

Sharkansky, Ira, and Augustus B. Turnbull III, "Budget-Making in Georgia and Wisconsin: A Test of a Model." In Ira Sharkansky, *Policy Analysis in Political Science.* Chicago: Markham Publishing, Co., 1970, 225–238.

Sheridan, Richard G., "Budget Bytes" (Ohio's Capital Improvements Budgeting Process). *Urban Fiscal Ledger* 3 (May/June 1986), 8–10.

Sheridan, Richard G., "Fiscal Resources and Public Programs." In William O. Reichert and Steven O. Ludd, eds., *Outlook on Ohio: Prospects and Priorities in Public Policy.* Palisades Park, N.J.: Commonwealth Books, 1983, 53–69.

Sheridan, Richard G., *State Budgeting in Ohio.* 2nd ed. Cleveland, Ohio: College of Urban Affairs, Cleveland State University, 1983.

Snyder, Sheryl G., and Robert M. Ireland, "The Separation of Governmental Powers Under the Constitution of Kentucky: A Legal and Historical Analysis of L.R.C. v. Brown." *Kentucky Law Journal* 73 (1984–1985), 165.

Sobul, Michael, "How Federal Cuts May Affect State and Local Finances." *Urban Fiscal Ledger* 3 (January/February 1986), 6–10.

Sokolow, Alvin D., and Beth Walter Honadle, "How Rural Local Governments Budget: The Alternatives to Executive Preparation." *Public Administration Review* 44 (September/October 1984), 373–383.

Tucker, Harvey J., "Budget Strategies: Cross-Sectional View Versus Longitudinal Model." *Public Administration Review* 41 (November/December 1981), 645.

Turnbull, Augustus B., III, "Politics in the Budgetary Process: The Case of Georgia." Unpublished Ph.D. dissertation, University of Virginia, 1967.

Turnbull, Augustus B., III, and Patricia Irvin, "The Florida Appropriations Process—An Overview." In Thomas C. Foss and Thomas D. Sutberry, eds., *State Budgeting in Florida: A Handbook for Budget Analysts*, Tallahassee: Florida State University, 1984.

U.S. Advisory Commission on Intergovernmental Relations, *The Question of State Government Capacity*. Washington, D.C., January 1985.

Van Der Slik, Jack, and Kent Redfield, *Lawmaking in Illinois: Legislative Politics, People and Processes*. Springfield, Ill.: Sangamon State University, 1986.

Vaughn, "Constitutional Law—The Governor's Item Veto Power." *Missouri Law Review* 39 (Winter 1974), 105–110.

Walters, John Nelson, "Comment: The Illinois Amendatory Veto." *The John Marshall Journal of Practices and Procedures* 11, no. 2 (Winter 1977–1978), 417–440.

Wildavsky, Aaron, *The New Politics of the Budgetary Process*. Glenview, Ill.: Scott Foresman, Little, Brown & Co., 1988.

Wildavsky, Aaron, *A Comparative Theory of Budgeting Processes*, 2nd ed. Boston: Little, Brown & Co., 1986.

Wildavsky, Aaron, *Politics of the Budgetary Process*, 4th ed. Boston: Little, Brown & Co., 1984, 63–126.

Wildavsky, Aaron, "A Budget for All Seasons? Why the Traditional Budget Lasts." *Public Administration Review* 38 (November/December 1978), 501–509.

Willoughby, William Franklin, *The Movement for Budgetary Reform in the States*. New York: D. Appleton & Co., 1918.

Yondorf, Barbara, and B. J. Summers, "Legislative Budget Procedures in the 50 States." *Legislative Finance Paper #21*. Denver, Colo.: National Conference of State Legislatures, January 1983.

Index

About the Editors
and Contributors

EDWARD J. CLYNCH is Professor and Head of the Department of Political Science at Mississippi State University. His research interests include state budgeting. He has published numerous articles on this topic in professional journals.

THOMAS P. LAUTH is Professor and Head of the Department of Political Science at the University of Georgia. His research interests include state budgeting. He is the co-author of *Compromised Compliance: Implementation of the 1965 Voting Rights Act* and co-author of *The Politics of State and City Administration*.

GLEN HAHN COPE is an Associate Professor at the Lyndon Baines Johnson School of Public Affairs, University of Texas at Austin. Her research interests include state and local budgeting. She has published numerous articles on these topics in professional journals.

ELLEN M. DRAN is a research associate with the Center for Governmental Studies at Northern Illinois University. Her research interests include how Illinois disguises its fiscal position with accounting smoke and mirrors.

H. SYDNEY DUNCOMBE is Professor Emeritus of Political Science at the University of Idaho. His research interests include budget success, budget theory, impacts of revenue scarcities on budget practices, cutback management and budget uncontrollability. He has published numerous articles on these topics in professional journals. He also served as State Budget Director for Idaho.

GLORIA A. GRIZZLE is Professor of Public Administration and Policy Sciences at Florida State University. Her research interests include strategies for improving budgeting decisions and the character and determinants of legislative and executive budget deliberations. She has published numerous articles on these topics in professional journals.

MERL M. HACKBART is Professor of Finance and Public Administration at the University of Kentucky. His research interests include state government innovations and processes. He is the author of *Program Evaluation and Review: The Kentucky System.* He is State Budget Director for Kentucky.

F. TED HEBERT is Professor of Political Science and Director of the Center for Public Policy and Administration at the University of Utah. His research interests include budgetary process and he is the co-author of *The Politics of Raising State and Local Revenue* and the co-editor of *Congressional Budgeting: Politics, Process, and Power.*

JAMES E. JERNBERG is Professor and Director of Graduate Studies at the Herbert Humphrey Institute of Public Affairs at the University of Minnesota. His research interests include the role of legislative bodies in the budgetary process. He participated in the study team which wrote *Tribune of the People,* a study of the Minnesota legislature.

JACK KING is a Ph.D. student in public administration at Northern Illinois University.

RICHARD KINNEY is Professor of Political Science at Boise State University. His research interests include budget success, budget theory, impacts of revenue scarcities on budget practices, cutback management, and budget uncontrollability. He has published numerous articles on these topics in professional journals.

CAROL W. LEWIS is Professor of Political Science at the University of Connecticut. Her research interests include state and local budgeting. She is co-editor of *Casebook in Public Budgeting.*

JERRY L. McCAFFERY is Professor of Financial Management and Budgeting at the Naval Postgraduate School. His research interests include budget reform and state budgeting. He is the author of *Budgetmaster* and the co-author of *Government Response to Financial Constraints: Budgetary Control in Canada.*

SUSAN A. MacMANUS is Professor and Chair of the Department of Political Science, Public Administration, and International Affairs at the University of South Florida. Her research interests include state and local budgeting. She is the author of *Revenue Patterns in Cities and Suburbs* and *Federal Aid to Houston.*

IRENE S. RUBIN is Professor of Public Administration at Northern Illinois University. Her research interests include revenue issues and changes in budgeting over time. She is the author of *New Directions in Budget Theory* and *Policies of Public Budgeting: Getting and Spending, Borrowing and Balancing.*

STEVEN C. WAGNER is Assistant Professor of Political Science at Washburn University. His research interests include the influence of state-local governing structure on revenue policy.

MARCIA LYNN WHICKER is Professor of Public Administration at Virginia Commonwealth University. Her research interests include state budgeting. She is the author of *Economic Policy Making in the United States*.